Routledge Revivals

The English Bible as Literature

The religious associations surrounding the Bible make it difficult for the general reader to appreciate, in its full purity, the value which the Scriptures bear as literature, and as an epic in no way inferior, in cultural worth, to the greatest works of Greece and Rome. Dealing as it does with elementary passions and principles, the English Bible is, in the author's view, the greatest book of all the ages. This book, first published in 1931, will be of interest to students of literature and religious studies.

The English Bible as Literature

Charles Allen Dinsmore

Routledge
Taylor & Francis Group
ROUTLEDGE REVIVALS

First published in 1931
by George Allen & Unwin

This edition first published in 2015 by Routledge
2 Park Square, Milton Park, Abingdon, Oxon, OX14 4RN
and by Routledge
711 Third Avenue, New York, NY 10017

Routledge is an imprint of the Taylor & Francis Group, an informa business

Publisher's Note
The publisher has gone to great lengths to ensure the quality of this reprint but points out that some imperfections in the original copies may be apparent.

Disclaimer
The publisher has made every effort to trace copyright holders and welcomes correspondence from those they have been unable to contact.

A Library of Congress record exists under LC control number: 31006060

ISBN 13: 978-1-138-91718-7 (hbk)
ISBN 13: 978-1-315-68917-3 (ebk)
ISBN 13: 978-1-138-91720-0 (pbk)

THE ENGLISH BIBLE AS LITERATURE

BY

CHARLES ALLEN DINSMORE

LONDON
GEORGE ALLEN & UNWIN LTD
MUSEUM STREET

FIRST PUBLISHED IN GREAT BRITAIN, 1931

Printed by offset in Great Britain by
Billing and Sons Ltd., Guildford and Esher

PREFACE

THE Bible in recent times has passed through two distinct phases and is entering upon a third. There was a period when it was regarded as an infallible authority, the divine element was emphasized and the human overlooked; then came the age of the critic with his eager search for authors, dates, and documents; his main contentions having been established, his battle is losing its heat and absorbing interest. Now we are entering upon the era of appreciation. Educators are beginning to realize that Hebrew literature is not inferior to Greek and Roman in cultural value. One can here study the best of a racial literature, unified by a developing thought and a continuous quest into an epic, the world's noblest epic. With the 'Iliad' it shares the very distinct advantage of coming from a comparatively simple society where the important issues of life are seen in their fundamental principles and may be stated with clarity and simplicity.

Many of the books published to promote the appreciation of the Scriptures classify their contents according to literary types. The disadvantage of this method is apparent. It is analytical and fails to communicate the total effect of the writings. The power of all great literature lies in the impression whicn the drama or the story as a whole makes upon the mind. The compelling magic of any one of Shakespeare's tragedies is not in the artistry and insight of isolated passages, but in the atmosphere and spirit of the whole. The sublimity of the 'Divine Comedy' is not to be readily found in its brilliant episodes, it is felt as one follows the entire mystic journey from lowest hell to the vision of God. What distinguishes the greatest books from the great is precisely the fact that the whole is more than the sum of all the parts. A book is a living thing and is not seen at its best on the dissecting table. Therefore the author begins with Genesis and follows with considerable consistency the unfolding thought and high spiritual adventure of this vast Epic of Redemption, discusses the different types of writing as they are met and brings out the permanent spiritual truths of the individual books. The effect is cumulative and tends to make the Bible a living book.

Another purpose has been to show the unique and sovereign greatness of our Standard English Version. It is unlike any other book in our language and in charm and power is above them all. Its diction is neither Hebrew nor English, but a thing of peculiar excellence, born of the genius of two remarkable races, modified by the influence of Greece and Rome. More than any book in the world, it is the product of many centuries and many minds. Dealing with elemental passions and principles, its glory is that it expresses them in forms of final beauty. This is brought out by comparing the best in the English Bible with the best in other literatures.

In Part I the author tries to answer the question how a people so insignificant in numbers and political importance could write a literature so significant. They assembled the world's first history; they produced a body of religious lyrics of universal appeal;

first among the nations they passed from magic to prayer and from ritual to righteousness, they followed hope as did no other people, and their extraordinary succession of men of high genius culminated in the supreme figure of the ages. The peculiarity of their natural endowments and the disciplinary process to which they were subjected is a most fascinating study.

I wish to express my deep gratitude to Professor Charles C. Torrey for reading the proof of the whole book, and to Professor Frank C. Porter for reading the New Testament section and to Professor Robert S. Smith for reading the Old.

CHARLES ALLEN DINSMORE

NEW HAVEN, CONNECTICUT

CONTENTS

PART I

THE GENIUS AND DISCIPLINE OF THE HEBREW PEOPLE

THE ENGLISH BIBLE AS LITERATURE

PART I

THE GENIUS AND DISCIPLINE OF THE HEBREW PEOPLE

THE ENGLISH BIBLE AS LITERATURE

CHAPTER I

THE MARKS OF A SUPREME BOOK

The Authorized Version of the Bible is a piece of literature without any parallel in modern times. Other countries, of course, have their translations of the Bible, but they are not great works of art. The only other translation that can be compared with the Authorized Version is the Vulgate; and that is written in a language now foreign to everybody.... It is more than a translation, it expresses the religious thoughts and emotions of Englishmen as well as of Jews and early Christians.

A. Clutton-Brock

THROUGH space we travel by many vehicles; through time we journey most easily by the magic of a good book. Of these there are many, but they differ in worth and durability, Some are for the day; others are for the ages. Some are so ephemeral that they are like 'a snow-fall on the river, a moment white, then melts forever.' Others shine like the stars forever and ever.

What are the marks of an immortal book? Emily Dickinson once wrote: 'If I read a book and it makes my whole body so cold no fire can ever warm it, I know it is poetry. If I feel physically as if the top of my head were taken off, I know this is poetry.' These vivid words are a poet's intense way of saying that poetry, and all vital literature, affects us profoundly. How well I remember the day I finished reading

Hugo's 'Les Misérables'! I walked on air, a golden glow suffused earth and sky, my ears were unstopped and I heard the dynamos of the world purring in the deep places. Every novel of George Eliot was a spiritual milestone in my early pilgrimage; while the very splendor of God rests upon the day I casually opened Dante's 'Divine Comedy.'

No book is great to us unless it affects us in a deep and permanent way. But our individual judgments may be mistaken; some trivial thing may release our emotions. If we find, however, that a volume which gives us mental and spiritual elevation has in like manner moved competent minds in many generations, and of many races, then we conclude that it is one of the world's great books.

Now, what is there in these deathless books which causes them thus to stir the minds of multitudes in every century? We find in all of them a clear, fresh, powerful vision of human life. They tell the story of men and women in their great moments; they reveal the grandeur and the degradation of our humanity. Never do the greatest books deal with abstractions or speculations, but always with truth as it is revealed in human experience. Always their theme is man, his sins, his sufferings, his sources of comfort and redemption. The great books often deal with some one aspect of life, as 'The Scarlet Letter,' or 'Romola,' but life is always the stuff of which they are made. The immortals always see life steadily, and usually they see it whole. They have broad horizons, amazing penetration of thought, and amplitude of diction.

We find also that what makes these books powerful is their delineation of passion and their appeal to passion. Literature is measured by the quality and force of its emotional effect. 'Mankind,' says Goethe, 'is always advancing, but man is always the same.' The elemental emotions — love. hate, revenge, thirst for God — these are permanent, and upon these unchanging feelings the enduring literature rears its stately structure.

One is also impressed with the vividness of the imagination of the immortal writers. 'When you describe a thing,' wrote Tchekhov to Gorky, 'you see it, and touch it with your hands. That is real style.' The characters in the immortal books are as living as historical figures. Achilles is as much a part of Grecian history as Pericles, Mephistopheles is as vivid a memory as Bismarck, Hamlet is as well known in England as Gladstone.

But the manner of the supreme books is as memorable as their matter. In their sentences is the rhythm of great music, the grace of a polished shaft, the glitter of a flight of silver arrows. Truth unadorned does not live in the memory of men, but truth shaped and glowing with beauty. Truth plus beauty equals immortality, is the algebraic equation of literature.

Long before we feel the power of the book as a whole, our attention is arrested by the magic word, the grace of the perfect sentence. We do not look for these on every page, but ever and anon in a good book we expect to find a word that fits as a jewel in its setting, a sentence that shines with the authentic fire of genius. In all the masterpieces there are phrases which condense a whole lifetime of experience, like that sentence Dante heard in Paradise, 'And his will is our peace'; or that give utterance to an emotion, in a form which cannot be improved, like

> We are such stuff
> As dreams are made on; and our little life
> Is rounded with a sleep;

or some conviction, like 'They also serve who only stand and wait.' It is by these 'winged words,' these sentences glowing with celestial beauty, that the kings of speech reveal their royal blood.

After much searching I have found no better description of the characteristics of the pages that do not perish than that given by John Morley: 'Literature consists of all the books — and they are not so many — where moral truth and human passion are touched with a certain largeness, sanity and attraction of form.' Of the few books which meet the terms of this definition, there are three which hold incontestably the first rank as world classics. They are Homer's 'Iliad,' Dante's 'Divine Comedy,' and Shakespeare's Dramas. Many would add to this list Plato's Dialogues, the dramas of Æschylus, Sophocles, and Euripides, and Goethe's 'Faust.' Aside from the worth of their thought, the Dialogues, considered as literature, have neither the variety of form nor the scale of emotional effect attained by the first three classics mentioned. The Greek dramatists may see life steadily, but they do not interpret an epoch like Homer or see it in as complete a compass as Shakespeare. Goethe has not yet been tested by enough centuries to be acclaimed a fourth in so great a company. The three mentioned are the highest expression in literature of the ancient, the medieval, the modern world. Each is concerned with human life in its decisive and crowded moments; each is the voice of an epoch, the picture of a civilization; each displays wide ranges of elemental emotion; all have a splendor of thought, a sweep of imagination, a superlative mastery of the resources of language, that place them upon an unapproached eminence. In them all 'moral truth and human passion are touched with a certain largeness, sanity and attraction of form.'

My purpose now is to show to the reader how easily the English Bible — and by English Bible I mean the King James Version, and the Authorized Revisions — simply through its literary qualities takes a conspicuous position in the group of the world's greatest classics. Of course we cannot evaluate literature as we do real estate, or with confidence assign relative rank to documents of the spirit. Yet standards of judgment are not wanting, and superlative merit is not easily concealed. I wish to bring out the greatness of the English Bible by comparing it with these classics.

If the substance of great books is the extent and importance of the moral truth taught, and the powerful portrayal of human passion, surely no book compares with the Bible in aggregation of truth and variety of passion. In the 'Iliad,' the events of less than fifty days are recorded. There are four days of fighting, followed by twenty-two days of funeral. Against a somber background there shine forth a few figures so resplendent that the 'Iliad' was used as a Bible by the Greeks to teach valor, magnanimity, hospitality. But the Scriptures hold in view the developing succession of centuries and show life under an immense diversiformity of conditions. In scope of truth and range of emotion, the 'Iliad' compares with the Bible as a broad-flowing river compares with the ocean.

Like the Bible, Dante goes down into the deep places of Satan; he also reads the mystery of life in the face of God. He is deep and high, but he moves in a strange world, the divine fire in him is often dimly seen under the encasement of medieval theology. His 'Comedy' lacks the universal appeal of the Scriptures. It is for all time, but not for all people.

The crowded stage of Shakespeare discloses a multiformity of emotions comparable with the Bible. No one surpasses him in envisaging the austere grandeur of the moral law, and in splendor of diction he is worthy of all honor. But his sight is very dim when he peers into the Supreme Mystery. He is world-wide, but there are heights which he cannot attain.

Neither Homer, nor Dante, nor Shakespeare touches so many chords of human passion, delicately and powerfully, or interprets so wide a compass of experience as does the Bible.

Or, apply another standard. It is perfectly fair to compare books of genius by the characters they create or the dramatic power of the situations involved. As the heroes of these famous books pass before our imagination they stir us profoundly: Agamemnon,

Achilles, Ulysses; Dante, Francesca, Latini, Beatrice; Othello, Lear, Miranda, Hamlet — a glorious company; but no more interesting than Jacob, David, Saul, and the great company of saints and heroes. When our thoughts turn from these to the divine portraiture of Christ, there is no question as to which way the balance turns. No literature has a character of such perfect proportions. And if the test is the powerful presentation of plot and the tragic moment, there is Calvary and the long centuries of spiritual adventure leading up to it.

Quite apart from questions of inspiration, the English Bible has the advantage of all other classics in the fact that a library of sixty-six books is gathered into one volume. While the other masterpieces are the product of one mind, or of a small group of minds, our Scriptures were written by many men, under many conditions. They were dictated by the genius of one race and then moulded by the genius of another. They present life as it appeared to successive generations and to successive strata of intelligence. The 'Divine Comedy' issued from the brain of one man, the 'Iliad' may be the minstrelsy of one poet or of a syndicate of poets, but the English Bible is the production of a multitude of minds stretching in succession over nearly three thousand years, representing many temperaments and many points of view. Like John at Patmos, we hear the voice of many waters, yet unified as the clear note of a trumpet. It is the Holy Ghost speaking in divers portions and in divers manner through many men, in many centuries, in many countries.

Or, if we make the basis of comparison the magic word, the enchanted phrase, the sentence of perfect grace, only Shakespeare would be mentioned and his treasure-house is far smaller than that of the Scriptures.

But we have not yet disclosed the deepest secret of the literary effectiveness of the Bible. In any real book, a large part of its power lies in the nature of its background — in the atmosphere in which the characters live and move and have their being. It is just this lack of background that condemns much of our modern work. The greatest writers do not neglect it. Dante makes his marvelous pilgrimage against a scene first of the terrifying gloom, and then of the ineffable glory of the eternal world. In all of Shakespeare's tragedies the actors seem to be playing their part before the high throne of inexorable justice. Even in Homer, the issue of the battle on the plains of windy Troy is determined by the councils on Mount Olympus. In all of the sovereign books which the world will not let die, the characters live and do their deeds in the atmosphere and against the awful curtain of the Eternal.

Now in the Scriptures the Eternal is the background, even more intimate and solemnly impressive than in the other classics we have mentioned. Never for a moment is the gloom, or the glory, of the background forgotten; the shadow or splendor is on every page.

But the source of greatest power lies deeper than this. Not only are the actions performed and the words spoken as in the presence of the Most High, the Background becomes intensely personal and steps upon the stage as the chief actor in the drama. He is the absorbing center of attention from the beginning to the end. At first he is an Invisible Presence, hearing all, directing all. His authentic message comes through the mouth of his prophets, 'Thus saith the Lord.' Again he speaks directly: 'Come, let us reason together: though your sins be as scarlet they shall be white as snow.' Until finally the Word becomes flesh, and dwells among us, we behold his glory, full of grace and truth. Henceforth every thought is on him, whose glory filleth all in all. The ancient Hebrew could make God speak so directly to the hearer or reader because he held with such intensity the conviction that the voice which spoke in the depth of his soul was the veritable utterance of God. These writers could represent the Eternal as speaking and acting through man with the sincerity and simplicity of utter belief. Therefore their words have power. Both Homer and Milton use this device. The Greek poets represent the gods as speaking on human topics, but the real God — the Eternal Fate — preserves an awful silence. The speeches of Jehovah in 'Paradise Lost' are pompous, theological, and artificial, they are stage machinery. Tennyson may represent the Two Voices engaged in earnest debate, but he cannot speak as the mouthpiece of God. Whittier in perfect sincerity can sing:

> I know not where his islands lift
> Their fronded palms in air;
> I only know I cannot drift
> Beyond his love and care.

But these lines, confident and beautiful as they are, do not carry the convincing and comforting power of 'I will never leave thee nor forsake thee.' What modern writer could assert the divine forgiveness in such tremendous words as those of Israel: 'Though your sins be as scarlet, they shall be white as snow.'

Now regarded merely as literary machinery — quite apart from religious value — the genius to see life vividly and to see it steadily against the background of the Eternal Righteousness, the ability to introduce God as an authentic voice speaking constantly through the drama, warning, directing, encouraging, and finally to make his grace and glory assume human form and bring the drama to its culmination of victorious agony in one supreme moment; considered, I say, merely as literary art, this tremendous drama, this divine human comedy, makes the plot of the 'Iliad,' or of 'Hamlet,' seem very insignificant.

If we add to this the fact that this incredible story is told with such simplicity and utter sincerity that multitudes in every generation and in every age hear through its pages the very accents of the Holy Ghost, and feel the immediate presence of the Eternal, then I think we are justified in saying that in the whole range of the literature of power this volume is unique.

If the tests of great literature are the scope and quality of the humanized truth presented, the variety of emotions vividly and truthfully delineated in a manner at once generous, sane, and attractive, then the Scriptures certainly stand with the world classics. But if we add to these its effect on its readers, its power to liberate them from the drudgery of the commonplace, to add new territories to the domain of their consciousness, to move so powerfully on all their feelings as permanently to change their character, and to do this not to a few elect minds, but to all classes and conditions of men everywhere and in every age, then I think that we may claim for the English Bible a place not inferior to that occupied by the very greatest books of the Western world.

CHAPTER II

AN EPIC OF REDEMPTION

East and West met long ago in the matchless phrases translated from Hebrew and Greek and Latin into the English Bible; and the heart of the East there answers to the heart of the West, as in water face answereth to face. That the colonizing Englishmen of the seventeenth century were Hebrews in spiritual culture, the heirs of Greece and Rome without ceasing to be Anglo-Saxon in blood, is one of the basal facts in the intellectual life of the United States to-day.

BLISS PERRY

IT is usually affirmed that the Bible is an inspired book. Properly speaking, persons, not books, are inspired. We are closer to the facts in stating that the Bible is the record of an inspired race; it is a literature attesting and preserving a unique movement looking toward redemption. Its books are made the Book, its variety becomes unity, because one increasing Purpose gathers the many into one. It differs from all other sacred books of the world in that it is the only one which reveals God as the chief actor in the drama of human life, working through the centuries for the moral and spiritual redemption of mankind. The Koran was written by one man at a definite period of time; the Bible was written by a multitude of writers, of different temperaments, of diverse outlooks on life, separated from one another, often by many centuries, not consciously writing sacred scripture, but doing the day's work and serving their own generation. This heterogeneous mass of tradition, statutes, folk-lore, song, and history, is shaped, united, illumined by an increasing and divine Purpose, making a library of sixty-six books into one Book.

The background of every writer is Palestine, the modes of thought are Oriental, yet a Semitic book has been clothed in English dress, and we find the characteristic style of our Scriptures to be a blending of the best in the East with the best in the West. It has a movement and cadence of speech which is unmistakable, in whatsoever connection it is quoted. No book is more thoroughly at home in our literature, none more influential over our thought and speech.

This Oriental volume is not only domesticated in English literature, it occupies a supreme place, not merely because it is venerated as sacred, but because of its literary excellence.

THE AUTHOR

If the increasing movement, beginning with our first parents and culminating in Christ and the Church, is a manifestation of the Divine Will, then the author of the book is God. But of its human authors we may say that it was written by the genius of the Hebrew people, and modified by the successive influence of the Greek, the Roman, and the English. A few of the books, such as Ruth and Jonah in the Old Testament, and Romans and Corinthians in the New, were conceived and shaped by an individual mind, yet a mind representative of the race. But the stories, the psalms, the prophecies, even the histories, were fashioned by the intuitions and the taste of many generations, and selected, preserved, and canonized by succeeding generations. The *material* of all the books was observed, thought out, shaped, written, and preserved by a Hebrew, and represents the pure gold of the spiritual experience of a great people seven times refined in the fires of pain.

The form as it comes to us in the Authorized Version is not the work of any gifted individual, but is the result of the labors of many men in many generations. Thus the English Bible is the literature produced by the genius of the Hebrew people, refashioned by the genius of the English stock, after that stock had been enriched by the finer spirit of Greece and Rome. It is a world book written and shaped by the divinest spirit of many races, many generations.

THE PERIL OF MISINTERPRETATION

The greater the book, the greater the disaster if it is misinterpreted. Unquestionably misunderstanding of the Scriptures has brought much tragedy to believers, and has been a serious bar to progress. A Hebrew singer destitute of scientific knowledge, yet with eager eyes open to the world, chants the praises of God. Quite incidentally using the current thought of his day, he exclaims: 'The world also is established that it cannot be moved.' This poetic rhapsody of an ancient singer was quoted over a thousand years later as an authentic dictum of the Holy Ghost and used to condemn the researches of Galileo. The wonderful hymn of creation in the opening chapters of Genesis is used in the closing years of the nineteenth century to confute scientific thought. The Hebrews, but two generations from slavery, with utter ruthlessness exterminated their enemies — men, women, children, and cattle — yet the savagery of an uncouth people is defended as a direct command of a God of love. To clothe the crude conceptions of a primitive people with the sanction of the Eternal God gives to the scribe authority to check the creative thinker, and is fraught with peril to a spiritual religion. Think of the terrible fears, the black agony, which has afflicted the Christian centuries because the theologians with their dry and practical minds gave literal validity to Oriental visions of a lake burning with fire and brimstone! An inspired seer rapt in the ecstasies of apocalyptic vision does not use language with the precision of one writing a legal code. Rhapsody must not be forced into the logical formularies of a dogmatist. Yet this has been the fatal defect of popular exegesis. Daniel and Revelation have been read as though they were as prosaic as Leviticus, and legends have lost their true glory when interpreted by the dusty minds of the scribes. Evidently the Bible is a collection of many types of literature, fable, folk-lore, poetry, allegory, law, history, ballads, and each teaches its lesson after its own method and in its own vocabulary. Each must be understood according to its own canon of interpretation. Prose must be read as prose, poetry as poetry; parable and allegory must not be mistaken for history.

The English Bible is the selected literature of a peculiarly gifted people, translated and domesticated in the language of another people. As literature it belongs to the domain of Art and must be judged by its standards and understood by its methods.

ITS TRUTH SHAPED BY THE IMAGINATION

Spiritually minded men of our day are intensely concerned with the relationship of science and religion, and to a less extent with the relationship of philosophy and religion. Now religion does have intimate business with science, for she must have the scientific spirit to validate convincingly her historic facts and her documents. Religion rests on the facts of history and the facts of consciousness, and therefore comes within the realm of psychology and of historical criticism. Religion also leans heavily on philosophy to aid her in the reasonable interpretation of faith. But the methods and the innermost spirit of religion are much more nearly related to art than to either science or philosophy, and especially to that branch of art which is concerned with poetry.

To a conservative mind accustomed to consider religion prosaically, and to think of the Bible as a book of infallible law, it may seem revolutionary to assert this close relationship of religion and its literature to poetry, but consider carefully how close the kinship is; closer than to either science or philosophy. Poetry, and indeed, all great art, is the imaginative shaping of reality. Prose is performing its best office when it achieves precision of statement; it addresses primarily the understanding and the judgment. Poetry, on the other hand, takes the facts of experience, and fashions, colors, and unifies them, by the creative imagination. The religious mind acts precisely as the mind of the poet. Reality is too vast, too mysterious, to be apprehended by the understanding only, so our imagination shapes our thoughts of God and of destiny; we visualize the Redeemer and his Cross according to our experience, until we feel the truths of our religion and can sing them.

The material composing the Scriptures has been conceived as an artist would conceive it, and handled as an artist would handle it. Every artist, be he poet, painter, or orator, arranges his material to produce a certain impression. His concern is not with exactitude of detail, but with releasing the energy and glory of an idea.

Most of the facts of experience related in the Scriptures were apprehended and transfused by the spiritual imaginations of men who were essentially of a poetic temper. The story of Creation was told by a poet of superlative ability; such facts as he knew were arranged to bring out a single sovereign truth. The origin and nature of sin is not stated philosophically in the early chapters of Genesis, but visualized by the creative imagination. The experience of Israel from the beginning is not given to us in the achromatic light of history as we conceive it in these scientific days; the facts have passed through the imagination of many generations, and were finally arranged, as an artist arranges his material, to create a desired impression. So the events narrated of Jesus were molded by the minds and hearts of the early Church and so set down as to bring out vividly the truth that Jesus was the Christ, the Son of God. And the hopes of the future as conceived by the prophets and apocalyptical writers were surely dyed and fashioned by the imagination.

Religion and great poetry make their appeal

primarily to the emotions, and must be experienced in order to be known. Scientific facts and laws are known by experiment, but religion deals with values which are apprehended only by the prepared mind. The poet, the saint, the musician, each says, 'I know,' and his knowledge is valid; but it is different from the knowledge which the scientist claims and which is reached by other methods.

Religion and art speak with the same kind of authority. The influence of 'Hamlet' over us does not depend upon the historic accuracy concerning men and dates, or even that it is the work of Shakespeare. Its authority rests upon its fidelity to the truths of human experience; it dramatizes powerfully in the life of one man the forces and entanglements which are common to the many. Its authority is the authority of truth, recognized by intuition and felt by the heart.

Religion, also, like all art, works to a model, imperfectly in the Old Testament, perfectly in the New.

The writings in which religion speaks to us are not legal documents to be prosaically interpreted; all the facts of importance have passed through human experience; they have been brooded over, shaped by the imagination and the emotions, until they reveal the deep experiences of men. They are true as Hamlet is true, true to life. The critical scholar can give us much information regarding actual events, dates, and authorship, but his scholarship can go no further. The power and the glory of the Scriptures are known only to those who read with a devout heart and a sensitive imagination.

When the King James Version was printed in 1611, the translators did not have the key to Hebrew poetry, nor understand its nature; therefore the volume was printed in the form of prose. By the time of the English revision the structure of Hebrew verse had been ascertained and the Psalms were printed in poetical form; in our American translation the oracles of the prophets and some of the emotionally heightened passages of the New Testament are put in the fashion of verse. It is true that the Bible contains much that is driest prose, genealogies, long stretches of history, laws and ritualistic regulations, yet in the vast sweep of its movement from Genesis to Revelation it presents the story of divine revelation with the power and splendor of great poetry, and the diversified material is so unified by a controlling idea that we inevitably think of it as a Drama, an Epic of Redemption.

DRAMA OR EPIC, WHICH IS IT?

At first thought one is much inclined to classify it as a drama. There is a prologue, the tragic sin, the unfolding plot culminating in Calvary, the founding of the Church, the whole closing in an epilogue describing a new heaven and a new earth. And through it all God is the chief actor meeting every situation, sometimes tragically, always victoriously.

Yet a second thought shows it to be more like an epic, an Iliad of struggle, an Odyssey of a hero sailing over the deep until he comes to his home. We have Humanity — the giant with a wounded heel — going forth from Paradise to high adventure and desperate battle to final victory.

There are these distinctions to be borne in mind. The drama deals with the tragic moment which is significant because of what has been done in the past; we discern the cause in the effect. In the epic, on the other hand, it is the future which makes the present significant. The doings of Æneas from Troy to Italy are trivial enough, but they have meaning because in them are hidden the destinies of imperial Rome. There is indeed tragedy in the Scriptures, in those awful moments when sin brings forth its fruits; yet the prevailing interest is not in the past but in the future. Abraham's story is significant because in his loins are a great people. The profoundest meaning of the Cross is its effects in the future: 'And I, if I be lifted up, will draw all men unto me.'

In the great epics the hero is under supernatural guidance. The key to all actions is the purpose of heaven. The real battle of Troy was fought on Olympus. Neither Odysseus by his craft, nor Æneas by his pious virtue, brought his adventures to a successful issue. It was the will of the gods which prevailed. In the Bible, the interest is not centered in the battling spirit of man, but in the nature and purposes of the Most High. Not man's greatness, but God's grace, is the dominant note. 'Thine is the kingdom, and the power, and the glory' — is the ever-recurrent refrain.

Moreover, in the drama, the virtue most admired is fortitude. The hero takes arms against a sea of troubles; in the epic the required virtue is obedience. Man is the instrument, the servant, the child of God. Again, the interest of the drama centers in the moment of the collision; in the epic the interest is not absorbed in one dramatic moment, but follows the hero through a series of adventures.

Because in the Bible the meaning of events lies not in their dramatic relation to the past, but in their bearing upon the future; because the connecting thread is not the achieving valor of man, but the unfolding character of God; and because the virtue most exalted is not heroic self-reliance, but loving obedience to a Grace that works its purposes in and through us, I think we are justified in calling the book an Epic of Salvation.

THE BIBLE BELONGS TO THE LITERATURE OF POWER

De Quincey has given us the convenient distinction between the literature of knowledge and the literature of power. We read an encyclopedia to learn facts, we read 'Paradise Lost' to receive emotional elevation. The literature of knowledge is ephemeral, for when we have gathered its information we forget the book; the literature of power is permanent, for if we would recover the mood, feel again the coveted power, we must read the book.

We indeed go to the Bible for knowledge — knowledge of the experiences of men of former times with the living God, knowledge of the historical Jesus, the founding of the Church, and the beliefs of the Apostles; but usually we read the Scriptures not for knowledge but for power — to quicken our sense of God, to feel the comforting presence of Christ, to renew our enthusiasm by catching again the ancient vision, and to have created within us those high moods which give freedom and infinite peace. As a source of spiritual renovation for peoples of all temperaments and degrees the Scriptures easily head the list of the books of power.

Like all literature, we know it only when we catch its vision and feel its emotions. We do not know the 'Iliad' because we are familiar with the debate whether Homer was a single minstrel or a group; we may spend several years in analyzing the poem, assigning to the different parts their dates, correcting the errors in the text, learning much of Troy and Mycenæ; we may know a great deal about the Iliad, but we do not know the Iliad until we catch its innermost spirit, feel its exquisite beauties, and glow with its emotion. So our scholars with infinite patience and with great success have been studying the Scriptures. They have been improving the text, discriminating between the documents, assigning dates and authorship. All this is of great value, yet it is only preparatory to something of greater value. Professors do not really teach the 'Bible as Literature' when most of the time is spent on questions of documents and authorship. Literature is known only when one appreciates those qualities which give to the writings enduring vitality. The purpose of the following pages is to point out the sources of power, the secret of the enchantment of the English Bible; to show how the miracle happened, and to feel the wonder of it.

CHAPTER III

HOW DID A LITERATURE SO GREAT COME FROM A PEOPLE SO SMALL?

Lo, it is a people that dwell alone,
And shall not be reckoned among the nations.

Numbers 23:9

But the land, whither ye go over to possess it, is a land of hills and valleys, and drinketh water of the rain of heaven: a land which the Lord thy God careth for; the eyes of the Lord thy God are always upon it, from the beginning of the year even unto the end of the year.

Deuteronomy 11:11, 12

In the beginnings, as the human race multiplied on the face of the earth, families naturally gathered together in the great river bottoms, for here water was abundant, unfailing, and the soil was rich. Consequently, in the fertile valleys of the Nile, the Euphrates, the Tigris rivers, we find the earliest and most powerful civilizations; and the romance of our modern times is the discoveries we are making in the buried cities and tombs of these ancient peoples. The more we know, the stronger is our wonder at the wealth, the power, the highly complex social organizations existing thousands of years before the Christian era. It is conjectured that in the days when Babylon was at the height of her power, the soil of the Euphrates valley would yield one hundred bushels to the acre and produce two crops a year. Soil as rich as that of Mesopotamia and Egypt would naturally support teeming populations and powerful dynasties.

A DISQUIETED PEOPLE

Lying between these two river bottoms of immense fertility is the land of the people of Israel — a small territory, about the size of the State of Vermont, the position important to spiritual history being only about twenty miles wide and forty-five miles long. As Egypt and the Assyrio-Babylonian Empires were rivals, contending for the dominion of the known world, the Hebrew people were as secure as a grain of wheat between the upper and nether millstones. Northern Israel, living on the chief highway of war and of commerce, was as safe as tent-dwellers on a crowded road. Even Judah was but little removed from the pathway of the world's armies. The land was not fertile enough to support a population sufficient in numbers to withstand such powerful enemies; the rivers of Zion flowed gently, and the land drank its water from the uncertain clouds. The conditions of the times made it inevitable that Israel should be a disquieted and a suffering nation. But the mountains of Judah were an excellent place to breed and train men. The soil was poor enough and mountainous enough to nurture heroic spirits. The land stretched from the heat of the Dead Sea, 1292 feet below the level of the Mediterranean, to wind-swept Jerusalem, 2582 feet above. One standing on Mount Zion and looking down into the valley of the Jordan has a feeling that he is on the top of the world, and often the clear air from the desert, drifting over the heights, produces a mystical effect of light which creates a spiritual elevation out of which prayer and ecstasy are born. The heat of the valleys of the Nile and the

Euphrates is oppressive, unfavorable to strenuous intellectual activity. Whenever virile races shall develop in a more favorable environment, among the mountains or by the sea, we may expect a distinct forward movement in the concerns of the mind. And so it proved. The river valleys cradled civilization, in the mountains of Judah and by the shores of the Ægean Sea it took an immense step forward in the higher interests of the mind. The strength of the hills, the tang of the upland air, the broad horizons energized the wills, stimulated the imaginations, shaped the character of the sons of Israel.[1]

But their environment, while it stimulated individual genius, set limits to the enterprise of the nation. Being few in number, the Hebrews could not become a conquering nation like the Babylonians; unlike the Phœnicians, they had no love for the sea and therefore clung to their hills and failed to become a commercial people; unlike the Romans, they showed no ability in the organization of large bodies of men; they were also lacking in the artistic capacities of the Greek. Extraordinarily vital as they were, both environment and talent confined the outlet of their energies to religion. Forbidden to make graven images with their hands, their intense minds could, nevertheless, conceive vivid mental images which would find expression in metaphor and parable. They seem foreordained to religion and its literary expression.

[1] Nomadic life in the desert through many generations had already made the stock virile by its stern discipline.

INBREEDING

Heredity as well as environment shaped their peculiar genius. Before this genius broke out in its splendor there had been a long period of preparation. The Hebrews, according to their traditions, were subject to a very significant process of inbreeding, a process which made them — in the words of Professor Huntington — 'biologically religious.'

Our knowledge of breeding among animals teaches us that each new stock originates in the pairing of individuals possessing some marked common peculiarity. Close in-and-in breeding is then practiced until the strain becomes stable and certain of transmitting its distinguishing characteristics. Provided the stock is healthy, this inbreeding of good blood is fertile in excellent results. But close inbreeding, persisted in too long, results in degeneracy. Like methods produce like results among men, who, after all, belong to the animal kingdom and are amenable to its laws. Where the blood is vigorous and healthy, the intermarriage of near relatives is likely to result in the reproduction of greatly strengthened family peculiarities. If the qualities are good, the inbreeding is beneficial; if they are bad, it is disastrous. It is the common opinion that the marriage of close blood relations produces degenerate offspring. This depends on the vitality of the strain. Closely related degenerates produce children still more degenerate; but, if the stock is vigorous, qualities of exceptional strength mingling create increased power.

Professor Ellsworth Huntington, in his 'Pulse of Progress,' [1] writing upon consanguineous marriages,

[1] Huntington, Ellsworth: *The Pulse of Progress*, pp. 174–93.

quotes Sir Marc A. Ruffer's 'Studies in the Paleopathology of Egypt':

> Dr. Ruffer selected for study the Eighteenth Dynasty which began when Atmose I drove out the Shepherd Kings. A man of unusual strength he married his sister; their son, Amenhotep I was highly venerated for his conquests. One of his wives was his sister and their daughter, Aahmes, married her half brother, Thutmose I. From this union was born the noted queen Hatshepsut, Egypt's greatest queen. She was succeeded by Thutmose II, a step-son who married her daughter whose relation to his wife was that of half-brother, cousin, and husband. Yet he was one of the greatest of the Pharaohs, and the product of five unbroken generations of brother-sister marriages.

Professor Huntington also cites the case of Charles Darwin, who married his cousin, and of the five sons, four became distinguished.

The racial distinctiveness of the Hebrew strain seems to have been developed by a like biological process of inbreeding and selection. According to the Scriptural accounts, the original Hebrew stock was not only religious but of that sturdy pioneer type which will devotedly leave all for a great adventure of faith. Abraham heard God's whisper and had the valor of soul to obey and go into a strange land. He not only broke from the old home, he broke with the prevailing religious customs of his day and renounced human sacrifices. This peculiar religious temperament is now strengthened and perpetuated by the well recognized biological process of consanguineous mating. His wife, Sarah, was his half-sister. Isaac and

Jacob both go back to the ancestral country and stock for their mates, Isaac married the daughter of his uncle; Leah and Rachel were Jacob's own cousins. When Esau took two Hittite women in marriage, Isaac and Rebecca 'were grieved in their minds,' for alien blood was come into the family. Even if these patriarchal traditions represent, not individuals, but the movements and characteristics of tribes, they record the marriage customs which were practiced in ancient times and which moulded the nature of subsequent generations. After the patriarchs there follows a period of obscurity when the Hebrews dwelt in Egypt. Here breeding in-and-in must have been a common practice, for when the curtain lifts we find that Amram is married to his father's sister,[1] and that Moses, Aaron, and Miriam are their children. These records show that as with the Egyptians, so with the Hebrews, marriage with near relatives — half-sisters, cousins, aunts — was according to social custom. If adventurous faith was in the original strain, the practice of breeding in-and-in would intensify and fix distinguishing characteristics. In the exodus, the desert experiences sifted out the weak of body and the weak of faith. In the land of Palestine, the dependence of the country upon the rain from heaven would accentuate the people's dependence on God and thus strengthen their trust in Him. In the long process of the conquest of the land, the blood of the sons of Jacob was mixed with the blood of the inhabitants. But even thus it does not follow that the pure strain of the ancient blood was not preserved in certain families —

[1] Exodus 6:20.

just as in our country, although vast numbers of immigrants have come among us, yet many among us are as untainted by any alien strain as any noble lord in England who traces his pedigree back to the Conqueror. It is significant that Amos, Micah, Jeremiah came from small villages, where the blood would likely be the most pure and the bent of the ancestral stock preserved.

SELECTION

This stock also experienced a severe process of selection. After the succession of Northern Israel under Jeroboam, those minds in the North country most loyal to the ideas represented in Jerusalem would inevitably gravitate toward that center, while on the other hand the more worldly of the inhabitants of Jerusalem, unsympathetic with the growing strictness of worship in the temple, would be attracted to the larger liberty, the easier practices of the North. Thus the people of a pronounced religious temperament would gather around the temple, and their blood would be likely to be the least contaminated. Judah, occupying the hill country, kept the stock relatively pure. With this tribe were the temple, the ark, and the least contaminated blood. Then to Jerusalem came the Babylonian invasions of 597 and 586 B.C. — a still more vigorous sifting of the seed, for the best of the population was carried into captivity. Here they remained for some two generations. The less religious became identified with the country in which they found themselves, but those in whom the fires of religious faith burned most brightly more and more withdrew within themselves, feeding the inner flames as they sacrificed worldly considerations for their faith. Then came the opportunity to return to the home of their fathers. Again the divining rod of divine judgment passes through the people and the elect — those possessing the most ardent racial loyalty, the preponderating religious interest — would be willing to encounter the hardships of the return, and endure the discouragements of the rehabilitation of the city of their fathers. Searching as was the sifting of the captivity and the return to select the peculiar wheat with which to sow the mountains of Judah, another test, scarcely less severe, is applied. After the return there had grown up the practice of intermarriage with the inhabitants of the land. The blood was being mixed. Then came Ezra and Nehemiah, compelling the faithful to put away their foreign wives that the ancient strain might remain uncontaminated.

Did ever the training of nature and experience act more effectively to bend the souls of a people toward religion? A strong tendency in the original stock, by a prolonged practice of inbreeding, becomes a dominant interest, the organizing center of the national life. Then by a rigid process of selection those in whom the religious passion and purpose are most pronounced are picked from the rest, closed about by strictest customs, and isolated that they may make their peculiar contributions to the race. Small wonder that this stock, so selected and trained, should flow into such splendor of genius. A tendency becomes a peculiarity, a peculiarity becomes a talent, and talent develops into genius. As Professor Huntington has so well stated, a people so severely sifted becomes 'biologically religious.'

The Puritan migration to New England offers a partial analogy. England was winnowed for some two generations for a certain kind of wheat to plant on this new continent. The strong-minded religious individualist was the pattern selected, and for about one hundred and fifty years was isolated in a rigorous country until a type had been formed and had multiplied. If, instead of a revolutionary war which opened a continent to the ambition of the sons of the Puritans for land and for an enlarged prosperity, there had fallen upon them another religious persecution from some foreign foe, forcing the strongest and most religious of the Puritan settlements to move further west solely in the interest of their faith, and if for over five hundred years they had been kept in subjection to a foreign power so that neither commerce, nor war, nor political discussion afforded an outlet for their energies, but the overshadowing interest was the church and its services, then their experiences would have been like those of the Jews and a permanent biological type would have been established. But Puritanism as an exclusive discipline was given a little less than two centuries before it was scattered and new motives gave life diversity. The Jews were subjected to a rigid selective process of not less than two thousand years, which so sifted the people as to produce Jesus and Paul and John. Let a group of artists isolate and discipline themselves for two millenniums, and it is probable that from them there would come art altogether unique and superior. By a system of inbreeding, segregation, persecution, and sifting, the religious bias of the first Abrahamic migration becomes a biological characteristic, a bent becomes a talent, and the talent flowers into a succession of geniuses. Nomadic tribes become a nation, and a nation becomes a church.

HOME TRAINING AND POLITICAL OPPRESSION

The genius of this people was shaped and preserved by inbreeding and rigid selection; it glowed and flamed because of the extraordinary discipline to which it was subjected in the homes of Israel. No people ever transmitted their history, their laws, their culture by a more faithful practice of home instruction. They took literally to heart the words of their law-giver: 'Thou shalt teach them diligently unto thy children, and shalt talk of them when thou sitteth in thy house, and when thou walkest by the way, and when thou liest down and when thou riseth up. And thou shalt bind them for a sign upon thine head, and they shall be for frontlets between thine eyes. And thou shalt write them upon the door-posts of thy house, and upon thy gate.' [1]

From the beginning the Hebrews were surrounded by enemies. There was the constant pressure of the tribes beyond Jordan, the Philistines competed with them for the possession of the land, they also fought among themselves. In those early days they were fighting with equals and their songs were songs of battle. Such conflicts would naturally produce such literature as

[1] Deut. 6:7–9.

Saul hath slain his thousands,
and David his ten thousands,[1]

the intense passion of Deborah's song, or the dirge of David over Saul and Jonathan. In this respect their experience and its literary expression were not unlike that of other nations of antiquity.

But a spiritual literature that will compel the attention of the world must issue from depths profounder than are stirred by sporadic border conflicts. Out of the deeps must come the cries which never cease their appeal. And the soul of Israel found God and uttered words of deathless power because it was awakened and kept awake by a series of tremendous crises. It is a fact of psychology, confirmed by history, that when an individual or a nation struggles desperately for a great end, the spiritual power of the individual or the nation becomes exalted; and when the spirit of man becomes exalted, it believes mightily in the worth of altruistic passion, it is convinced that the universe is on its side, that the right will not ultimately be defeated. It was out of extreme spiritual agony brought about by the stress of contemporary events, that the prophetic soul of Israel emerged and shone. Sorrow bravely met is a stimulus of a lofty faith.

Judah first felt the elemental emotions, asked the great questions, and listened intently for the Divine answer on account of the experiences of Assyrio-Babylonian invasions. Here was a foe who altogether outmatched her. She was helpless in the presence of a titanic power, and she was thrown back, not upon the strength of her own resources, but upon God. It was

[1] I Samuel 18:7.

this menace from the northeast that awoke the spirit of the prophets; it was the Babylonian captivity which gave the people the strictest spiritual discipline. There their poets learned to sing in a strange land and to brood on things to come. Out of the ferment of those sad days and the anguish of the Maccabean period came their Psalms of incomparable power. It is true that Proverbs, Ruth, Jonah, the 23d Psalm were written in quieter times. Emotion was 'recollected in tranquillity,' to use Wordsworth's description of poetry, but there must always be great living before there can be great literature. One cannot understand the nature of the Scriptures who fails to realize that they are the reaction of an intense and gifted people to eight hundred years of foreign oppression — Assyria, Babylon, Persia, Greece, Rome, all in succession laid a heavy hand upon this devoted people.

It is interesting in this connection to contrast the experience of Israel with that of Greece. Israel could not have a state, therefore she developed a church; she could not rule, therefore she wrote. The steady menace of an unconquerable foe influenced her genius as well as her politics. Israel was like a sapling sprouting under an enormous boulder: to reach the sunlight it must shape itself to the immovable mass above it. The huge rock is the explanation of the direction and form of the growing tree.

With Greece the training was altogether different. The sea lured her to commerce and fashioned her in hardy independence. When the might of Persia was turned against her she resisted successfully. Had the menace continued, the Greek states would have clung more closely together, their excessive individualism would have been restrained, and the discipline of danger would have developed the virtue of coöperation. The glory that was Greece would not have ripened so rapidly, although it probably would have longer endured. But the pressure was removed and the mind of the Greeks could express itself in freedom. Their superabundant energy, their zest of life, their faith in liberty and in themselves, carried them into nearly every domain of human interest and made them undisputed masters in many regions of thought and activity. Under the inspiration of liberty their extraordinary intellectual power unfolded itself in times of peace and abundance. But liberty degenerated into excessive individualism, which ultimately rent and destroyed a great people.

The genius of the Greeks flowered in the days of prosperity; the genius of the Hebrew revealed its splendor in adversity. One developed best when all external restraint was removed; the other when the pressure was most unbearable. Philosophy and art flourish in the secure days of peace; faith and hope are strongest when challenged by extreme danger. As religion grows out of a sense of dependence, the insecurity of the Hebrews, both from the uncertainty of the rains and the constant menace of empires with whom they could never successfully cope, was essential to their training as spiritual leaders of the world.

We have endeavored in this chapter to consider as concisely as possible the effects of heredity and environment in fashioning the destiny of the Hebrew people. The religious tendency of a branch of the

D

Semitic race was intensified and strengthened by a rigid process of inbreeding and selection until it became a passion, a genius. This unique folk lived a precarious life on a battle-swept bridge connecting two ambitious empires. But it was for the most part high, and mountains make for vigorous and sturdy men. Religion is nourished by a sense of dependence, and during most of their history this proud, fierce people was suppressed and humiliated by vast empires with whom they could not cope — Egypt, Assyria, Babylon, Persia, Greece, and Rome. Therefore they rested back on the purposes of the Eternal, and their vigorous natures found outlet in vision, in psalms, in prophecy. The brute strength which broke Moab, Ammon, the Philistines, and the Hittites could not obliterate Israel, for her life was in a spiritual realm of ideals and hopes which the swords of her enemies could not destroy.

It is proper now to consider in detail that quality of their genius which separated the Hebrews from other nations.

CHAPTER IV

THE MENTAL AND SPIRITUAL CHARACTERISTICS

WHICH DIFFERENTIATED THE HEBREWS FROM OTHER PEOPLES OF THEIR TIME

These people have a secret, they have discerned the way the world was going, and therefore they have prevailed.

MATTHEW ARNOLD

I will stir up thy sons, O Zion, against thy sons, O Greece.

Zechariah 9:13

Great things are done when men and mountains meet.

WILLIAM BLAKE

IT is a commonplace in modern thought that the mind of man has passed through stages of development. Like Milton's tawny lion, 'pawing to get free his hinder parts' from the imprisoning earth, the story of the mind is its struggle to emerge from primitive ignorance to selfhood and freedom. In this upward movement, the coming of the Hebrew people marks a distinct step. They were the first nation that achieved a sense of selfhood; the first that was organized around a structural idea.[1] This is a large claim; let us try to show that it is valid.

CONTRAST BETWEEN THE HEBREWS AND THE EGYPTIANS

The Egyptians preceded them, and the accomplishments of that people had been indeed marvelous. The

[1] Many of the ideas in this section were suggested by H. O. Taylor's *Ancient Ideals.*

excavations at Fayum have disclosed flint instruments which Professor Petrie claims belonged to a people living in the Nile Valley 12,000 B.C. The earliest fixed date in history, 4241 B.C., finds the Egyptian using a calendar of 365 days. By 4000 B.C. they had ascertained the uses of copper dug from Sinai; they had attained a stable government by 3400 B.C. Four hundred years later, by substituting papyrus for the clay tablet, and using a reed dipped in soot and water in place of a sharp engraving metal, they gave to writing a decided impetus. Their extraordinary practical genius is attested by the pyramids and by the ruins of those temples whose marvelous columns ranged in colonnades so profoundly impressed the Greeks. Yet with all their brilliant achievements the Egyptians never outgrew the Primitive Mind. Their genius was severely utilitarian and lacked the higher form of intelligence which weaves ideas together in their true relationships. Skillful in the arts, they were incapable of producing a noble literature: oldest of civilizations, they wrote no history. Egyptian stories are interesting because of their antiquity, but they are not conceived as a whole or shaped by the imagination. We find in their literature proverbs of great worldly wisdom, but the Egyptian mind reasoned poorly when it attempted to lift itself above material things into the supersensible. Although not lacking in ethical character, their religion was preoccupied with the life after death. This of itself would tend to give undue prominence to the priestly caste and to the formulas of magic. Righteousness was not enough: the soul must be protected by some magic formula to safely tread the halls of judgment. In her five thousand years of history Egypt produced only one man, judging from the writings which have come down to us, who possessed the higher philosophical mind. In the Pharaoh Ikhnaton spiritual insight and expression attained remarkable elevation. He actually broke for a time the seemingly invincible power of the priesthood of Amon, built a new capital at Amarna for the higher faith, and set noble standards of virtue. Had the soul of Egypt been rich in spiritual qualities, a succession of high-minded men, such as appeared in the prophets of Israel, would have given her spiritual freedom. But Egypt was too primitive and earthborn to live in that loftier atmosphere. No successor to Ikhnaton appeared and the people settled back contentedly into the old grooves. We must not forget that it was in Egypt that the monotheistic idea first found literary expression, but it died at birth in uncongenial surroundings. There were not in that land enough men of the higher consciousness to apprehend it, and to pass the vision on through subsequent generations.

The Egyptian never outgrew the primitive mind with its fears, its magic, its shrewd wisdom incapable of becoming philosophy or a spiritual faith. The constraint which held the multitudes and the generations together was the force of external conditions — social, geographical, political interests. No commonly apprehended ideal, or spiritual principle, organized the people into a whole. No inner loyalty to an ultimate truth made them one, or fashioned their civilization. They were held together like the waters of a dam, and not like the fibrous matter of a tree.

THE PRIMITIVE MIND OF THE ASSYRIANS AND BABYLONIANS

Contemporary with the Egyptian civilization and perhaps prior to it was the mighty Empire supported by the fluvial soil of the Tigris-Euphrates valley. How fertile the land was it is difficult for us now to conceive, but Theophrastus, who succeeded Aristotle as the head of the Peripatetic School of Philosophy, wrote in his 'History of Plants': 'In Babylon the wheat fields are regularly mown twice, and then fed off with beasts to keep down the luxuriance of the leaf; otherwise the plant does not run to ear. When this is done the return in lands that are badly cultivated is fifty-fold; while in those that are well farmed it is a hundred-fold.'[1]

So blighted is the country to-day that it is with difficulty that we can imagine its former productivity. But it supported an immense population whose eyes were ever turned toward the west as the land of their hopes. The Assyrians were a fiercely brutal race of warriors. Their art was characterized by coarse vigor and unimaginative energy, and in literature they had no intellectual or spiritual contribution to make to mankind. Their civilization need not detain us. Their southern neighbors, the Babylonians, were made of finer clay. Babylonian influence on the laws, the mythology, the literature of other nations was widespread. The men of Babylon, however, never passed beyond the primitive mind. They never grew mature enough to cast out magical incantations from religion, or to be obedient to a lofty spiritual ideal. Hammu-

[1] De Burgh: *The Legacy of the Ancient World*, p. 18.

rabi, indeed, was one of the world's great men, and his code set a lofty standard, yet no successor of comparable genius followed him. The stock was not fertile in men of the higher spiritual consciousness, and no one built upward from the mighty law-giver's foundations as the prophets built upon the work of Moses. The stories of the Babylonians were crude and brutal and their vast mythology had slight spiritual significance. In religion, ritualistic scrupulousness was quite as efficacious with heaven as moral integrity.

Like Egypt, Assyria and Babylon were wanting in that creative imagination which sees visions and clothes them in forms of beauty. The peoples were held together by physical necessity, and by political, geographical, and social bonds. When their material energy was overcome there was no remnant to preserve the soul of the people. They were a body without a unifying spirit.

Nations like individuals are ultimately judged, not by their material possessions but by their aspirations. The ideals of a people are the measure of their worth. It is significant that neither Egypt, nor Babylon, nor Assyria had structural ideas which, penetrating through the life of the people, fashioned a unified civilization. Such national constructive principles first appeared in history with the Hebrews and after them with the Greeks.

THE HEBREWS SPIRITUALLY MORE MATURE

That strange civilization which claimed to spring from the loins of Jacob was weak where Egypt and Babylonia were strong. The Hebrews were not builders like the inhabitants of the Nile Valley, nor possessed of the practical inventiveness of the people dwelling on the banks of the Euphrates; but they had in abundant measure what these older civilizations never attained. They exhibited an inner spiritual vitality which enabled them to create a literature of permanent world significance; they produced a notable succession of men of spiritual genius who traced unerringly the main thoroughfare along which the world is moving; they were prolific in poets of such sensitiveness and elevation of mind that they have sung the soul's loftiest aspirations and profoundest experiences in forms of ultimate beauty.

The mind of Egypt and Babylonia was confused when it looked above the material to the spiritual world. The higher consciousness of Israel was not confused. It perceived and laid hold of a principle which became organic in the nation's life. This has differentiated Israel from other nations; it created in those who came under its spell an inner loyalty which unified and sustained them when all political, social, and geographical bonds were destroyed. In the line of mental and spiritual development in which the western world claims heritage, the Hebrews were the first people to conceive an ideal of such practical and transcendent excellence that it moulded their history and still lived on when the political bonds of the people were loosened. A nation outgrows its childhood and comes to maturity when it attains to a sense of selfhood, and selfhood means a national consciousness, and a national will that recognizes governing idcals and chooses between them.

An example will illustrate what I am trying to enforce. The United States of America is something more than a multitude of people living together on a bit of earth continental in its reach. Geographical boundaries and political necessities do indeed bind us together, but our real and most glorious unity lies in a national spirit which permeates us as a people and shapes all of our institutions. That national spirit is the product of what Lincoln called a 'proposition,' or which others would denominate an 'ideal' or a 'principle.' This apprehended 'proposition,' this 'ideal,' this 'principle' is the constructive force which unifies a multitude of minds of many generations into a nation.

The three elements which are necessary to constitute a nation are territory, people, and an organizing national spirit. Land and population are not enough: a common spirit, born of loyalty to a common ideal, must subdue the multitude to an organic unity. The structural ideal which has given America a soul, which has shaped her history, which is written deep in her constitution and is the passion of her songs, is *individual liberty under the proper restraints of law;* the ideal that every man shall have a fair chance to be what his Creator intended him to be. It has never been perfectly realized, but its influence is the most potent force in our civilization. This spirit will live in memory and in literature when our physical fabric is disintegrated.

So Israel attained to that degree of spiritual and mental selfhood that she projected an ideal, obeyed it, lived by it, and bequeathed it to the world. In the early days she was much like the surrounding tribes. She had a national God who was her confidence in battle and whose favor she sought to keep by ritualistic honors. But the cry of her prophets marked the birth-pangs of an emerging truth. And this truth, held by her superior minds, became the life that preserved the people, and the vital element which made her literature enduring.

The feeble folk whose capital was Jerusalem were the first people to move upward from the primitive mind into selfhood; to be unified not by material bonds but by spiritual loyalties; to catch the vision of a truth so glorious that its splendor matured them into the greatness of the things of the spirit.

The truth which gave the first soul to a people was this: *the Supreme Power is a Personal Spirit, graciously and earnestly, through individuals and nations, especially Israel, carrying forward his purpose of the ethical redemption of mankind.* There are tremendous implications in this simple sentence. A people holding such a conception will have an historical consciousness; they will have an inextinguishable hope and a firm belief in the Providential ordering of events.

THE CAUSE OF THIS SUPERIORITY

Now it is important to ask how all this happened. What mental characteristic did this little people have which so differentiated them from the nations of their time, that they of all others first apprehended truths which so completely satisfy the religious needs of humanity? Religion was the absorbing interest of all the dominant peoples of the ancient world. Witness their temples, their art, their elaborate ritualistic systems. The Jew was not peculiar in this respect. All peoples were eager to find the true God and to enjoy his favor. What trait in this exclusive, limited, provincial people led them so inevitably to the ultimate truth in religion? What is the secret of their discovery of the true God?

There are two methods by which God may be known, and two only. The first is through nature and her processes and the second is through man and his experiences. The nations of antiquity habitually sought for the Divine in nature and her forces. They deified the energies, especially the reproductive energies, of the world about them. Their gods and goddesses were natural powers personified, some beautiful, some monstrous. Even Ikhnaton, the philosopher king of Egypt, poet and reformer, who was far above his age in spiritual elevation, took for his highest symbol of God the splendor of the sun's disk. No symbol could be nobler or more gloriously suggestive, with its ineffable radiance, its beneficent and all-pervading energies. In light the material world becomes so tenuous and finely spun that it almost dissolves into the spiritual. Yet light, for all its dazzling luster, is still a physical and impersonal symbol; it is the material order at its loftiest point, but still it is material. An impersonal symbol easily causes faith in a personal God to fade away, and upon a subpersonal God no religion can flourish. Moreover, the daily rounds of the sun suggest routine rather than an increasing purpose. The Primitive Mind, whether living on the hills of Samaria, or by the waters of Egypt and Babylon, unaccustomed to introspection, yet keenly aware of the passions of the flesh and the besetting forces of the world, would naturally think of God through the powers which were most in evidence. Therefore the popular representations of the gods were forms suggestive of natural forces. The superior minds of every people doubtless rose above these crude conceptions, but in Israel there was a succession of spiritually minded men who kept the torch aloft and made the loftier views to prevail. The prophetic spirit of Israel was not unmindful of nature as a revelation of the Most High; the heavens declared the glory of God, the clouds were his chariot, and the flames of fire his ministers, but when it most earnestly sought the face of God, it turned not outwardly to nature, but inwardly upon itself. Not in the earthquake, wind, or fire, but by a still, small voice Jehovah spoke. It interpreted God, not predominantly through natural symbols, but through man's own moral and spiritual nature. To the loftiest consciousness of Israel God was intensely personal, he was a Spirit. A bull-calf, representing the productive energies of nature, might be a sufficient symbol to the common mind; but the prophets heard a voice speaking in the depths of their consciences, demanding purity, justice, and mercy. Recognizing the inner compulsion as divine, they conceived of the Eternal in the terms of their own highest being. Finding him in the spirit, they thought of him as Spirit. Not nature, but man was the chosen and habitual avenue through which the spiritual genius of Israel sought to know God. And the people responded. They learned, as other nations did not, that the authentic word of the Lord is the burden laid upon superior minds and hearts, rather than the half-articulate cries of frenzied oracles.

THEREFORE THE HEBREW WROTE HISTORY

Finding God's revelation of himself in man, of course the Hebrew was greatly concerned with man's experiences; for man's experiences, seen over long ranges of time, would make the clearest disclosures of God's character and purpose. Therefore he would preserve the records of the past, and would ultimately develop an historical sense. Ask an American why he believes in God and he will give you arguments drawn from philosophical reasoning, or what he considers such. Not so the true son of Israel. He would point instantly to history. He would say: 'Jehovah led our fathers out of Egypt, he gave us this goodly land, through us he will establish judgment among all nations. We know there is a God because we see a living hand in the deliverance of our people. He smote the oppressor and gave liberty to the weak, therefore we know him to be just and merciful.' Because of this deep-rooted belief that the Most High is best known through a process of human experience the Hebrews have given us the only continuous and interesting history that has come from ancient times. 'No people,' writes Renan, 'can boast with confidence of possessing so complete a body of history or archives so regularly kept.' To the Hebrews must be given the honor of first conceiving the value of the orderly arrangement of the records of the past, both for wisdom and for inspiration. Out of Israel came the first great historical writings, for history in their thought was a manifestation of God.

I am not so ignorant of the literature of Egypt and of Babylonian and Assyrian civilization as to be unaware that this generalization — that the Hebrew found God through man and his experiences while surrounding nations looked for him in nature and her process — is a very broad one to which there are many exceptions. Devout souls in every people found refuge in a deity compassionate and righteous, the multitudes of Israel turned very easily to the worship of Baal and the nature gods. But it is undoubtedly true that there was among the sons of Jacob a mighty succession of spiritual and ethical geniuses whose distinguishing characteristic was their habit of interpreting what is highest in the universe by what was highest in themselves. They thought of the Eternal through the noblest symbol they possessed — the personal spirit of man at its best. Therefore they developed a more ethical and spiritual religion than the stronger nations about them. Finding God in man and in the experiences of man they wrote history, and discerning God in history they turned toward the future with expectation of the fulfillment of a divine purpose.

THEREFORE THE HEBREW HAD HOPE

This conviction that the Eternal reveals himself through man and his experiences not only gave to the prophetic spirit of Israel a sense of the value of history, it also gave significance to the future. If God's providential ordering was made manifest in the days gone by, it was because he was working towards a determined end; there is a far-off divine event; something better further on. This brave, hopeful forward look is not characteristic of either Confucius or his contemporary Buddha. But a sense of the future was woven into the traditions of the Hebrew people. When sin came into the world the promise was given that the seed of the woman should bruise the serpent's head. Through Abraham all the nations of the earth were to be blessed. Two centuries before Confucius or Buddha, Isaiah in Jerusalem had perceived that a divine plan was unfolding through national events, but it was reserved for the Second Isaiah to adequately and magnificently state a philosophy of history. Afterward, in Daniel, we find a most powerful visualization of it in the image depicting several dynasties, whose feet of clay were smitten by the stone which grew to be a mountain filling the earth.

There are hints of the progress of humanity both in Æschylus and the Greek philosophers, but it was the Jews who fixed in the thoughts of men the idea of a moral goal which explains the movements of history and the tragedies of individual experience. 'These people,' said Matthew Arnold, 'have a secret, they have discerned the way the world was going and therefore they have prevailed.' No other literature of either ancient or modern times is so radiant with hope and dominated by it as is the literature of the Hebrews.

THEREFORE THE HEBREW BELIEVED IN A WORLD PROVIDENCE

Out of this consciousness of historic values and this forward look grew the firm conviction of this people in the progressive providential government of the world. From them we have received it. Our faith that God overrules the affairs of men for the accomplishment of his own purposes did not come to us from Babylonia, or from Egypt, or from Confucius who looked for a prince to restore the past, or from Buddha who would annihilate the future; it did not come to us as a heritage from Greece, where Homer taught the interest of Zeus in the victory of the Greeks over the Trojans, but gave no hint of a divine purpose which was using them to carry forward a larger plan for mankind; it came to us in direct line from Israel, and her history from Abraham to Christ, and from Christ to the present, is our strongest proof of its validity.

THE GREAT SUCCESSION

And Israel was able to make this bequest because she was extraordinarily prolific in men of unique spiritual endowments. Her genius did not blossom in isolated individuals and then fade. Her great men came in groups and in a steady succession for many centuries. They wrote down their vision and the people were sufficiently awake to cherish their writings as sacred. Moreover, these men conceived a personal and individual God more intensely than was true of the philosophers and thinkers of other peoples. They heard his voice, they felt his presence, his hand was heavy upon them. In every nation creative minds have framed a conception of the Ultimate Reality as both spiritual and benignant. Israel's uniqueness lies in the vividness of the impression and the tenacity with which it was held by a great body of spiritually gifted men. The stock was strong yet sensitive, enabling its representative men to believe with a fierce energy, almost a fury of faith, which glowed hot and glowed long. Their passionate intensity made it possible for the elect remnant to rise superior to all misfortune and persevere in the face of every disaster. Ardor made religion vital, a superior ethical sense kept it from going the way of the cults of Moab and Ammon.

CONTRAST WITH THE GREEKS

Let us still further make clear to our minds the distinctive characteristics of the Hebrew people by contrasting them with the Greeks, their successors and rivals in influence upon the world.

Somewhere in the second millennium before Christ, fair-haired warriors of the Indo-European races issued from the North into the peninsula which is now called Greece. Spreading over the islands of the Ægean, they came into vital contact with the advanced civilization of Crete. The mingling of the crude blond barbarians with the more cultured Minoan races resulted in a breed finer than either. By the time that Israel was cleft in twain by the secession of the northern tribes (937 B.C.) the Greek people and race were well established in the Greek peninsula and the islands of the Ægean Sea. Of these two remarkable people — the Hebrew and the Greek — the former came earlier to maturity.

As Israel was profoundly influenced by the mountains, so the Greek was influenced by the sea. It was the sea that bound the different city-states together; it was the sea, thick-studded with islands, which lured the Greeks to adventure and formed them into a virile and conquering people. When the Babylonian legions were beleaguering Jerusalem (597 B.C.) the Greeks had extended their civilization to the Euxine, to Sicily, to North Africa, and had wrenched the trade of the Eastern Mediterranean from the Phœnicians. Soon after the second temple was completed on Zion, the Persians invaded Greece. Marathon and Salamis so stirred the soul of the fierce democracy of Athens that immediately her genius expanded into the fullness of its splendor. For about a century and a half the glory that was Greece shone in its perfection; then came Alexander, the attempt of Hellenism to supplant Judaism in Jerusalem itself, the revolt of the Maccabees, and the conquest of Greece by Christianity.

We have dwelt thus long upon the outlines of Greek history because from Athens as well as from Jerusalem flowed a large stream of influence which affects modern civilization. With the coming of these two great peoples the human mind cast off many of its primitive habits of thought and moved up into higher regions of activity. With them the new world began. The two had some characteristics in common, but their divergences were radical and numerous. We understand each better by contrasting it with the other. These two people, whose histories were so nearly contemporaneous but not commingling, were alike in that mental and spiritual vitality which makes new paths for the mind. Like the Hebrews, the Greeks also came under a unifying ideal. Although they lived under separate and often intensely antagonistic governments, they cherished a loyalty to common cultural ideas. In spite of bitter rivalries, their unity was recognized through a common outlook on life. Greece had a soul which for generations held together her discordant members.

But the divergences between the two people were more numerous and pronounced than their similarities. The words of Zachariah 9:13, 'I will stir up thy sons, O Zion, against thy sons, O Greece,' represent a recognized dissimilarity. Together they were the earliest civilizations of the world to be shaped by a constructive ideal; but that of the Hebrew was righteousness, and that of the Greek was truth with beauty. The Greek fixed his mind upon humanity and its multitudinous concerns. The moral aspects of life did not exclusively interest him; his mind ranged largely over every domain — art, literature, politics, philosophy, science. Nothing was alien to him. His motto was 'Know thyself,' and to know himself he sought to know his world. His ideal was the attainment of the fullness of life.

The Hebrew turned his thought toward God and his ways. His chief concern was to be right with the Eternal. Consequently he revered authority. His God was the God of Abraham, Isaac, and Jacob. The law was sacred. The Greek, on the contrary, interested in man and the fullness of life, was the first to realize the worth of individual liberty and to guarantee it in his institutions. He knew that the human spirit must work according to its own law, if the imagination is to express itself in art or the intellect in philosophy. The full life means the free life. Because in Athens the human mind was phenomenally free 'to follow knowledge like a sinking star beyond the utmost bound of human thought' it moved rapidly and accomplished amazing results in a short time. Poets with their inspiration, instead of priests with their dogma and formulæ, were the leaders of the spiritual life of the people. Being a humanist, the Greek considered it the supreme wisdom to keep his head clear, to think straight. By reason he hoped to subdue his world and achieve knowledge. The Hebrew prayed for a clean heart to give him understanding. Reason to him was an unsuitable instrument, for 'out of the heart are the issues of life.' Truth came to him through revelation, not by the searchings of the mind. His motto was not 'know thyself,' but 'know thy God.' The Greek would elevate man by enlightening him; the Hebrew by changing his heart. The one stressed knowledge, the other love. Indeed, the notable failure of the classical world was its blindness to the true value of the instincts and the emotions. The Hebrew went more deeply into human nature and released a mightier power for redeeming universal humanity when he selected love rather than knowledge as the center of his attention. The elect few may be governed by reason, but the vast majority of men are controlled by those emotional forces which lie below the conscious intellect. Failing to rightly assess the value of the instincts and the emotions, the Greek failed to know himself. 'Nothing too much' is a pallid and ineffective philosophy compared with one demanding love to God and man with the whole heart. The genius of Hellas, being concerned with all the interests of man, is rich in variety. The literature of the Hebrews, concerned only with God and his purpose, is so severely unified that its books early became a book. The Greek turned the feet of humanity into the paths by which the world is conquered and its beauty released. The Hebrew, by persuading men to look upward and forward, led them into the way everlasting.

CHAPTER V

THE LITERARY QUALITIES OF THE HEBREW MIND

Whoever can express *himself* with the full force of unconscious sincerity will be found to have uttered something ideal and universal.

JAMES RUSSELL LOWELL

Perfect sincerity and transparency make a great part of beauty, as in dewdrops, lakes, and diamonds.

HENRY D. THOREAU

WE have seen in the preceding chapter the mental characteristics by which the Hebrews attained their faith — they interpreted God through man and his spiritual experiences. This caused them to think of the Eternal as a personal spirit; it also interested them in history and gave them the expectation of something better further on. Thus they arrived at their truth, but by what magic did this primitive people write such wonderful literature? How did a group of lowly folk in the mountains of Judea set a standard of the sublime in letters which more cultivated ages have failed to equal? How did men so early in the world's history give such ultimate expression to profound truths? How did a people so exclusive write a universal book? Spiritual truth never has been stated elsewhere or since in forms so imperishable.

What qualities of mind and soul made them such consummate literary artists? We must recognize. first of all, that religion of itself, because it brings man face to face with the Eternal, and includes life's most significant experiences, is a powerful incentive to elevated and emotional expression. Religion by deepening the soul of man has been the prolific and fostering mother of music, architecture, letters, drama, and all the arts. Atheism writes no hymns; agnosticism does not burst into song; skepticism constructs no institutions. The singing and building eras of the world are periods of stalwart belief. A noble faith, caught in the tragic experiences of the world, may be expected to utter elemental emotions and final truths in sentences which cannot be improved. Assuming, then, that religion is a powerful stimulant to the emotional and imaginative nature, let us examine more in detail those qualities of the Hebrew mind which help us to understand its literature.

THE INTUITIVE MIND

There are three quite clearly marked stages in the development of the racial mind. In the first, primitive man looked directly at the objects and facts about him and felt them. To express what he saw and what he felt he used sounds and symbols which best conveyed his meaning. His language was in consequence vivid, picturesque, simple, and, being close to nature, was concrete. Such freshly minted words, not yet worn by much usage, hold the original picture in bold relief. They fulfill excellently Milton's statement that the words of poetry should be 'simple. sensuous, passionate.'

In the second stage the mind reflects on facts and experiences. Behind the object or the deed it perceives a meaning; it acts intuitively and largely through the imagination.

In the third stage the mind unites facts and experiences into a system; it sees not only objects and their meaning, but joins thought with thought and discerns their relationship. With interest in ideas and their relationship philosophy is born, and abstract words creep into the language.

The Hebrews in Old Testament times passed through the first and entered the second stage; they never attained the third. In their Scriptures there is no philosophy or metaphysics, no linking of thought to thought in a reasoned argument. The frequent 'therefores' of their writings are used to enforce a moral obligation, not to draw a logical conclusion. The sentences are connected by the ever recurring word 'and.' Every reader of the English Bible has noticed the frequency of this conjunction. Perhaps he has also noted the almost complete absence in the Old Testament of qualifying clauses. Affirmations are unmodified by subordinate parts of the sentence. Instead, sentences are continually strung together by the connective 'and.' This is a mark of a mind that works intuitively; seeking clearly one thing after another, but not given to analysis or subtle reasoning. Throughout the Old Testament the Hebrew mind is distinctively intuitional in its operations. The Jew saw facts and their significance; it was the Greek who, in the Western world, was first concerned with ideas and their relationship. In later history the Jewish strain has shown its capacity for philosophical reasoning in Spinoza, and its ability to think abstractly in

Einstein. But intuition, not ratiocination, was the characteristic of the Hebrew mind in Bible times. This is best seen by contrasting Jesus, who was the fulfillment of the Hebrew genius, with Socrates, the exponent of the Greeks. Before he drank the hemlock, Socrates reasoned about the nature of the soul and of the life hereafter. Being a philosopher he reached conclusions by argumentation. Jesus, in the account we have in the Synoptics, never arrived at truth by philosophical deductions. His mind quickly perceived truth without conscious reasoning. He saw, he affirmed. His statements lie side by side as jewels in a casket; they are never strung together in logical sequence or set in any system of thought. He was the Son of Man, but he thought with a brain which was Hebrew in its characteristics. He was the fulfillment of the literary genius of his people as well as the fulfillment of their prophetic spirit. Not until we come to Paul do we find the Oriental mind working along the lines of Western thought. In his epistles he argues with the subtlety of the Greek and the passion of the Hebrew. The writer of the Fourth Gospel casts his prologue into the mould of Greek philosophy, represents Jesus debating with the Pharisees and unfolds a thought through a long paragraph in a manner utterly foreign to the method of the first three Gospels. In the Epistle to the Hebrews the ideas are developed in clauses of considerable length and are related to one another by appropriate transitions. Luke, in writing the stories of the life of Christ, weaves together with artistic skill his sentences so as to give the desired effect. In these four writers the shadow of the Western world falls upon the pages of the Scripture. The insights of the Jew are here shaped by mental habits of Greek training. Paul in a single sentence truly characterized the distinction between the two peoples: 'Seeing that Jews ask for signs, and Greeks seek after wisdom.'[1] The Greek mind was naturally philosophical and sought truth through reasoning; the Jewish mind was direct in its operations, and must either see truth at a glance or not at all.

This intuitive character, seen in sentence structure, is just as clearly evidenced in the complete works of any individual author, excepting the writers of short stories. No one of the voluminous Hebrew writers conceived his work as a whole and shaped it into an artistic unity. Such unity is not in Job nor in Isaiah, much less in inferior men. Their works are all glimpses at truth, flashes of insight. No one would think of attaching a poem on the strength of Behemoth to 'Paradise Lost,' or of inserting a poem on the shortness of life into 'Macbeth.' The great English writers have an artistic unity and imaginative form which discourage accretions from alien sources. But Hebrew literature is fragmentary, it is a grouping of insights, and therefore easily lends itself to alien additions, perplexing to critics.

This mental characteristic is stamped on the book as a whole. The Bible is a book of glimpses into the Divine Secret, not a complete disclosure of the Divine Plan. It is a book of flashes of revelation, not a full solution of the Divine Riddle. The Hebrew saw

[1] I Corinthians 1:22.

truth; he could neither harmonize nor explain it. Had it been otherwise, instead of a living Bible we should have had another outdated philosophy. God was not found by the searchings of reason, but in the facts of history. This sententious habit of the intuitive mind explains many features of the Bible. It makes it an inexhaustible treasure-house of texts, for it expresses profound truths in the smallest possible compass. It gives a tone of authority which is lacking in a reasoned conclusion. The prophets speak with certainty as those who know. The mind that perceives intuitively is easily persuaded of direct inspiration, the vision is so clear, the inner voice so insistent. This emboldens them to say 'Thus saith the Lord,' and even to represent the Most High as speaking directly through them, thus creating a literary method of incalculable power, which has been lost to the prophets of to-day. No sane writer of these times would dare speak for the Almighty with such absolute conviction.

If the Hebrew mind was intuitive in its operations, it was not wide in its interests. It was only in the sphere of religion that it saw more clearly than others. The Hebrew had no bent for the plastic arts; the scientific habit was alien to him; as he could not reason abstractly, the delights of philosophy could not be his; unlike the Roman he had no talent for political life, nor capacity for military organization or discipline. Even his poetic gifts, in which he was preëminent, gave of their best only under the influence of the religious feelings. His God was a jealous God who valued only one aspect of life.

PECULIARITIES OF IMAGINATION

The great Hebrew writers had the Oriental imagination at its best — penetrative, creative, colorful; not luxuriant, but intense. It did not linger long on the loveliness of nature: it moved eagerly and directly to God, the source of all — 'Seek him that maketh the Pleiades and Orion and turneth the shadow of death into the morning, and maketh the day dark with night.'[1] The genial imaginative sympathy which gave Shakespeare delight in all the varied aspects of life was not theirs. Neither did their imagination run easily to the graceful sports of fancy. Shakespeare, in the exuberance of fantasy, exclaims:

> Night's candles are burnt out, and jocund day
> Stands tiptoe on the misty mountain-tops...[2]

Far more soberly the Hebrew prophet saw the morning break: 'The sun of righteousness... with healing in his wings.'[3] Imagination so solemn will find its congenial domain in religious poetry.

They thought, as poets do, in pictures. Ideas never seemed to come to them as abstractions, neither did they express them in general terms; they thought in figures and spoke in metaphors. Therefore they taught moral truths by analogy and parables which the imagination could lay hold upon and the memory retain. Being a Hebrew of the Hebrews, our Lord spoke readily in similes — 'The Kingdom of heaven is like a grain of mustard seed,' 'it is like a net,' 'it is like leaven'; or in metaphors — 'Ye are the light'

[1] Amos 5:8. [2] *Romeo and Juliet*, Act III, Scene 5.
[3] Malachi 4:2.

of the world,' 'ye are the salt of the earth.' Not being given to philosophical thinking, the Hebrew spoke in words concrete, definite, and picturesque, and concrete nouns joined to active verbs give to style masculine vigor. The Hebrew language, Herder reminds us, 'is a sea of verbs where action ever rolls surging into action.'

Here are a few examples of ideas put with the utmost possible force. Instead of declaring, 'Exact justice must be done,' the law says, 'Eye for eye, tooth for tooth.' [1] How vividly is the fact of heredity stated: 'The fathers have eaten sour grapes, and the children's teeth are set on edge.' [2] A prosaic mind might speak of the immutability of character; the poet-prophet exclaimed: 'Can the Ethiopian change his skin, or the leopard his spots?' [3] 'Thou shalt labor' is a poor substitute for 'In the sweat of thy face shalt thou eat bread.' A preacher quite recently took for his text: 'They that take the sword shall perish with the sword,' [4] and then he said, 'That is, violence is suicidal.' Thus he changed a thought vividly expressed in concrete form, into language abstract and much less forcible. The very life of literature is the power to put truth in expressive imagery. Shakespeare's pages are crowded with figures of speech — 'Out, out, brief candle!' 'All the world's a stage, and men and women merely players!' When the troubled soul of Hamlet leaves his body, Horatio puts the darkness of death, the victory of the spirit, the compassion of God, the joy of heaven, in an im-

[1] Exodus 21:24. [2] Ezekiel 18:2.
[3] Jeremiah 13:23. [4] Matthew 26:52.

mortal picture: 'Good night, sweet prince, and flights of angels sing thee to thy rest.' These words fulfill precisely Coleridge's definition of poetry, as 'the best words in the best order'; they express in perfect form a great hope. But, 'Yea, though I walk through the valley of the shadow of death' is not inferior and voices a more common mood. It has been said that one might as well try to wrench the club from the hand of Heracles as a word from one of Homer's lines. This is even more true of innumerable passages of the Bible. Did not a Jew nearly three thousand years ago put the world's yearning for permanent peace into an imperishable picture, shaped in a single sentence, 'They shall beat their swords into plowshares and their spears into pruning hooks'?[1] If a Hebrew wished to declare the moral uses of great men, he would call before the memory a scene whose every detail was associated with emotions of safety and comfort. 'And a man shall be as an hiding place from the wind, and a covert from the tempest; as rivers of water in a dry place, as the shadow of a great rock in a weary land.'[2] And again, 'The mountains (that is, great men) shall bring peace to the people.'[3] This satisfies Huxley's definition: 'A good style is the vivid expression of clear thinking.'

VISUALIZED EMOTIONS

Furthermore, the Hebrew vitalized his writings by describing emotions through pictures of the physical appearance of one experiencing the emotions. He revealed the feeling by showing how the sufferer

[1] Isaiah 2:4. [2] Isaiah 32:2. [3] Psalms 72:3.

looked. Instead of saying, 'The man was disappointed,' he said, 'His countenance fell.' He enforced the notion of despair by painting a picture of one in great physical distress. For example, in Psalms 69:1–3, 'Save me, O God; for the waters are come in unto my soul. I sink in deep mire, where there is no standing; I am come unto deep waters, where the floods overflow me. I am weary of my crying; my throat is dried; mine eyes fail while I wait for my God.'[1] Shakespeare uses the same method in the famous scene where the ghost speaks to Hamlet. In place of the declaration, 'I will send horror into thy soul,' he piles up the visible symptoms of horror:

> But that I am forbid
> To tell the secrets of my prison-house,
> I could a tale unfold whose lightest word
> Would harrow up thy soul; freeze thy young blood;
> Make thy two eyes, like stars, start from their spheres;
> Thy knotted and combined locks to part,
> And each particular hair to stand on end,
> Like quills upon the fretful porpentine.[2]

The absence of drama in Hebrew literature has often been noted. But if these ancient writers produced no formal drama, they were not wanting in dramatic imagination. Ideas were personified and uttered their voice. Wisdom is a woman crying in the street. Mercy and truth meet together: righteousness and peace kiss each other. The mountains and the hills break forth into singing and all the trees of the field clap their hands. The Hebrew not only per-

[1] Gardiner: *The Bible as English Literature*, p. 116.

[2] Act I, Scene 5.

sonified external nature and the objects of his thought, he had a habit of personifying his moods and of carrying on a dialogue within himself. Soliloquy was a very favorite device. The temptation of our Lord [1] is a conspicuous example of this. We are not to suppose that Satan came in visible presence and conversed with Jesus. It is not thus that men are tried. The debate was within the Master's innermost spirit and is related dramatically.

Our English writers often employ this method. But the Hebrew had a practice of making his characters think aloud, which is not according to our custom. They 'say in their heart' very plainly what their motives are. Where a modern author would analyze the purposes and feelings of a character, the Biblical writers make him state dramatically what is in his mind. Thus the rich man in the parable reasoned with himself and said: 'Soul, thou hast much goods laid up for many years.' [2] After the flood Jehovah 'said in his heart, I will not again curse the ground,' [3] and Saul is made to state clearly a motive which he probably would not have admitted to himself.[4] In the book of Job, the friends speak consistently with their characters, and the voice of God out of the whirlwind gives the poem such dramatic power that, were it not for its lack of action, it might be classified as drama. No Hebrew writer may have been equipped to elaborate an extensive tragedy. Perhaps he was too sincere and intense. But the narratives of the Old Testament are replete with dra-

[1] Matthew 4:1–10.
[2] Luke 12:16–19.
[3] Genesis 8:21.
[4] I Samuel 18:17.

matic scenes, such as the soul struggle of Moses in the Tent of Meeting,[1] Saul in the witch's cave at Endor,[2] and the portrayal of the character and activities of Elijah.

Certainly the Hebrew had extraordinary ability in stating the significant in dramatic form, but his dramas were short, for he was eager to express the heart of the matter. Yet on the whole his intense emotion did not permit him to disengage his imagination from personal feeling and enter sympathetically into opposing minds. He did not easily see all sides of a question. It was just this lack of sympathetic imagination which made him so fiercely intolerant. Yet what abundant materials for great tragedy his history afforded! What tremendous effects Æschylus could have produced with Saul for a theme! The stalwart youth suddenly crowned King of Israel, and in the end dying by his own sword after a night of terror in a witch's cave. Then there was the sin of David with Bathsheba whose fateful results occupy the greater part of Second Kings. Again, there is Rizpah keeping the carrion birds from the bodies of the seven sons of Saul.[3] Even though he saw events and persons dramatically, the main reason why the Jew did not write tragedy was because he did not look at life tragically. To him God's ways may be strange, but they are right and good. 'He knoweth the way that I take,' exclaimed Job, 'and when he hath tried me, I shall come forth as gold.'[4] 'Where sin abounded, grace did much more abound,'[5] asserts

[1] Exodus 33:12 ff. [2] I Samuel 28. [3] II Samuel 21:10.
[4] Job 23:10. [5] Romans 5:20.

Paul. The cry of despair is often heard in the opening of the Psalms, but in the end there is peace and the joy of faith. No people who see the black clouds of trouble against a sky bright with divine benignity can linger in tragedy. The Greek poets could write their powerful dramas because to them the background of life was dark with inexorable fate.

The chief note of the Hebrew religion was rejoicing. There was one day of atonement with its fasting and sacrifice; offsetting this there were some twenty days of festival joy and some forty other days commemorating God's work in delivering his people.

> Weeping may tarry for the night,
> But joy cometh in the morning.[1]

This was their faith.

In this connection it is worthy of note that Hebrew literature, its noble prophecies, its more spiritual Psalms, its blazing apocalyptic visions, its supreme words of comfort and hope, grew directly out of tragedy and disaster. In this it contrasts quite strongly with the literature of the Greeks, which was for the most part the fruitage of prosperity. Out of the victory of the Greeks over the Trojans came the songs of Homer; after the defeat of Persia came the brilliant day of Æschylus, Sophocles, Euripides; in the fullness of Athens' glory Socrates questioned and Plato philosophized with a mind serene. Even Demosthenes spoke when there was a chance for victory; destruction was not inevitable.

More than any other literature in the world the

[1] Psalms 30:5.

Hebrew is the outgrowth of tragic experience. The fiercer the storm, the deeper it sent its roots downward to lay hold of the foundations of the world. The genial sunlight was not its inspiration. Poets and prophets wrote their great works down in the depths near the elemental flames.

TRUTH CONCEIVED EMOTIONALLY AND PRACTICALLY

There is another mental characteristic of the Biblical writers which claims attention: they conceived truth emotionally for practical ends. Their perceptions passed quickly through their minds to the heart and will, and there glowed ardently. The Greek, on the contrary, could contemplate truth far more temperately. To him it was a proposition of the reason and was open to debate, but to the Jew 'a truth to the reason was a law to the will.' It was the word of Jehovah; it came to him as a direct command. It was not something to be contemplated, it must be obeyed. Cicero, trained in the method of the Greeks, speaks thus:

> Right reason is the true law, congruent with nature, universally diffused, unchanging, everlasting; which imperatively commands to duty and forbids fraud; which nevertheless, while it requires rectitude, leaves me free to obey or disobey. No authority exists to repeal this law, or to detract anything from it.[1]

These truths which the Roman states philosophically the Hebrew puts in the form of sententious command:

[1] *De Republica*, Liber III.

I am God and there is none else.... Be ye holy, for I am holy.... Behold I set before you life and death, therefore choose life.

Feeling truth thus keenly and personally, his speech would have a natural rhythm. Great writing, whether in prose or poetry, is always informed with the subtle and pervasive music of genuine emotion which charms the senses and makes an easier pathway for truth to enter the mind. When the intellect only is expressing thought, the sentences may be clear, but they will be unmusical. Touch the heart and into utterance steals a penetrating melody. Thus the prophets spoke in natural poetry, and eloquence turned easily into rhapsody. When Paul is framing an argument, his style is without beauty; touch his feelings — as in the thirteenth and fifteenth chapters of I Corinthians — and his sentences shape themselves into delicate cadences; heart speaks to heart, and the truth glows with unfamiliar light. Lucidity characterized all of Lincoln's utterances, but his words came charged with a new energy when his emotions were deeply stirred, as at Gettysburg and in the Second Inaugural. The Hebrews wrote literature because they put so much of the heart element into their work. And this natural rhythm of deep feeling has, by rare good fortune, passed over into the English Bible. The chief criticism of our modern versions is that the translators so often obtain novelty of expression by destroying the emotional value of the thought.

CONDITIONS MODIFYING HEBREW LITERATURE

Let us now turn for a moment to consider some of the conditions favorable to literary excellence under which the Hebrew writers worked.

All great art requires that the artist look directly at his object and express his own impression in his own way. In so far as he is imitating some other craftsman, or is governed by a tradition that is not entirely congenial to him, he will become insincere and will lack originality. One conspicuous reason why the Greeks and the Hebrews were such consummate writers in their own distinctive domains was that they looked directly on life. They were early in the field; and as Lowell has wittily remarked: 'It is the early risers of literature who gather phrases with the dew on them.' Whatever mists of tradition, or memory of standards alien to their own, may have at first dimmed their sight were soon brushed away. After the Persian War, the Greeks forgot Egypt and saw with their own eyes and expressed their own conceptions. So the Old Testament writers had few models to copy. No commanding literature had preceded them to make them slavishly imitative of methods foreign to their own genius. They established their own standards, told their own stories in their own way, sang of what interested them, wrote their own history, and believed in a religion which grew up on their own soil and was the expression of their own habit of looking at their world. This fresh, direct outlook on life and experience gives to these early writers a spontaneity and perfect sincerity which go far in explaining their attractiveness. When one expresses his own insights and feelings with the full force of utter sincerity, he is in the way of saying what is true and universal.

A modern writer works under serious handicaps in this respect. He has behind him the notions and literary conventions of many peoples. His ideas come to him from many sources; many standards obtrude themselves into his thought, making him critical and self-conscious. The established traditions of centuries serve to repress the spontaneous workings of his own brain and heart. Before him is the immense body of literature from Chaucer to Kipling; beyond that is Dante and the Middle Ages; beyond shines the grandeur of Rome and the glory of Greece. If he writes on religion, he is not looking into his own heart and transcribing at first hand what God has done for him, using forms of expression fashioned by the experiences of his race. His faith is borrowed, and its facts and beliefs come from another continent and from a remote civilization. If his subject is philosophy, the ideas of the thinkers of thirty centuries restrain him from originality. And if he is a poet, the melody of many singers mingles with his own notes.

The genius of the Hebrew was weighed down by no such ponderous inheritance; he looked with young eyes upon his own experience and that of his fathers. He could be original because he was the first in the field.

> Who can see the green earth any more
> As she was by the sources of time?
> Who thinks as they thought,
> The tribes that roamed on her breast,
> Her vigorous sons? [1]

[1] Matthew Arnold: *The Future.*

Vigor also would be given to his writing from the fact that he was looking on a small world. No poet to-day could sing the praises of London or of Boston as the Jew sang of Jerusalem. His vision would be too comprehensive, his standards of comparison too numerous. He could not persuade himself that his city was the center of the world, nor that the purposes of the Almighty flow exclusively through the politics of his municipality. But such a conviction gives lyrical intensity to one's words.

The prevailing theme of the Scriptures — God and his purposes — gives to its pages the grand manner which Matthew Arnold declares characterizes all the superior books. High seriousness tends naturally to simplicity of speech. One speaking earnestly upon a topic of eternal importance is not loquacious, neither does he use high-sounding words or artificial ornamentations. When a grave and lofty soul is profoundly moved it speaks simply and usually with restraint. A great editor once advised a young reporter, who had taken a column and a half to describe a small fire, to study the first chapter of Genesis in order to learn brevity. The parables picture profoundest truths in a few sentences. One of the most significant books of the Old Testament, Jonah, contains only 1328 English words.

This direct utterance of sincere and sensitive minds which felt the pressure of momentous themes goes far in explaining how a primitive people could write such marvelous literature. Many of these writers had style in the sense in which Arnold used that much abused word: 'Style, in my sense of the word, is a peculiar recasting and heightening, under a certain condition of spiritual excitement, of what a man has to say, in such a manner as to add dignity and distinction to it.' One source of the literary power of the Bible lies in the fact that lofty and gifted men, under the spiritual excitement kindled by contemplation of tremendous truths, spoke with a seriousness and deep emotion which recast and heightened the simple words of the plain people into sentences of unforgettable beauty. Clear thought, simple words, striking imagery, genuine emotion: these are the gold of literature.

It is interesting to note further that although these men used their instruments so artistically, yet nowhere does the artistic temperament, with its vagaries, its excessive egotism, its sensitiveness, obtrude itself. The writers are too intently concerned with God to long fix their minds on their own hurts.

We shall deal more at length in subsequent pages with the technique of the Hebrew literary art, but we wish to close this chapter by mentioning two methods which are fundamental in giving power to the book.

First, these writers for the most part practiced in their writings the principle which came to its fullness in the incarnation. The word had flesh: truth was incarnated in individuals. They did not state opinions, but told the story of men and women, and nothing is so interesting as human experience.

Secondly, in this supreme epic of redemption God is always on the stage; he speaks directly and with a power no other art could give. The Greeks, indeed, represent the gods as active in human affairs and as conversing with men, yet no dramatist ever had the audacity to make that dread Fate which was above the gods lay aside his silence or his awful mystery. But Hebrew prophets and poets in simple sincerity declared, 'Thus saith the Lord,' or present him speaking in his own proper person. No one since that day could do this naturally and therefore with persuasive power. Hence the Bible has a unique tone of authority.

CHAPTER VI

HOW THE HEBREW WRITINGS BECAME AN ENGLISH CLASSIC

Among the qualifications of a good translator, the first, undoubtedly, is that he shall be penetrated by a sense of the surpassing value of his original, and a corresponding sense of the importance of his task. This will preserve him from flippancy and meanness by imbuing him with earnestness and humility.... He will conform to the genius of his own tongue while endeavoring to transfer to it the treasures of another; and, besides possessing naturally, he will cultivate, in every proper way, a sensitiveness to that music of the phrase, which, in the case of the Bible, is but another name for the music of the heart.

ALBERT S. COOK

IN opening this chapter I wish to make a statement which may seem startling, but which I hope in the following pages to substantiate as sober truth. The statement is this: the English Bible in the standard versions is a finer and nobler literature than the Scriptures in their original tongues. Some Hebrew scholars may dissent from this affirmation. Others may declare that no translation of a masterpiece can equal the original. This last objection we may answer by calling attention to the fact that the Bible suffers least from translation of any of the works of human genius. Dealing as it does with the elemental emotions and common needs of men, its peculiar power is little affected by passing from one mobile language to another. A bit of literature whose charm is in its form, like most of the poetry of Poe, cannot carry its special value into another tongue. But the great books, whose power lies in their disclosure of fundamental truths and passions, find in every developed language appropriate words for the same experiences. Especially is this true of the English translation of the Bible. Tyndale declared that 'the properties of the Hebrew tongue agreeth a thousand times more with the English than with the Latin. The manner of speaking is both one, so that in a thousand places thou needest not but to translate it into the English word for word, when thou must seek a compass in Latin, and yet have much work to translate it well-favoredly, so that it have the same grace and sweetness, sense and understanding with it in the Latin as it hath in the Hebrew.' In our translation of the Old Testament we come nearer tasting the savor and feeling the emotions of the original than did the men of the first century reading the Septuagint, or the Roman reading the Vulgate. For a translation to be understood and felt, the people receiving it must be akin in temper to the people who produced the original. And the truth is that the characteristic qualities of the English mind are very similar to those of the Hebrews. Our great writers, like theirs, have moral earnestness, prophetic passion, simplicity of speech; and the Anglo-Saxon likes the energetic, emotional, poetic, and forcible in statement.

Not only do our standard versions preserve in an extraordinary degree the best qualities of the original, they have a unique and superior beauty of their own created by the contributions of many men and many races. Greece and Rome and England have all brought their glory and honor into it.

Sometime in the third century before Christ, the

Jews of the Dispersion, being unfamiliar with the tongue of their fathers, demanded a translation of their Scriptures into the more familiar Greek language. The translation was made and called the Septuagint — the Seventy — because of the legend that seventy-two scholars had completed the task in seventy-two days. This translation had a distinct influence on the diction of our New Testament. Of the one hundred and sixty direct quotations from the Old Testament made in the New, practically all came from the Septuagint. This translation changed the old order of the Hebrew Scriptures from the Law, the Prophets, and the Writings to the arrangement with which we are familiar. The New Testament diction would have been quite different had its authors been acquainted only with the Old Testament in Hebrew. Something of the flavor, the delicacy, the charm of the Greek language was thus added to Hebrew thought. The flexibility of the Greek tongue is manifest in the grace of Luke's stories of the Christ Child. It is the Greek power of uttering abstract thought that has given us the marvelous Logos chapter which opens the Gospel of John.

Then Rome made a still greater contribution. In A.D. 383, the reigning Pope commissioned Jerome, a richly gifted man, ardent in temperament, delicate in taste, accurate in his knowledge of the Hebrew, Greek, and Latin tongues, to translate the New Testament into the Roman speech. This he did and then continued his work until he had translated most of the Old Testament and some of the Apocryphal books into Latin. For more than a thousand years the

Scriptures were read and the Psalms were sung in the majestic, rhythmical speech of the Latins. Medieval scholars, under the spell of Cicero's flowing style, imitated his rhythms, especially those affecting the endings of sentences. These subtle cadences of the Latin passed over into our English Bible. Every one of the early translators of Holy Writ had his taste formed by the Latin Vulgate, and the stately music of the Roman tongue haunted his memory. Thus something of the majesty of Rome gives sonority and dignity to our English Bible.

Now we come to the contribution which the English language makes to the Scriptures, a language whose flexibility, range, and vigor of utterance give it a sovereign place among the vocabularies of the world.

The King James Version was published in 1611. Mark the date. In that year Shakespeare was retiring from the stage and taking up his residence in Stratford, Ben Jonson was writing his rare works, and John Milton was three years old. The period is the golden age of the English language, as concerns poetic and vigorous diction. We have interesting testimony of the joy of an English poet in the capacities of the newly formed language in 'An Epistle on the Excellency of the English Tongue' by Richard Carew, who was in his fifty-sixth year when the King James Bible was published. He writes:

The *Italian* is pleasant but without sinews, as too stilly fleeting water; the *French* delicate but over nice, as a woman scarce daring to open her lips for fear of marring her countenance; the *Spanish* majestical, but fulsome, running too much on the *O*, and terrible like the devil in a play; the *Dutch* manlike, but withal very harsh, as one ready at every word to pick a quarrel. Now we in borrowing from them give the strength of consonants to the *Italian*, the full sounds of words to the *French*, the variety of terminations to the *Spanish*, and the mollifying of more vowels to the *Dutch;* and so, like bees, gather the honey of their good properties and leave the dregs to themselves. And thus when substantialness combineth with delightfulness, fulness with fineness, seemliness with portliness, and courrantness with staidness, how can the language which consisteth of all these sound other than most full of sweetness?

Again, the long words we borrow, being intermingled with the short of our own store, make up a perfect harmony, by culling from out which mixture (with judgment) you may frame your speech according to the matter you must work on, majestical, pleasant, delicate, or manly, more or less, in what sort you please. Add hereunto, that whatsoever grace any other language carrieth, in verse or prose, in tropes or metaphors, in echoes or agnominations, they may all be lively and exactly represented in ours.

Since that time our language has been enriched by multitudes of scientific and philosophical terms, but in the days of Queen Bess and of James, it was more intensely vitalized in concrete, virile, picturesque words than at any period since. It is significant that the three loftiest monuments of the English literary genius — the King James Bible, Shakespeare, and Milton — all should appear in the same century. This miracle was possible because the English language for all literary purposes was then at its best.

What was the definite contribution which the genius of our race made to the authorized Scriptures? As we inherited the truth and the passion, the broad outlook, the high seriousness — that is, the substance of the Bible — what we added was a peculiar charm of style, the perfect phrasing of truth so as to bring out all of its emotional values.

As God at sundry times and in divers manners has sent to the world great poets, reformers, and prophets of righteousness, so once he sent a translator of peculiar genius — William Tyndale, the first translator of the New Testament and portions of the Old from the original languages into our tongue. As he set the standard of style which has made the English Bible the glory of our language. we shall linger for a moment to consider more at length his service, remarking in passing that his influence on the Bible did much toward shaping the English language and setting a high standard in English letters.

Tyndale's peculiar contribution to the English Bible is that indefinable something we call charm. If we try to break that illusive word into its elements, charm certainly includes lucidity of expression, the natural rhythm of deep emotion, the inevitable euphony of intense sincerity, the perfect phrase which allows the thought to be revealed, not in utter nakedness, but trailing all its clouds of glory. The first translator might have been unduly influenced by the monotonous sonority of the Vulgate; he might have shorn the Scriptures of half their power, and forestalled our modern versions by using unmusical colloquialisms. But his excellent taste saved him.

Here is an example of Tyndale's ability to use the best words in the best order. His version reads: 'In the world ye shall have tribulation; be of good cheer, I have overcome the world.'[1] Tribulation is a beautiful Latin word set in the center of a group of Saxon words — the keystone of a Saxon arch. The word tribulation falls into the cadence of the preceding words and compels a pause, ere the line is broken to new meanings and accents.[2] The whole sentence has the effect of fine music. Change 'tribulation' into 'trouble,' as some recent versions do, and the effect is lost. I do not for a moment mean to affirm that Tyndale consciously worked for this effect — he was too much in earnest — but instinctively he made a perfect phrase.

Accuracy was of course his first aim and simplicity next, but nevertheless, feeling both in the Hebrew and the Greek that beat of natural emotion which makes language rhythmical, he endeavored to convey the beauty and the passion as well as the sense of the original.

But the secret of the magic of Tyndale's style lies deeper than his taste for words and sentence structure. His mind had a strong affinity for the minds which wrote the sacred books. The power of a translator really comes, not from his intellect, but from the depth of his personality. The choice of a word or of a rhythm is not a matter of thought; from the depths of one's being comes a compulsion which forces words to fall into their places by a sort of inevitability. No one can translate a great piece of literature who is not one

[1] John 16:33. [2] A. C. Deane: *How to Enjoy the Bible*, p. 54.

in spirit with the original author. He must catch the same vision, quiver with the authentic passion, enter into the innermost soul of the writer. The heart must feel what the hand writes. Tyndale may have lacked the creative imagination of some of the prophets, or of Paul and John, but his was the passion of both prophet and apostle. He could translate the Bible because first he experienced it. The moods of high seriousness and intense moral earnestness, out of which came the sacred books, were his habitual moods. William Tyndale was an incomparable translator of the Bible, because, like the chief writers of the Old and New Testaments, he was a God-intoxicated man, simple in faith, desperately in earnest. He could not only render the words of Paul, he could transmit his spirit. In plain and vivid sentences he reproduced the gospel thought, and caused the rhythm of the gospel passion to beat again in our English speech. Perhaps I cannot better state the peculiar note in Tyndale's translation than by claiming for it the quality which John Morley asserts belongs to good writing. Style, he says, 'is agitation rigorously restrained, the touching and penetrative music which is made prose by the repressed trouble of grave and high souls.'

Tyndale set the standard of translation so high that all subsequent translators who stand in the great succession of the English Bible had the good sense to follow in his footsteps. Our Bible contains eighty per cent of Tyndale's Old Testament and ninety per cent of his New Testament translation. After him came the gentle Coverdale, who made the first complete translation of the Scriptures and smoothed out many of his predecessor's rough sentences. For example, Tyndale had written, 'For none of us liveth his own servant; neither doth any one die his own servant.' Coverdale greatly improved this by rendering, 'None liveth to himself, and none dieth to himself.' Tyndale had written: 'In the beginning was that word, and that word was with God, and God was that word... all things were made by it, and without it was made no thing, which was made.' This is certainly less euphonious than our present reading.

To Coverdale, it is claimed, we are indebted for the introduction into our language of those fine expressions, 'loving-kindness and tender mercy.' Two years after Coverdale's version a friend of Tyndale, John Rogers, produced what is known as Matthew's Bible by uniting Tyndale's work with Coverdale's translation from Ezra through the Apocrypha. In 1539 came the Great Bible, largely the work of Coverdale. Then some twenty years after, the Calvinists in Geneva made a translation whose prime aim was literalness. It won extensive popularity because it was small in size, printed with chapter and verse divisions, and in language was terse and idiomatic. To meet the activity of the Dissenters the Archbishop of Canterbury appointed a commission, upon which were nine bishops, who produced what is known as the Bishops' Bible, a stately folio suitable to be read in the churches, but marking no special advance. To offset the Protestant versions the Catholics issued a translation in English of the Latin Vulgate which is known as the Douai Bible. Its aim certainly was not simplicity, for the style is often pompous as in the sentence, 'that at the name of Jesus every knee should bow, of the celestials, the terrestrials, the infernals'; it is often quite unintelligible, as, for example, 'Beneficence and communication do not forget for with such hosts God is promerited.' [1] But its effect is seen on the King James Version in these improvements; instead of 'just and perfect men,' the Catholic translation gave us 'just men made perfect.' In place of 'let not man put asunder that which God hath coupled together,' we have the familiar words 'what therefore God hath joined together, let not man put asunder'; and 'he hath sent away the rich empty' becomes 'the rich he hath sent empty away.'

We come now to the King James Version. In 1604 the Hampton Court Conference was summoned by the King to consider the Puritan petition against many of the rites and ceremonies of the Church of England. His Majesty was in no conciliatory mood and 'soundly peppered' the petitioners with stinging and vindictive words, but he did listen approvingly to the suggestion of Dr. John Reynolds, the Puritan spokesman, that a more accurate translation of the Scriptures be prepared. With unaccustomed wisdom he selected fifty-four of the most learned scholars of the nation, representing the different phases of religious opinion, to undertake this task. Of these forty-seven actually engaged in the work. For three years the undertaking was delayed for lack of funds, although doubtless the appointed scholars privately

[1] Hebrews 13:16.

were preparing themselves for their labors. In 1607 they assembled for the great adventure. Three centers were appointed, Westminster, Oxford, and Cambridge; at each were stationed two companies of, according to the plan, nine scholars each, one to translate the Old and the other the New Testament; the Bishops' Bible was to be the basis, but other versions were to be consulted. Each scholar was to bring his notes, and when an agreement was reached by one company, the result was to be communicated to the others. For two years and nine months they worked steadily, then a final board of revision, two from each company, met daily for nine months, and in 1611 this noblest book in the English tongue, the composite result of the best learning of Christian scholarship for three generations, was launched on its beneficent career.

With its advent a splendor fell on English prose; a new standard of expression was introduced and a nobler rhythm. A distinguished English writer refers to it as a miracle. Listen to his words: 'I grant you, to be sure, that the path to the Authorized Version was made straight by previous translators, notably by William Tyndale. I grant you that Tyndale was a man of genius, and Wyclif before him was a man of genius.... But that a large committee of forty-seven should have gone steadily through the mass of Holy Writ, seldom interfering with genius, yet when interfering, seldom missing to improve: that a committee of forty-seven should have captured (or even, let us say, should have retained and improved) a rhythm so personal, so constant, that our Bible has the voice of one author speaking through its many mouths; that is a wonder before which I can only stand humble and aghast.'[1]

To make their work perfect these translators spared no pains to find the most expressive phrase. They incorporated here a word and there a sentence from Swiss, German, Latin, Spanish, French, and Italian translations, so that as the Book now stands it bears some mark of nearly every civilization in Europe since the days of Christ.

This commingling of the spiritual contributions of many men and many races, of the ancient and the modern mind, of Oriental sublimity with Occidental vigor, has resulted in a Biblical diction, unique in rhythm and effect, which is neither characteristically Hebrew nor Anglo-Saxon, but a new creation.

But revisions later became necessary. The new light from archeology, the discovery of ancient and better manuscripts, the knowledge of the principles of Hebrew poetry demanded recognition, and in 1870 the Convocation of the English Church voted to proceed with the task. Fifty-four English scholars and thirty-four American, representing nine denominations, were chosen. Final decisions, however, were to rest with the English. In 1881, the first edition of the New Testament was published, and the whole Bible in 1885. The changes suggested by the Americans were placed in an appendix for fourteen years, during which time no other than the editions printed by the university presses of England were sanctioned. In 1901, the American Standard Revision, incor-

[1] Sir Arthur Quiller-Couch: *The Art of Writing*, p. 149.

porating the changes originally proposed by the scholars on this side of the Atlantic, was issued. These revisions aimed simply to make more accurate the King James Version, and in this they were successful, but unfortunately the Greek scholars seemed to have little ear for the cadences of speech and needlessly sacrificed virile English to meticulous precision. This is less true of the Old Testament translation which in literary excellence is much superior to the New.

CHAPTER VII

THE DICTION OF THE ENGLISH BIBLE

Style must be considered as a way in which the perceptions and emotions are persuasively conveyed: a piece of prose becomes stylish as its writer succeeds in exercising persuasion over good intelligences and well-tuned nervous systems, in relating words so that their overtones stir the memory, and then in organizing their mere mechanical sounds, and the mere grammatical relations they have with one another, so that whenever possible these may assist the senses to a kind of harmony with the mind while it deals with the meaning.

E. G. TWITCHETT

As in the original tongues the Scriptures represent many periods of time and the manner of many writers, we find in them necessarily many varieties of diction. But in passing through successive translations these differences would become obscured. The edge of distinction would be blurred until there would be a marked uniformity in mode of expression throughout the books. Neither the Greek, Latin, nor English translators tried to preserve the stylistic idiosyncrasies of the writers. Consequently the diction of the English Bible has a character of its own, and a quotation from it is easily recognized. This characteristic diction is never used by modern writers, except by those whose minds have been saturated with Scriptural thought and emotion, and then only in moments of extreme emotional elevation. It is unique, it is a source of singular power, and is worthy of careful study.

In the communication of mind with mind language serves two functions. It conveys thought and it conveys feeling. Words primarily are used to express intellectual concepts, and the best words are the ones which utter the conceptions with clearness and precision. But words are like worlds; they are dead unless they have an atmosphere. Pure thought may have currency among celestial beings and mathematicians, but among ordinary mortals every thought is charged with an appropriate emotion. Language falls short of its full power unless it communicates the emotion as inevitably as it communicates the ideas. Music is the ordained vehicle to express pure emotion, those feelings which cannot be uttered in words, and it is the harmonies of speech which excite the emotions. Words not only denote thoughts and things, they release feelings. They convince the mind, they also stir the heart. It is the musical qualities of words, skillfully arranged, which charm the senses at the outer door of attention, while the thought passes through to lay its message before the executive in the inner office.

The diction of the English Bible has this power of enchantment in a most remarkable degree. The sheer beauty of its phraseology arrests the attention and then lingers in the memory like haunting strains of music. The charm lies partly in the quality and succession of sounds and partly in the rhythmic beat. Let me give a few examples of passages where regard for the melodies of speech have added either to the persuasion of the thought or to its hold upon the emotions and the memory. Tyndale had written, 'when this corruptible hath put on incorruptibility, and this mortal hath put on immortality, then shall be brought to pass the saying that is written, Death is consumed into victory. Death where is thy sting? Hell where is thy victory?'[1] In the Authorized Version incorruptibility is changed to incorruption, hell to grave, and 'O' is inserted before 'death' and 'grave,' thus improving the cadence of the sentence and its power to utter exultant emotions. It is a most noble sentence, for the triumphant feelings of the Christian are expressed as adequately as the thought upon which they are based. Sir A. Quiller-Couch has called attention to the effect of the *O*'s and of their combination with the liquid consonants, *m* and *n*, in the despairing cry of David: 'O my son, Absalom, my son, my son Absalom! Would God I had died for thee, O Absalom, my son, my son!'[2] This harmonious arrangement of the dominant vowel O with consonants upon which the voice may linger effectively utters the prolonged wail of a broken heart. If it had been Adonijah who had rebelled and been slain, the passage would not have become classic.

The Bishops' Bible in Isaiah 53:3 reads, 'He is such a man as hath good experience of sorrows and infirmities.' Such a sentence could scarcely be remembered, much less sung. But 'a man of sorrows and acquainted with grief' is fit for oratorios and sings its way into the heart. Moffatt's, 'a man of pain who knew what sickness was' gives us a thought bereft of its carrying power.

From the New Testament one or two examples of the skillful arrangement of sound to convey emotions by overtones must suffice. Through the Sermon on

[1] I Corinthians 15:53–56. [2] *On the Art of Writing*, p. 171.

the Mount there is 'the penetrative music which informs great prose.' Take the words of Matthew 5:25, in one of our modern versions:

> Therefore I tell you, do not trouble about what you are to eat or drink in life, nor what you are to put on your body; surely life means more than food; surely the body means more than clothes!
>
> Look at the wild birds: they sow not, they reap not, they gather nothing into granaries, and yet your Heavenly Father feeds them. Are not you worth more than the birds? Which of you can add an ell to his height by troubling about it? And why should you trouble over clothing? Look how the lilies of the field grow.

Compare this matter-of-fact, cacophonous, almost pert manner of speech, a manner which makes the thought seem to come from the lips only, with the same thought expressed in language whose very music gives comfort and reveals the deep feelings of the heart:

> Therefore I say unto you, Take no thought for your life, what ye shall eat, or what ye shall drink; nor yet for your body, what ye shall put on. Is not the life more than meat, and the body than raiment? Behold the fowls of the air: for they sow not, neither do they reap, nor gather into barns; yet your heavenly Father feedeth them. Are ye not much better than they? Which of you by taking thought can add one cubit unto his stature? And why take ye thought for raiment? Consider the lilies of the field, how they grow.

This last sentence in the two translations is especially significant for our purpose. We know that the sensibilities are stirred in proportion to the vividness of the picture held in the mind. To ask one to consider 'how' lilies grow presents only a vague concept to the attention. But 'Consider the *lilies*, how they grow,' introduces a clear image. It is definite, it is arresting, and having a picture in our mind we can turn to some detail of it. The difference between literature and not-literature is the difference between 'Consider the lilies' and 'Look how.' Another popular translation is even more inferior: 'See how the wild flowers grow.' The definite image of lilies is blurred into the general notion of flowers. The old Hebrews wrote well because they filled the minds of their readers with the concrete, the objective, and this quality the Authorized Version preserves.

John 14:27 is an unimprovable expression of spiritual comfort: 'Let not your heart be troubled, neither let it be afraid.'[1] The gentle command unfolds itself in words of perfect and consoling melody, while thought and sound come to a pause in the strong falling accent of the last syllable — afraid. The reader has the sensation of resting on the Everlasting Rock! The cadence brings a feeling of security. The revisers destroyed this effect by substituting 'fearful' for 'afraid,' and, the sentence ending on a rising accent, the sound and the reader's emotions are left suspended in the air. Thus a perfect word of comfort loses its perfect form by the change of accent.

The same instinct for the perfect phrase is seen in the sentence, 'Come unto me, all ye that labor and are heavy laden, and I will give you rest.' The thought stops with a falling accent on a firm short

[1] A. C. Deane: *How to Enjoy the Bible*, p. 40.

word. The cadence of the sentence communicates a sense of rest. But, 'Come unto me, all who are laboring and burdened, and I will refresh you,' fails to convey the same confidence to the spirit. 'Refresh' is a weaker word than 'rest,' and the sentence ends with an unaccented word.

The other sensuous attribute of the Biblical style besides its perfection of phrase is the subtle beauty of its rhythm. This rhythm is partly inherent in the Hebrew sentence itself. As already stated this ancient people had minds which worked intuitively. Their sentences were simple and short, rarely, except in Deuteronomy, going beyond a single clause. Being about the same length they fall into natural rhythm, and this tendency is accentuated because strong emotion characterizes the writers, and emotional utterance is usually rhythmical. The translators caught this natural cadence and preserved it. They could not well escape somewhat modifying it, for the medium they used was different. The cadences of the Anglo-Saxon are not the cadences of the Hebrew. Consequently there was produced a rhythm of peculiar beauty which is neither Oriental nor Occidental, but a *tertium quid.* A unique charm which is neither Hebrew nor Anglo-Saxon but is formed by the mingling of the thought and emotion of one race with the language of another. This resultant is a thing apart, singular in literature and of rare attractiveness. It achieves effects which are foreign to any other style. Mr. T. Watts-Dunton says of it:

> The meeting of the Anglo-Saxon and Hebrew minds created a new movement which is neither Hebrew nor

English; it is neither verse nor prose. Its naïveté and pathos in the historic parts, its variety, splendour, sublimity in the lyrical portions, are above all the efforts of English poetic art, above all the rhythms of the modern world. It is a form of art in itself in which artifice has been abandoned. This rhythm runs through the Prayer-Book and reaches its highest in the Psalms. It is fortunate that prose was used as a medium, for if the translators had tried to reproduce the Hebrew art the result would have been artificial.

Again, calling attention to the musical possibilities of the English language, he says:

Among Western people there is but one who could have uttered such music as this: 'By thine Agony and bloody Sweat; by thy Cross and Passion; by thy precious Death and Burial; by thy glorious Resurrection and Ascension, and by the Coming of the Holy Ghost, Good Lord, deliver us.'

Let me give a few illustrations of sentences in which the simplicity and majesty of the Hebrew mind, mingling with the sweet rhythms of our English speech, have produced paragraphs which are of unique beauty. Take the sentence, 'The heavens declare the glory of God, and the firmament showeth his handiwork.' [1] This is marvelously beautiful. For depth of spirituality, sublimity of thought, simplicity of emotional expression, it is unmatched. There is nothing quite like it in Milton, or Burke, or Webster. It is not an English sentence; it is not the product of our Anglo-Saxon genius. Neither is there anything

[1] Psalm 19:1.

quite like it in Hebrew. It is the diction born of the union of two great races.

Contrast this with the same thought expressed in the familiar hymn by Joseph Addison, no mean poet.

> The spacious firmament on high,
> With all the blue ethereal sky,
> The spangled heav'ns, a shining frame,
> Their great Original proclaim.

This is second class compared with the majestic sweep of the Nineteenth Psalm. Twenty-one words are used where the Bible requires but thirteen; the rhyme detracts from the majesty of the affirmation; the adjectives add feet to the meter, but nothing to the picture, and 'great Original' is a poor substitute for 'God.' The expression natural to the genius of our tongue lacks the severe majestv of combined Hebrew and English form.

Or recall the opening sentences of the Ninetieth Psalm:

> Lord, thou hast been our dwelling-place in all generations.
> Before the mountains were brought forth,
> Or ever thou hadst formed the earth or the world,
> Even from everlasting to everlasting thou art God.

These words are the natural and perfect expression of experienced faith resting confidently in the Everlasting. An English poet — Bickersteth — has put the same thought after the manner of our own literature.

> O God, the Rock of Ages
> Who ever more hast been,
> What time the tempest rages
> Our dwelling place serene.

Before the first creations,
O Lord, the same as now,
To endless generations,
The Everlasting Thou.

This is decidedly inferior to the Psalm in moving power and in firmness of phrase. It has only two more words, but the iambics and the rhymes fail to give the thought the dignity and comforting strength found in the words of Scripture.

Let me give another example. Clutton-Brock, editorial writer on the London 'Times Literary Supplement,' and one of the most eminent literary critics of this generation, said, almost in his last breath, when a friend read Saint John's description of the descent of the New Jerusalem, 'That is the supreme example of the sublime.' Listen to the opening words: 'I John saw the holy city, new Jerusalem, coming down from God out of heaven, prepared as a bride adorned for her husband.'

No Englishman ever wrote anything like that! In its substance throbs the unquenchable hope, the glowing passion, the serene faith of the Hebrew; its form is the simple music of our Anglo-Saxon tongue.

Thus our English Bible is more than the translation of a great literature into an alien speech. It is a good book made better by the patient labor of many minds, many races, and many translators. Greece is in it, and Rome, and England. The best in the Orient and the best in the Occident, the best of the ancient and the best of the modern world, have met together to produce a book as unique in diction as it is incomparable in thought and passion. It is the

English language at the acme of its literary power, heightened and intensified by emotions which our race never could have originated.

CONTRAST WITH MODERN VERSIONS

Perhaps I can best illustrate this extraordinary emotional expressiveness of the diction of our Bible by contrasting the Authorized Versions with some of our modern translations. This I wish to do with all fairness of spirit, for most of these new renditions correct errors in the standard versions and by their original phrasings bring out obscured meanings of the text. They are valuable as commentaries and are to be so used. But as helps in the art of worship many of them are decidedly inferior to the Authorized Versions. Their colloquialisms do not fit into life's solemn moments like the strong musical phrases of the familiar text.

But some of these versions are avowedly and in places ridiculously colloquial. These scholars search the alleys and listen in the bleachers for slang. Their plea is that much of the New Testament was written in the speech of the common people. The original Greek, they say, was colloquial, therefore the English translation should be colloquial to produce the effect made on the first readers.

I suspect there lurks a fallacy here, for when great truth is uttered with a glow of fervent conviction it never comes forth sprawling and shapeless. When uncommon men under the pressure of strong emotion use common language they use it in a most uncommon manner. When Lincoln uttered the immortal sentence, 'With malice toward none, with charity for all,' the vernacular of the market place throbbed with the 'touching and penetrative music' which informs great prose.

Jesus used the vocabulary of the plain people, but with such restraint of emotion that his words survived the generation that heard them, like the music of old ballads. There was a grace in his speech which these translators have failed to catch.

Paul, the author of the Fourth Gospel, and the Seer of Patmos, had their prosaic moments when their language is pedestrian enough, but under strong emotion familiar words clothed themselves with unfamiliar beauty. The true translator must catch the cadence of this intense passion or he fails at a most vital point. If he is conveying a truth or a scene, he must at least use words which do not clash with the purpose of the author. Here is an example in which an awkward touch mars a pathetic incident.

The strong son of God stands at the tomb of Lazarus whom he loved. To portray the Eternal Word touched with the sorrows of death is a most difficult artistic problem. John simply says, 'εδάκρυσεν 'Iησοῦς. Tyndale translates this 'Jesus wept.' In two words we have an unforgettable picture and feel pathos that is too deep for words. A modern version improves Tyndale by stating, 'Jesus shed tears'! Could anything be more wooden, more utterly unimaginative than that? Crocodiles shed tears! To deliberately obliterate the cadences of natural emotion from the great passages of the New Testament is to ignore the simplest principles of translation. A translator must at least try to produce the effect which the original writer intended.

If the Bible were merely an ancient Hebrew classic, then the demands of translation would be met if the translator correctly rendered the words and communicated the antique flavor in a form close to the original. But the Bible is more than a classic. Most men do not read it in the same spirit in which they read Homer. They do not go to it to delight their imaginations by contemplating strange Oriental scenes, or to enjoy mental companionship with its writers. The multitudes go to the Bible, not for knowledge, but for power; they go to renew their sense of spiritual realities, and to catch again the vision splendid. This book passes beyond a classic and becomes to men a Word of God, because it voices those ultimate truths which give to life its meaning. These are the truths upon which our faith rests, which bring comfort to our hearts, and keep burning the fires of hope. They are as final to religion as the primary colors are to painting, or the line and the circle to geometry. The men who first expressed them endeavored to state them in the fullness of power; they were passionately concerned to have these truths produce their full effect in reaching men's minds and hearts.

Now I maintain that the translator of the Bible has not accomplished his task if he simply conveys to his readers the thought of the original author, or even if to this be added a good imitation of the foreign form and savor of language. He must so use our idiom that the truth shall come to us with no less force than it came to the original readers. The light must pass through the prism of his sentences without losing any of its healing rays. 'Bright is the ring of words,' says Stevenson, 'when the right man rings them.' The prophets, the chief poets, the Master himself were artists in their use of words. Bright was their ring; vibrant with sincerity, with ardor, with truth. To translate these golden thoughts into wooden words which strike the mind with a dull thud is certainly not commendable. To deaden the bright ring of truth for the sake of novelty is, to say the least, a mistake. Most of the original writers were as conspicuous for their gifts of expression as for their nobility of thought. If they spoke of rest the thought was clothed in the restful harmonies of speech, and not in sharp accents suggestive of a cavalry charge. The style fitted the truth.

One reason why the English Bible has held its sovereign place is because a succession of translators have given most painstaking care to interpret the ultimate truths and emotions of religion in a form so adequate that they should have their full power. The translators so fashioned their sentences that the generations have felt that here is something unimprovable, permanent; here is the very glory of truth, here is the majesty of its power.

Consider for a moment some of these ultimate sentences: 'Come unto me all ye that labor and are heavy laden, and I will give you rest. Take my yoke upon you and learn of me, for I am meek and lowly in heart, and ye shall find rest unto your souls.' [1]

Walter Pater, thinking of the divine appeal this

[1] Matthew 11:28–29.

passage makes, exclaimed: 'How can man explain that? There is a mystery in it — a something supernatural.' And Middleton Murry, continuing Pater's thought, writes:

> There the language itself has a surpassing beauty. The movement and the sound of the first sentence is exquisite, I have no doubt a thousand times more beautiful than the Greek, which I have forgotten, if I ever knew it. But still, but still — would it be so very different in its effect in the Greek? I doubt it. In whatever language that sentence was spoken to you, your depths would be stirred.... Apply your coldest test to it, and it remains great style; and when a man appears who can use it again, perhaps the face of the earth will be changed, for assuredly there is a mystery in the love which finds expression in it.[1]

It is indeed great style, for it is a great call from the depths of a heart of infinite love, and such a call carries its own music with it. In whatever language it is spoken it has the cadence of the heart. Our Authorized Versions communicate this supreme emotion in the most delicate harmonies of our speech. You cannot change a single word of it and retain the full emotional effect of the thought. It is a perfect expression of the Gospel invitation.

Change this into a modern rendering: 'Come to me, all of you who toil and are burdened, and I will let you rest. Let my yoke be put upon you, and learn from me, for I am gentle and humble-minded, and your hearts will find rest, for the yoke I offer you is a kindly one, and the load I ask you to bear is light.' Here we

[1] *The Problem of Style*, p. 129.

have the invitation, but not the inner harmonies of its passion which bring it persuasively into the mind.

'Behold the Lamb of God, which taketh away the sin of the world'[1] — is a trumpet note of salvation. From sheer beauty it haunts our memory. It is a gospel sentence. All the passionate yearning of Israel for a redeemer beats in John's exclamation. Change this into 'Look, there is God's Lamb, who is to remove the world's sin,' and you turn an incomparable proclamation into a newspaper headline! The translator has not thrown a particle of new light on the thought, but he has awkwardly cut off all its locks of power.

'For God so loved the world, that he gave his only begotten Son, that whosoever believeth on him should not perish, but have eternal life,'[2] is perhaps the supreme verse of the Bible. The essence of the Scripture is crystallized in a sentence. A translator must do more than correctly transfer the thought from Greek to English. He must allow the thought to produce all the effect it was intended to produce. The form must be as perfect as the thought. The Authorized Versions accomplish this exacting achievement. An absolute truth is clothed in a form of absolute beauty. The majesty of the rhythm fits the nobility of the thought. A modern version reads: 'For God loved the world so dearly, that he gave up his only son so that every one who believes in him may have eternal life, instead of perishing.' The thought is preserved, but the divine note has vanished. Such a proclamation should not

[1] John 1:29. [2] John 3:16.

end with a qualifying clause, but with a strong affirmation — eternal life.

Perhaps the finest illustration of the power of the overtones to convey the emotion appropriate to the thought expressed is found in the pathetic story of the woman taken in adultery. To portray the reaction of Divine Purity in the presence of human shame, and this in a sentence, is an artistic task of supreme difficulty. The Authorized Versions, in describing our Lord's thought and actions, select words which subtly and inevitably suggest his pity. The delicacy of the phrasing reveals the compassion as well as the judgment. 'When Jesus had lifted up himself and saw none but the woman, he said unto her, Woman, where are those thine accusers? hath no man comdemned thee? She said, No man, Lord. And Jesus said unto her, Neither do I condemn thee; go and sin no more.'[1] Compare this perfect delineation of the emotional accompaniments of this strange scene with a modern improvement. 'Raising himself, Jesus said unto her, Woman, where are they? Has no one condemned you? She said, No one, Sir. Jesus said, Neither do I. Be off, and never sin again.' These two raucous, brutal words, *Be off*, change divine compassion into petulant annoyance.

In the days when the Oracle at Delphi was in the fulness of its power the words of the Pythoness were given to the public in noble hexameters. The form was made worthy of the god. Time passed, the quality of the interpreters diminished, the accents of the god no longer flowed in stately rhythm, the verse was

[1] John 8:10, 11. King James Version.

poor and often ungrammatical, and cynics said, 'Apollo cannot even speak good Greek!' Then the oracle was discredited. Thanks to the labors of generations of devout scholars the elemental truths and emotions of the Scriptures have been translated into our tongue without detriment to their power and beauty. They come to us bringing all the meaning and the feeling they were intended to convey. The simplicity and grandeur of the truth is matched by the simplicity and grandeur of the phrase. No book can be accepted as sacred whose style is not on a level with its thought.

But our admiration for the excellencies of the Biblical style must not prevent us from being wisely critical. The Scriptures are made up of many books, and not all of them are literature. Much of the writing is inferior. The Hebrew language was a primitive language, and never attained to that maturity of development permitting it to express the finer shadings of thought. There are effects produced by our best English writers of which the Old Testament authors were incapable.

Whole sections of the historical narratives are written in an immature and inferior manner. Many of the Psalms are as far from being literature as many of our modern church anthems. Some of the prophets have only a single verse that arrests attention. Only occasionally did Paul reveal his tremendous capacity to express thought in a memorable manner. Much of Daniel, Ezekiel, Revelation, consists of grotesque imagery constructed without a particle of inspiration. The 'Iliad' is not all literature, neither is the 'Paradiso,' nor the Shakespearean dramas; so the Bible has many areas of desert. But in those passages which belong to the ages, truth comes forth clad in a beauty worthy of the Word of God. For the Biblical style is not an ornament to the truth, as one's dress may decorate his body; it is the body itself sustaining and expressing the vital spirit.

PART II

LITERARY VALUES OF THE OLD TESTAMENT BOOKS

CHAPTER VIII

THE EARLIEST HISTORIES EVER WRITTEN

With regard to the speeches made by the various parties either when they were about to go to war or during the war, it was hard both for me, in respect to what I myself heard, and for those who reported to me from elsewhere, to remember the exact words: I have therefore written what I thought most appropriately to each occasion the various parties would say. At the same time adhering as closely as possible to the general sense of what was actually said.

THUCYDIDES

HERODOTUS is usually called the Father of History. Born in a wonderful century, when the genius of Greece was at its flood, he wandered about the world, urged by an immense curiosity to learn the thoughts and the ways of men. Vivid, impressionable, he traveled everywhere asking questions. Returning to Greece he had confidence enough in the charm of his narrative and the intelligent curiosity of the Greeks to recite his history at the Olympic games. So interesting were his tales that according to a credible tradition he was awarded, in the year 445 B.C., by the admiring city of Athens, a sum of money equivalent to about twelve thousand dollars in our currency. Tradition further states that among his fascinated listeners was a youth named Thucydides whose ambition to become a great historian was that day enkindled. With the coming of Herodotus and Thucydides, history as an art and as a department of literature was established among men. Yet four hundred years before Herodotus a Hebrew set down an account of the world from its beginning, and the story of his nation from the first pioneers to his own day. Later writers supplemented this primitive narrative until in the fifth century before Christ, some author shaped into its present form the first continuous history of the world ever written. Notice the significance of the dates. In 445 B.C., according to Eusebius, Herodotus received public recognition from the Athenians. The year 450 B.C. is the date assigned by competent critics to the final redaction of the history contained in the books from Genesis to II Kings. Even if the dates are only approximate, we are justified in affirming that the same period which saw the beginnings of history as interpreted by the Greeks saw the completion of a history whose chief narratives were written some four centuries earlier by Hebrew narrators.

We get a keener appreciation of the genius of the ancient Hebrew and an added sense of the uniqueness of our Scriptures when we realize that in the connected story running from Genesis through Kings we have the world's first written history. Genesis–Kings is indeed one book, shaped by some mind which was probably contemporaneous with Herodotus. But this man was simply a redactor. The body of the book, as we shall presently see, was written centuries before by men who were the pioneers in the art of history. Clio, the Muse of History, first made her voice audible through Hebrew, not through Grecian lips.

Naturally this narrative, coming from a date so early, is quite different from the histories of our own day, both in purpose and in method, for history writing, like every other art, is subject to the law of development. The first historians in any civilization have been neither critical nor painstaking in the investigation of facts. No one of them placed high value on accuracy of detail. They were tellers of good stories and their purpose was to charm the imagination by the artistic presentation of events. Froissart confesses that his chronicles were written with the sole aim of giving delight and pleasure. 'Before I commence this book,' he says, 'I pray the Saviour of all the world, who created everything out of nothing, that he will also create and put in me sense and understanding of so much worth, that this book, which I have begun, I may continue and persevere in, so that all those who shall read, see and hear it may find in it delight and pleasance.' Neither Herodotus nor Thucydides was painstaking in the minutiæ of accuracy. Their aim was the effective presentation of their material through art. From Thucydides to Gibbon, this ideal has prevailed in the noble succession of historians. Histories have been written under the ideals and according to the methods of literature, and have been esteemed for the interest of their story, the weight and splendor of their diction, the sagacity of their judgments. With the incoming of the scientific spirit when the nineteenth century was well advanced, history, like every other department of knowledge, was profoundly modified. Then came in the habit of scrupulous accuracy and the notion of growth and development under apprehensible laws. This seems to have been the line of progress: first the chroniclers of pleasant stories, followed by artistic and then scientific history. To the Hebrews belongs the credit of the conception out of which history grew. After them the

Greeks took a long advanced step when they distinguished between fact and fiction and gave reasoned interpretations to events, seeking for second causes instead of referring everything to the intervening will of God. These earliest Hebrew chroniclers must be judged by their own standards, not those of Greece; by their own times, not by the ideals of the twentieth century. Much misunderstanding of the earlier books of the Bible grows out of the fact that men forget that they are reading documents, many of them written over three thousand years ago by an Oriental people, far removed from us in all their habits of thought. Many critics would be less caustic if they bore more constantly in mind the fact that much of what they read from Genesis to the end of II Kings is the world's first continuous narrative, and is therefore to be judged by standards and appreciated for virtues quite different from those of modern histories.

WHY THE HEBREWS WROTE THE WORLD'S FIRST HISTORY

It is pertinent to ask why the Hebrews wrote the world's first history. This may be answered in part by asking another question: why did not the Egyptians forestall them in this honor, for of all people of ancient times they had abundant records and the longest existence. Their earliest known record dates from 2750 to 2651 B.C., and is inscribed on a stone preserved in the Museum of Palermo, and thus precedes the 'J' document by nearly two thousand years. It contains the account written by Egyptian scribes of the reign of five dynasties, gives the names of the festivals of the gods, and mentions significant events. We know that scribes and record-keepers held responsible positions at court and much of their labor is still preserved to us. Egypt had abundant materials for a history, yet no history. She had a sense of a long past, but no continuous story was produced shaping the whole into unity. She had records but not chronicles, much less history.

The reason why the Egyptians were not first in this field of history writing seems to be that while they had superior practical genius, they did not attain the mental maturity to conceive of their national life as a whole, and consequently did not bind their scattered material into the unity of a history. Moreover, the scribes were not free men, but servants of the Pharaoh. His deeds were recorded for his future glory; to uncover the heroic accomplishments of his predecessors might seem to minimize his own. These Pharaohs did not scruple to erase the names of their great predecessors from the monuments and substitute their own. It was certainly more to the scribes' interest to glorify the present than to preserve the memory of the achievements of former reigns. The opinion has also been put forward that although the Egyptians had a sense of an immemorial past they did not conceive it vividly. To them it was too vague and dim to excite curiosity. Also, as the ancient hieroglyphics became hard to read, the scribes found it much pleasanter to allegorize than to decipher them.

Consequently it was not until the power of the Pharaohs was a thing of the past and Egyptian scholars came under the quickening influence of Greece, that Egypt produced an historian. Some six hundred years after the writing of the first Hebrew narrative, Manetho, a native Egyptian, about the year 250 B.C., compiled two large works in the Greek language, one on religion and the other on the history of Egypt, of which only fragments have come down to us. Mark the dates. The earliest continuous narrative of the Hebrews comes from the ninth century; the first Egyptian from the third century before Christ.

In Babylonia the facts are quite similar. Here in the Euphrates valley cuneiform writing was in vogue four thousand years before Christ. The baked clay of Mesopotamia was an excellent medium for preserving data and records innumerable of business transactions, laws, lists of kings and facts occurring in their reign. These were collected in huge libraries. The materials of history were here in abundance, yet no Babylonian composed history until in the third century Berosus, a priest, wrote the history of his native land; but it was Hellenic culture, not the genius of his people that inspired him. One characteristic the Babylonians possessed which has given them literary eminence and effect among the nations: they had an unusual curiosity concerning the origins of things. Consequently their creation myths were elaborate, and have exerted a profound influence because they shaped Hebrew thought. The scribes made careful lists of the succession of rulers, codes of laws were scrupulously treasured. Again the materials of history, but no historian was forthcoming. The same is true of Assyria. Neither did history come from the ancient civilizations of India, for to their thinkers all temporal things are an illusion, therefore, why record them?

So the question comes back to us with added force: Why did the Hebrew write the first history? What inner compulsion or outer condition urged him to become a leader in this art?

The main reason has been elaborated in a former chapter. Israel was the first people to outgrow the primitive mind, to come under the moulding influence of a national idea. This people had a secret; they discerned that human affairs were developing under a divine purpose. World events to their prophetic minds were not like the rise and fall of waves, but were a current moving toward a definite goal. Believing in the future they were interested in the past, not only in its facts, but in their meaning. This insight of the Hebrew seers grew out of that mental characteristic which in my opinion is the key which admits us to the secret of their unique achievements, namely: they interpreted God through man and his experiences rather than through nature and its processes. They found the most convincing evidences of their God, not through the unprogressive cycles of the heavenly bodies, but in their own signal national deliverances. They had a motive for remembering these stirring events of the past, for these gave to their faith confidence for the present and for the future. Later the Greeks might write history to preserve the memory of glorious deeds, but the Hebrew wrote to increase the nation's faith and to teach to succeeding generations the strange ways of God.

Besides this inner compulsion to write the history

of what Jehovah had done to the fathers, the Hebrew had a peculiar gift. He was the best story-teller of antiquity. His imagination was vivid and his thought took shape in clear-cut, concrete images. When he thought of the past, it was not dimly, like the Egyptian, nor in vague, enormous, cloud-like forms like the Babylonians, but distinctly, with intense realism.

HOW THE HEBREWS WROTE HISTORY

The history we are considering, Genesis–Kings, is quite different from any with which we are familiar. A modern historian is exceedingly careful to establish his data, and plagiarism is with him a cardinal sin; so conscientiously he gives his authority for every fact and every quoted expression, disfiguring his pages with footnotes. Quite otherwise was the purpose and method of the Oriental historian of antiquity. To him, property rights in ideas were unknown. He as little thought of acknowledging the source of facts and expressions as a carpenter of our day would think of stamping on every board or nail the name of the mill or the mountain whence it came. The rights of the individual were in those days quite subordinate to the social whole. The story having been told belonged to the public, not to the author. 'It is the law of Oriental history writing, in fact, that one book should annihilate its predecessor. The sources of a compilation rarely survive the compilation itself. A book in the East is rarely copied just as it stands. It is brought up to date by the addition to it of what is known, or supposed to be known, from other sources. The individuality of the historical book does not exist in the

East; it is the substance, not the form, which is held of importance, and no scruple is felt about mixing up authors and styles. The end sought is to be complete, and that is all.'[1]

When the first Hebrew historian began his task he had much engaging material before him — old ballads, war-songs, folklore tales, oracles, which had come down through the generations; he had also some excellent biographies and reliable historical documents. Samuel had written 'a book and laid it up before the Lord.'[2] David had appointed a recorder and a secretary to keep the annals of his reign.[3] Nathan the prophet had written of the acts of David and Solomon.[4] Some writer of most unusual literary ability, who lived at or very near the time of David, had written a dramatic and intensely realistic account of David's sin with Bathsheba and its tragic consequences.[5]

These legends, chronicles, biographies, poems, which were at his hand, a brilliant writer shaped and combined into a continuous narrative for the glory of his country and his God. This first history was supposed to have been compiled in the latter part of the ninth century before Christ, about 825, when the spirit of Judah was glowing with patriotic and religious fervor.

[1] Renan, *History of Israel*, vol. III, pp. 50, 51.

[2] I Samuel 10:25. [3] II Samuel 8:16, 17.

[4] I Chronicles 29:29; II Chronicles 9:29.

[5] The writer of II Samuel 9–20 was not only a brilliant story-teller, he read beneath events to their spiritual significance. As good history, one need not hesitate to compare this vivid human document with the most charming pages of Herodotus. And yet the Hebrew wrote over five hundred years before the Greek historian.

It is called 'J' because it probably originated in Judah and uses the term 'Jehovah' or 'Jahveh' for God. The writer was a most excellent story-teller, simple and picturesque in language, and master of dialogue which moves quickly to the effect. He has been called the 'Sir Walter Scott of Judah,' for he preserved the legends of his country, enkindling the imagination and patriotism of his people. Fortunately, he had great reverence for his sources and embodied them in his narrative in their original form. Thus he preserves for us the flavor of the ancient folklore.

Less than a century later, when the influence of the great eighth-century prophets was being felt, some one in Northern Israel collected the traditions current in that territory. Being under powerful prophetic influences, the writer emphasized the dominance of the prophets over the kings. Being a hero-worshiper, he exalted Israel's leaders — Samuel, Deborah, Joshua, Joseph. Writing in the more bracing ethical atmosphere created by the religious enlightenment of the eighth century, he tones down the crude barbarism of the old stories, represents the patriarchs as still ignorant of the name and therefore of the secret of Jehovah, who first made himself known definitely to Moses in that dramatic moment at the burning bush. To him, God is a more remote being than is represented by his predecessor, 'J,' and the miraculous receives greater emphasis. This document is called 'E,' for it originated in Ephraim and uses the word 'Elohim' to designate God.

When the Northern Kingdom fell in 722 B.C., its literature became the heritage of the Southern tribes and some one combined these two documents into one composite narrative, which necessarily had some variations and inconsistencies.

With the menace of the Assyrian invasion, the prophetic spirit of Israel was aroused and its thoughts took a deeper channel, its utterance a deeper rhythm. The strange ways of God needed explanation, the simple theology of the fathers was inadequate to interpret the tremendous events now taking place. No thinking Israelite could write after the deportation of the ten tribes in 722 B.C. with the naïve simplicity which was natural before that date. When their history is again retouched we may be sure it will show a maturer mind with ampler sweep of thought and language. And so it proved. During the reign of Manasseh, while the prophetic party was in disfavor, it still served its cause by reëditing the history of the tribes and their ancient rituals so as to make them teach the distinguishing faiths of the prophetic school. This reshaping of the history and literature of the past in the interest of that larger vision, which disaster and persecution had revealed, was the cause of the religious reformation under Josiah in 621 B.C. As a result of the searchings of heart caused by the terrible calamities of the Assyrian invasion, we have the Deuteronomic Code, the reëditing of Joshua, Judges, Samuel, and the Book of Kings. This document, whose spirit is best shown in the Book of Deuteronomy, is called 'D,' and in chapters 5–11 the religious conceptions of Israel reach quite their highest point. Yet we see clearly the familiar process of religion reshaping facts to suit its own insights. With 'D' comes in a deeper note, and the style of the Old Testament narrative, heretofore popular, vivid and chiefly concerned with the story, now grows austere, elevated, and rhythmic through profound emotion.

In 586 B.C. there came a still more terrible calamity in the destruction of Jerusalem by Nebuchadnezzar, and the higher consciousness of Judah was turned into another channel. The State was destroyed, the people could be saved only by being organized into a Church. So the priest wrote history to bring out and to establish those ideas which have always been exceedingly dear to the priestly mind. History to priests means the account of the establishment of churchly institutions, the succession of holy orders, the origin and meaning of rites, the story of holy places.

This priestly history is called 'P' because of its origin and character. In this record we find the noble hymn to creation (Genesis 1), an account of the divine inception of the Sabbath, the origin of the rite of circumcision, the dramatic scene at Sinai where the priestly laws were given. It divides history into four periods, from creation to Noah, from Noah to Abraham, from Abraham to Moses, and from Moses onward.

The style of this writing attains great nobility in places and intones itself; yet for the most part it is diffuse, monotonous, and repetitious. Later 'P' was combined with the early prophetic histories into a simple narrative giving us substantially the Genesis–Kings history, although subject to modifying touches later.

What we have written shows that we are dealing

with stratified history. First, we have simple tales with their morals, issuing largely from the people in days of prosperity; then the tragedy of 722 B.C., the profounder thought, the more resounding style of the prophetic school; then the calamity of the loss of national independence, the exclusive absorption in religion, the rise of the priest to supreme power, and a history with a priestly bias superimposed on the narrative of the people and of the prophets.

From the standpoint of the modern historian, the most dependable and vital portion of this history begins with I and II Samuel. The writer lived near the events, legend had begun its work sufficiently to give glamour to the figures of Samuel, Saul, and David, but it had not obscured or greatly distorted the facts. Consequently we have truth told by a first-class raconteur. The Book of Kings also is based upon court records and authentic contemporary documents, but the author's treatment of them is contrary to our best standards, for his predisposition distorts the whole perspective. So intent is he on pointing a moral that his facts are but illustrations to support a thesis. Certainly he is not trying to do justice to his several characters — but perhaps we are doing him an injustice, for he repeatedly refers the reader to the sources in the Acts of Solomon, the Chronicles of the Kings of Judah, and the Chronicles of the Kings of Israel for the full story. All that he gives to us is his commentary. What he has written is not history, but homily.

If Herodotus, when he was in Egypt, had let his investigating curiosity lead him to Jerusalem, he might have passed an evening with a priestly author who had spent the day writing that supreme hymn of Creation found in the first chapter of Genesis and in whose eyes still lingered the far-off look of one returned from exalted thought. But he would have found a far more congenial spirit in the gentle humanist who was writing the Book of Ruth. Or Thucydides might have discussed the art of composing speeches to put in the mouths of important characters with an eager Hebrew who was then engaged in setting the Deuteronomic account of the speeches of Moses into the framework of the priestly document. Either of these famous Greeks might have encountered Nehemiah in Jerusalem, who would have looked at them with hostile eyes, and perchance have cast them out of the city. It was a period of aroused national consciousness both on Mount Zion and in Athens. As Genesis–Kings and the histories of Herodotus and Thucydides were practically contemporaneous, we may get fresh impressions of the virtues and defects of the Hebrew narratives by comparing them with the Greek.

GREEK AND HEBREW HISTORIES COMPARED

In the first place, it is to be noted that the Jew had no general era from which to date events. The Greeks reckoned from the Olympiads, the Romans from the founding of the city of Rome, but the Hebrews had no such definite standard for reckoning time. Again, Hebrew history is anonymous. No one knows the names of the men who so laboriously arranged the annals of their country, but the Greeks claimed each his own work. The prophets often signed and dated their oracles, but the historians, like the cathedral builders, sank their identity in their achievements. Moreover, the Greek histories were written by individuals; the Hebrew by the genius of the race. The Greek authors digested their material and stamped it with their own mentality; Hebrew history is a mosaic whose unity is that of the juxtaposition of different materials, not that of assimilation. Fortunately for all subsequent readers, the redactors who combined these different documents had great reverence for their material. If they had before them two accounts of the same event, differing and often contradictory, instead of eliminating differences and harmonizing them into a consistent narrative, they placed the two side by side — as, for example, the two stories of creation and the divergent tales of the first meeting of David and Saul. They not only preserved their original sources, they refused to pass judgment upon them and therefore preserved them in their inherited shape. It was the Greek historian, Hecatæus of Miletus (about 500 B.C.), who introduced the critical spirit into the writing of history. The opening words of his book, which we have in fragment, strike a new note, presaging the scientific method of a later day, when he writes, 'Hecatæus of Miletus thus speaks. I write as I deem true, for the traditions of the Greeks seem to me to be manifold and laughable.' Herodotus was also in the habit of criticizing and sifting his material. He would give a version of an event and then add, 'There is another story,' which he would then repeat. Nor did he hesitate to pass judgment on his narratives. 'But to my thinking,' he would say, 'this is untrue'; 'such is the tale, believe which you will.'

From the point of view of both literature and history, the habit of embodying the original sources of information in the body of the narrative has distinct advantages. Writing history by weaving together ancient documents gives to the reader the authentic voice and spirit of the past. Such a method takes the place of the historical imagination, one of the rarest of gifts. The ability to enter into the inner spirit of a distinct epoch or nation and make it live by veracious interpretation is given only to the very greatest. This Hebrew habit of composing history permits the distant times to speak for themselves through folklore, ballads, original documents. It is more than a substitute for historical imagination in the mind of the author, it is exceedingly effective in kindling the imagination of the reader. Old Testament history is like a scarf in which are woven jewels, some ancient and very precious; the Greek histories are one texture woven into a uniform piece. Genesis–Kings represents the genius and the limitations of a people; the histories of Herodotus and Thucydides represent the genius of a race illustrated and limited by individuals.

There is an intensity of moral earnestness glowing through the pages of the Old Testament history that is very conspicuous and unusual. Froissart, as we have already seen, wrote for the 'delight and pleasance' of his reader. Herodotus thus begins his history: 'These are the researches of Herodotus of Halicarnassus, which he publishes in hopes of thereby preserving from decay the remembrance of what men have done, and of preventing the great and marvelous actions of the Greeks and the barbarians from losing their due mead of glory, and withal to put on record what were the grounds of their hostility.' Remembrance, glory, explanation were the motives animating his history.

The dominant tone in Thucydides is impartiality and respect for facts. He holds the very highest rank among historians for his ability to relate events as they actually happened. A great advantage over the earliest Hebrew historian accrued to him because he wrote about the activities of his own time and of which he was a part. How careful he was to obtain the precise truth he records in the opening page of his history:

> Of the events of the war I have not ventured to speak from any chance information nor according to any notion of my own: I have described nothing but what I either saw myself, or learned from others of whom I made the most careful and particular inquiry. The task was laborious, because eye-witnesses of the same occurrences gave different accounts of them, as they remembered or were interested in one side or the other. And very likely the strictly historical character of my narrative may be disappointing to the ear. But if he who desires to have before his eyes a true picture of the events which have happened, shall pronounce what I have written useful, then I shall be satisfied. My history is an everlasting possession, not a prize composition which is heard and forgotten.

The Hebrew indeed wrote to preserve the memories of the past, but his purpose was not to honor the heroism of man: he would disclose the ways of God. He does not explain causes, far less does he seek to be just to his adversary. God is his hero and edification is his purpose, not precise, impartial statement. This intense religious interest induced the Hebrew to fashion a homiletical style of history peculiarly his own. His narratives for the most part are prolonged sermons, where facts are used, not artistically as the Greek would employ them, nor with scrupulous exactitude, which is the modern ideal, but to establish a conviction, to change the will. The historian's eyes were not on events, but on values. He was interested not in the details of an uncertain past but in the achievements of a glorious future. This earnestness grew out of an altogether unique sense of the active presence of God in human affairs for a vast moral end.

One limitation of the Hebrews shows very plainly in their history, and that is their lack of sympathetic imagination, enabling them to enter into the motives and experiences of other people. Herodotus possessed an intellectual curiosity which led him among other people and inspired him to understand and appreciate them. Thucydides also fairly stated the position and motives of the enemies of his country, but we feel a certain ecclesiastical hardness in the temper of the Hebrew historian which led him to condemn those of other interests, rather than to understand them. Being conscientiously exclusive in sympathies, he shut himself out from the possibility of writing history of the highest rank. The spirit of an ardent propagandist is not compatible with the balanced mind of an historian.

There is a characteristic, most important to notice, of both the Greek and Hebrew historians that did much to make their works readable and artistic, namely, their habit of putting exposition in the form of speeches uttered by the leading actors. Where a modern historian would write his reflections on an event and clearly differentiate his interpretation from the narrative, the Biblical historians, both in the Old and the New Testament, did not hesitate to construct explanatory speeches and put them into the mouths of the characters.

There is much to be said in favor of this method. It not only makes the history more readable, but in point of accuracy the interpretation given to an event by an author who has submerged himself in his subject and is as familiar with its characters and material as a gifted outsider could well be will probably come much nearer giving the reader a true conception of the spirit and meaning of an event than the more scientific method of presenting the bare facts to a reader less informed and less gifted with constructive imagination. The Old Testament historians all put speeches into the mouths of their characters. Only with them there is more restraint than with the Greeks. Usually a few short sentences serve to light up a situation. Only the Deuteronomist makes Moses deliver long orations and by this method he best gives the heart of the law and the deep emotion out of which it came.

We now come to a phenomenon of remarkable interest and related to the development of historical writing. The reader will recall a statement of Matthew Arnold already quoted: 'These people have a secret, they have discerned the way the world was going, and therefore they have prevailed.' This intuition of an unfolding purpose was latent in the very earliest Hebrew histories. With the eighth century prophets and the upheaval of thought brought about by the Assyrian invasion, the conviction that God was working out a providential purpose in history grew strong. In the Second Isaiah this faith broke into splendid utterance, and out of this fundamental and characteristic faith of the great minds among the Hebrews issued their inexpugnable hope of a glorious future for mankind. Quite apart from its religious implications, the conviction of a divine purpose in human affairs had its influence in shaping the writing of history.

Men may compose local and national chronicles with no other inspiration than a desire to narrate events, but the writing of universal history is impossible until men discover a supreme plan being worked out through the experiences of men. No polytheist or henotheist would dream of writing a unified story of the nations. Before there can be a universal history, two ideas must be firmly implanted in the channels of thought: the idea of the unity of mankind, and the idea of progress toward a goal. It was not until the men who gave substantial shape to the Genesis–Kings history, and their contemporaries, Herodotus and Thucydides, had been in their graves nearly three hundred years, that Polybius, a Greek of the second century before Christ, watching the steady advance of Rome, was convinced that 'the affairs of Italy and Africa joined those of Asia and Greece, and all moved together toward a fixed and simple point.' This conviction made him the first writer to attempt the construction of a universal history. But it was the Hebrew prophets who first sensed these conceptions and got them actively into the courses of history, and it was in this atmosphere of faith in a providential order that this Genesis–Kings record was composed. The germinal ideas of a universal history are certainly here.

This most ancient of histories is interesting to all sorts and conditions of men in all ages because it is largely a collection of biographies. After all, we are more concerned with human beings and their experiences than with anything else, and these histories are connected stories, often told with great artistic ability. They survived as oral traditions and were finally written down because they were so true to human nature. Moreover, these men and women are for the most part important; they change the course of affairs. We have here, then, history written from the standpoint of the importance of the uncommon and therefore the interesting man: the underlying conception being that when the unusual character appears, then events happen.

Abraham obeys the inner voice and the currents of history are changed; Moses chooses to suffer affliction with his people, and a nation is born; a Gideon appears and the land has rest; and at last the whole meaning of the process of the ages is summed up in the coming of the supreme man. This conception of the pivotal effect of the character and deeds of the great man is both ancient and continuous. In Homer, the issue of the Trojan War hangs upon the capricious temper of Achilles. In China's classic book of history, the Shu

King closes with these words: 'The glory and tranquillity of a state may arise from the goodness of one man.' And Paul was but expressing the viewpoint habitual to his people when he declared that by one man death came into the world, and by one man came also the resurrection of the dead. History written from the standpoint of the power of the great man is somewhat out of favor in these days. Climatic and economic influences are being strongly emphasized, one writer going so far as to affirm that a great man has no more effect on the course of events than an extra large piece of coal in the fire-box has on the direction of a locomotive. Undoubtedly, all the early historians neglected these potent forces, but they captured attention because their histories were extended biographies, and in the characters there is always some arresting quality, a noble generosity, an heroic recklessness, a stern fidelity which holds the interest of readers.

THE VALUE OF THIS HISTORY

It is permanently valuable because it gives to us the clearest and most abundant knowledge we have of how men lived and thought in those early civilizations. What these writers said occurred may not be what actually did occur, but these pages give us what the people learned from their experiences. And as A. Quiller-Couch has so well said in an introduction to the 'Oxford Book of Prose': 'We may reasonably agree, I think, that men's opinions about things — their speculations, memories, aspirations, glimpses of the unseen and infinite—are actually of more importance, of more meaning to mankind than any amount of ascertained fact.' The effect of facts upon humanity, the wisdom distilled from experience is not inferior in value to the facts themselves. The dates of battles, documents, and kings, the precise sequence of events in Palestine which the research of scholars is giving us is of high interest, yet surely it is of equal moment to know what this unique people learned from their history. They learned that God is not mocked; that sin sends its curse down through the generations; that righteousness exalteth a nation, and that sin is a reproach to any people; especially did they learn that a Power not ourselves is working for righteousness, and that from black disaster good may issue.

The important question for us to ask is, not whether all these alleged facts actually occurred, but whether the truth of history is brought out. Does God elect individuals and nations for specific tasks? Does he train and discipline them? This ancient history would not have lived were it not fundamentally true to human experience.

CHAPTER IX

THE HISTORICAL BOOKS OF THE OLD TESTAMENT

GENESIS: THE MYTHS AND LEGENDS OF A GREAT PEOPLE

> I will rejoice in thy word,
> As one that findeth great spoil.
> Ps. 119:162

THERE are certain supreme questions which humanity has asked in all times and in all countries. What is man? How did man and nature come to be? What is the origin of these customs and institutions which we have inherited? What of the future? These interrogations are as old as human thought and of perennial interest, and each generation answers them according to its light, according to its darkness.

Primitive peoples, rich in imagination but poor in knowledge, met these questions by telling a story. These picturesque interpretations we call myths. The word 'myth' has a forbidding sound to many: it seems to indicate falsity. To call a story a myth condemns it as untrue. On the contrary, it may be essentially and profoundly true, for the word simply defines the form, not the value of the answer. 'A myth,' according to the Century Dictionary, 'is a tale handed down from primitive times, and in a form historical, but in reality involving elements of early religious views, as respecting the origin of things.' It is not a fraud, not even a conscious invention, but a sincere attempt to give a reason in a vivid and intelligible manner. A myth is primitive theology, theology embodied in a tale that it may enter in at lowly doors.

The myths of a people are intimate revelations of character. Those of the Greeks are sensuous, yet touched with immortal beauty; the Babylonian are fantastic and bloody; the Scandinavian are monstrous and crude; the Hebrew myths are distinguished for their moral significance. Israel inherited the common traditions of the Semitic race and through the influence of her austere monotheism, and by a taste truly remarkable, eliminated the gross and repulsive elements. For example, both the Babylonian and the Hebrew wished to declare that man is like God. The former used imagery of crude materialism. He said Bel cut off his own head, and from the earth, moistened by the drops of blood, he made men, who therefore partake of his life and reason; the latter, according to one story, represents God by a fiat making man in the divine image, and in another as breathing into his nostrils the breath of life. In Genesis God is a friend and companion; in the Babylonian tradition he is an arbitrary despot. After the flood the rainbow of a great hope is hung in the sky, but the more ancient Semite saw only the bow of the Thunderer, which for a moment was laid aside.

One gets an added respect for the spiritual and literary sense of these Hebrews when he contrasts the noble account of the Creation in Genesis with that of our northern ancestors. Carlyle tells the story in his 'Heroes and Hero-Worship.' 'Consider only their primary myths of creation. The gods, having got the giant Ymer slain, a giant made by "warm wind," and much confused work, out of the conflict of Frost and Fire — determined on constructing a world with him. His blood made the sea; his flesh was the land; the rocks his bones; of his eyebrows they formed Asgard their god's dwelling; his skull was the blue vault of Immensity, and the brains of it became clouds. What a Hyper-Brobdingnagian business! Untamed thought, great, giant-like, enormous.'[1] Such were our ancestors!

The Egyptians were so concerned with the soul's destiny in the future world that we have only one account of their solution of the enigmas of the past. It was written about 305 B.C. but it represents the substance of a tradition as old as the pyramids. The supreme god formed himself out of primeval matter by uttering his own name, and, lo, his soul came into being; then he created two eyes to rule the day and night, and from the eyes of the sun-god fell tears, which when they touched his body became men and women. Thus the Egyptian expressed the conviction that man inherited life and reason from God.

The mythology of the Hebrews was superior to that of all the ancient nations in spiritual significance and in refinement.

The first eleven chapters of Genesis are quite palpably mythological. The stories of the Creation, the Garden of Eden, the origin of giants, the Tower of Babel, are sincere attempts to explain in a story form — which is the only form primitive man could well

[1] Quoted by Genung in his *Guide Book to Biblical Literature.*

use — the problem of the beginnings of the earth, of man, the Hebrew people, the confusion of tongues, the toilsome lot of humanity, the origin of the sabbath and other institutions.

But the greater part of the book is composed of the legends of the Hebrew people. A legend differs from a myth in this: a myth is an imaginative answer to a problem, a legend is a story which may have a basis of fact but whose kernel of truth has been shaped by the imagination of many generations into a tale expressing the popular feeling. In legends, also, the heroes are men rather than gods. Coming from the people, these folk-tales take us to the hearthstones and camp-fires and are the most intimate revelation of national habits, thoughts, and emotions.

We find in Genesis three quite distinct cycles of legends. First we have those gathering around the mystic figure of Abraham. These stories are simple, short, graphic. The ancient story-tellers, reciting from and trusting to memory, could handle only a few characters at a time and would naturally introduce only such conversation as helped forward the action; they also seem to have had no feeling for nature and they sketch no background. Neither are they concerned with the emotions of their characters.

The second cycle centers around the more complex character of Jacob. Abraham is on the whole a dim figure moving in the shadows of the past — the personification of unquestioning faith, rather than an individual. Isaac is but a hyphen connecting two greater than he, yet the Bible has no sweeter idyl than the story of his courtship of Rebecca, leisurely told in seven scenes. The author is using conscious art to create an atmosphere and make us feel the situation. 'And Isaac went out to meditate in the field at eventide, and he lifted up his eyes and saw.'

But Jacob is the father and prototype of the people. They were called after his name. About him gathered those stories which best expressed the nation's characteristics and experiences. He is the composite photograph of this unique people. Shrewd, patient, eager for material possessions, yet remembering vividly the ladder connecting earth with heaven, and halting upon his thigh because of his determined struggle to possess the secret of the angel of God. His biography shows more maturity in story-telling than was shown in the previous cycle. The separate scenes are still complete stories in themselves, yet they are joined together in a manner to form a consecutive whole.

The traditions concerned with Joseph are the ones most elaborately and artistically treated of any in the whole book. The different incidents are not strung together as are the legends of Abraham, but are so arranged as to fit into one another, making a developed plot. The growth of character is traced, motives are exposed, expectation is held in suspense until the climax, conversation is prolonged and delicately handled, more characters are introduced and are on the stage at one time.

A word about the uncommon interest and beauty of these stories in Genesis is fitting. It is not usual for the tales of one generation to be attractive to another: much less those of one civilization to another of quite different tastes and points of view. Yet these stories of the Hebrews have a fascination, undiminished after two thousand years, for all peoples. What is the cause? It is this. They were not fixed in permanent form until about the ninth century before Christ. As the coming of Abraham into the land of promise is usually dated about the year 2000 B.C., these tales would be current among the people for approximately a thousand years before they assumed their final shape. Mothers told them to their children at the tent doors at eventide; fathers by word of mouth passed on the traditions of the tribes to their sons. Thus by the moulding of generations every detail not of human interest was dropped; what was dramatic, memorable, true to universal experience, was retained. These stories thus are saturated with the vitality of many generations. Being formed by the imagination and experience of so great a multitude, their appeal is universal.

Genesis I

To interpret this extraordinary chapter aright, we must know its true nature. Evidently it is not a scientific account of creation, either in spirit or in language. It is not a direct revelation of God to the writer, for we can trace its ancestry to a common tradition of the time. It is not strictly in the Hebrew poetic form, for it lacks the system of parallel lines. Neither is it prose, for it is decidedly poetical in conception and bears the distinct marks of poetic art. Professor Moulton in the 'Modern Reader's Bible' points out that the parallelism is in the balance of the days.

First day, creation of light.	Fourth day, creation of lights.
Second day, creation of the firmament, dividing the waters.	Fifth day, creation of life in the firmament and in the waters.
Third day, creation of land.	Sixth day, creation of life on the land.

Each stanza ends with the refrain, 'and there was evening and there was morning'; four of the stanzas have the added refrain, 'and God saw that it was good'; the sixth balances the third by inserting, 'and it was so in the first part of the stanza, and the three refrains close the sixth.' Not only does the pattern show this noble chapter to be poetry, the material has been conceived and shaped poetically. Moreover, the whole theme is grasped poetically, the appeal is to the imagination. God spake and instantly the deed was done. That incomparable sentence, 'Let there be light,' is intense and lofty poetry, not scientific description. And through all the verses sweeps the rhythm of solemn emotion.

Notice the perfect art of the piece: the central truth is held in a commanding position throughout; no inferior sentiment is allowed to detract from the awful sense of God's instant and omnipotent power; the whole drama of creation is presented on a single page. In unity of thought, simplicity of language, brevity of expression, and in restrained and elevated emotion, it is unsurpassed. Only an austere monotheist of severe taste and deep feeling could have fashioned his wealth of material into such majestic beauty.

The spiritual values of this poem do not fall below its literary merits. The first five words, 'In the beginning God created,' are pregnant with faith and hope. They are the key-note of all that comes after in the Scriptures. If goodness, wisdom, might, are in the beginning, then they are in all the tragic processes of history, and they will be supreme at the consummation. All hope is here, What began good cannot end ill. 'Created' — that one word discards pantheism and naturalism. It takes God out of nature and makes him the supreme originating will.

In this hymn there are four insights of permanent worth: the universe rests ultimately on the will of a Power, righteous, wise, and good; in nature there is unity, order, and purpose; the world is good, and not evil; man, being in the image of God, has spiritual value and is designed to have dominion over nature — this was a revolutionary thought in the days of animal worship.

In Chapters II and III we are still dealing with primitive theology, but the center of interest changes from God to man. The questions answered are the origin of man, how sin came into the world, why the serpent is hated, the wearing of clothes, the wearisomeness of toil, the pangs of childbirth. This story of the Garden may not recount historical fact, yet it is true — true as Hamlet is true, true to life. Disobedience to law brought sin into the world, and all our woe and sin grows out of the folly of seizing immediate gratification in preference to the more remote good. Man's sin makes him self-conscious, timid, prone to blame another for his own fault. Inevitably it drives him out of Paradise and keeps him out. Scholars have very clearly established that we are here dealing with a different document from that which constitutes the first chapter and the first three and a half verses following. In the first chapter the original material out of which the world was formed was water; the second chapter is a desert tradition, for there is first the dry ground, then the rain, then vegetation. The conception of God walking in the Garden in the cool of the day is primitive and child-like compared with the august assertion that the Eternal created all things by the word of his mouth.

The literary ability of the writer is very pronounced. How much is told in a short space! We have rapidity of movement, simplicity of expression, insight into human nature, and fine artistic sense in the use of detail and effective dialogue.

We must not fail to notice a peculiar characteristic of this tradition. It has the forward look. No sooner has man sinned and lost his paradise than there comes the promise of redemption. The seed of the woman shall bruise the serpent's head. There is something better further on. This expectant hopefulness is absent from the mythology of the ancient world.

God's righteous will and man's obedient faith are the two poles of Israel's traditions. No wonder the people were inspired to moral greatness. Contrast the Hebrew with the Greek traditions. The gods of Olympus were scarcely respectable. Homer's heroes incited to valor and hospitality, but no Homeric hero would have dreamed of praying for his enemies as Abraham prayed for Sodom and Lot. Greek mythology may have enkindled the love of beauty, it certainly did not stimulate to purity. In the note of high moral adventure the traditions of America most resemble those of the Hebrew Scriptures. Lofty faith, heroic valor in the interests of supreme ideas, patience in disaster, these virtues are instilled in the minds of our children as they learn the folklore of their people. The traditions of the Greek taught valor, of the Hebrew faith, those of America inculcate love of liberty.

It is an interesting question why in English folklore there is such a notable absence of mythology and legend. Our fathers had intellectual curiosity, they were active in imagination and original in thought; why, then, do we not find at the beginning of English literature a group of stories explaining the origins of things? Probably the reason is that we came late into the world. When the English stock and lànguage were forming, and the minds of our ancestors were asking the big questions, then Christianity came to England with the whole body of Hebrew traditions, and these answers were so interesting, authoritative, and satisfactory, so much better than the English could have originated, that they were accepted, thus effectually checking the untrammeled working of the English mind on the meaning and origin of life. The legends of Arthur and his round table are our chief contribution to legend, and Christianity modified these by introducing the quest of the Holy Grail.

EXODUS: A WONDER-WORKING PROVIDENCE

The Book of Exodus is divided into two distinct parts. In the first eighteen chapters the center of interest is the dramatic career of Moses; from the nineteenth to the end we have a description of the giving of the law at Sinai. The whole atmosphere of the book is different from that of Genesis. There we met the traditions of a people shaped by later generations to set forth important truths. In Exodus we come in contact with more of historical fact. We call a narrative history when there is evidence to substantiate it. What evidence indicates that here we are dealing with a substratum of authentic facts? There is the racial memory of the Hebrew people, the persistent tradition that they had come out of Egyptian bondage. This is evidence of great value. Nations do not willingly trace their origin to enslaved ancestors, they usually claim to be descended from the gods; but this belief that they had been delivered from bondage by a series of extraordinary events was firmly wrought into the structure of their national life, they preserved its memory in their chief feast, the Passover, they celebrated their deliverance repeatedly in song and in psalm. The story of the Garden of Eden, having once been mentioned, is never referred to afterward in the Old Testament, but the exodus was an experience which left its mark upon the national memory. And the tradition that this escape was under a powerful leader — 'either Moses, or some other man of the same name — and was the result of many and amazing portents is entirely credible. Such an exodus could not have been conceived and carried forward to a successful conclusion except under the guidance of a man of unusual force as an executive and religious genius. None but a colossal man could have created such an extraordinary tradition.

Many scholars think the name 'Moses' to be of Egyptian origin, for there were Pharaohs of the name Thutmose or Thutmosis — *Thut* meaning 'is born,' and *mose* signifying 'the god': the god is born.

The Work of Moses

What was the precise nature of the contribution of this august man to his nation and the world?

He introduced into the courses of history a distinctive and effective conception of God. To appreciate how distinctive it was, it is well to compare it with the best ideas of contemporary people. In Egypt, the different Pharaohs of the early dynasties had formed a state religion around certain prominent deities, and thus worship had been systematized and stereotyped by the priests into formal ritual. Ikhnaton had endeavored to supplant this by a most exalted and spiritual monotheism. The Supreme was best symbolized in his mind by the splendor of the sun's disk. It was a glorious symbol, but it gave God an impersonal, cosmic character. It was Cod interpreted through nature. Yet this noble attempt to liberate the soul of Egypt came to naught, for the priests of Amon conquered in the end and the bright visions of the king were discredited. Nevertheless, in Egypt the pure in heart saw the true God and spoke the mystical language of faith: 'Thou sweet Well of him that thirsteth in the desert; it is closed to him who speaks, but it is open to him who is silent. When he who is silent comes, lo, he finds the Well.' Such lofty spiritual experience was not confined to a few educated individuals; on humble monuments Amon is called the God 'who comes to the silent.' The learned held an esoteric faith in the essential unity of the Divine Nature as a Being without name and whose attributes were personified by the gods of popular mythology. But these high conceptions, while they refined and satisfied individuals, did not change the currents of history.

According to Homer, Zeus was the father of gods and the king of men. He was more than a national god, for he controlled the Trojans as well as the Greeks. Yet he had no purpose for either. He carried in his brain no plan which he was realizing through the experience of nations. Moses came to a people in bondage proclaiming no vague abstract conception of a Something back of all the gods and the processes of nature; nor an Umpire watching with casual interest the changing fortunes of men, playing his favorites, but having no insistent purpose. This leader came to the people in the name of an intensely personal, eager, and jealous God, whose symbol was not the splendor of the sun's disk, but fire and whirlwind. This God has a purpose for the nation which he is earnestly concerned to carry forward. He is the God of battles and a man of war. Israel owes him allegiance because he has chosen them while they are a despised and weak people. This very act of selecting an oppressed folk shows him to be just, a God full of compassion and of mercy. That he can come down into Egypt and control for his sovereign purpose the natural forces of that land, the Nile, the locusts, the life of the first born, proves him to be a God above all the gods of the nations.

What a man or a nation thinks of God is of the utmost importance. To give to a virile people the faith in a God, personal, intensely interested in their affairs, jealous of his name, earnestly intent on a definite purpose, was to bring a distinct force into history.

Not only did Moses emphasize a purposeful and jealous God, he put tremendous stress on the ethical nature of religion. Morals existed before the decalogue, and the better minds of Egypt and of Babylon taught that men were judged according to the deeds done in the body. Neither was he the first to proclaim the duties enumerated in the Ten Commandments; reverence for God, respect for the rights of man, all coming from a generous heart, these are essential to the stability of any society. What Moses did was to unite morality and religion in the closest of bonds. His God was a jealous God, terribly in earnest, who demanded of his people righteousness above all else.

That the decalogue in its present form came from Moses we may not affirm, but the spirit of it came from him. He evidently laid but slight stress on ritual, putting primal emphasis on right conduct growing out of an honest heart. Morality according to him rested on religion, the law came from God himself. This of course was not a notion original with Moses. The monuments both in Babylon and in Egypt show the gods giving to the king the laws he promulgated. This was a conventional idea in the ancient world, in Israel it was a vivid conviction. A powerful dramatic scene is set to stamp it forever on the mind of the people.

We are not claiming that any of these ideas originated in the mind of Moses. Doubtless all of them were either taught or suggested in the faiths of contemporary people. The originality consists in the combination, on what is left out as well as what is put in. A piece of music is original, not because it creates notes never before heard: its newness lies in the unique combination of notes as old as the centuries. An architect does not design new lines and circles, but combines the old into new forms. So the Yahweh of Moses may have had no single trait in his character and religion which was unheard of in Moab or Philistia, but the ethical features of Israel's religion were simple and prominent, and they glowed with unwonted intensity.

We have mentioned that Moses brought to his people the conceptions of a purposive and morally earnest God. The idea was unique and powerful, but it would have faded long ago, as did the bright visions of Ikhnaton and many another noble philosopher, had not Moses organized a nation around this God-idea and then launched it into the currents of history. Many are the dreamers of dreams who see noble visions, but the men whose names are unfading are those who realize their dreams in institutions. John Fitch conceived and practically worked out the idea of steam navigation, but Robert Fulton established it in the ways of commerce. Many a wise man in Egypt may have had a conception of the Eternal as lofty as that of Moses. It remained a vision, a philosophy. Moses organized his vision into a nation and thus turned the streams of the world's affairs.

All this tremendous achievement was possible because he felt the Eternal, not in the splendor of the sun's disk, or in the fertility of the soil, but in his own fiery passion for freedom and righteousness.

Literary Characteristics of Exodus

The power of the book as literature grows out of the vividness and dramatic energy with which the career of Moses is portrayed. In Genesis we have many heroes; here the events of an epoch are centered in the experiences of one. No figure looms in the dim mists of the past with more stupendous proportion than he. Plutarch's men seem pigmies by his side, and their stories are told less powerfully. How intensely romantic it all is! A babe born in bondage, hidden in the Nile, reared in the court of Pharaoh, an exile in the desert, confronting the power of Egypt by summoning a superior might, founder and lawgiver of a great people, buried at last by the hand of God! It is a great story greatly told.

Those scenes where Moses demands of Pharaoh that he let the people go are highly dramatic. There is small reason to question that a succession of plagues made it easier for the children of Israel to make their escape from Egypt, but the events have been shaped by an imagination of unusual dramatic ability. Aaron simply lifts his rod and smites the waters and they become blood. Moses stretches forth his hand and darkness falls upon the whole land. It is not improbable that here we have the story as presented in a religious pageant, so closely related is it to drama.

One cannot conceive a more powerfully impressive way of teaching the sanctity of law and the covenant relation of the people with their God than the scene at Sinai: the smoking mount, the tables of stone written by the finger of Jehovah, Moses talking with God until his face shone with intolerable splendor!

The three equal divisions of the life of the hero into exact periods of forty years each has the touch of folklore — events so told are to be easily remembered.

In this book there are some famous chapters. The twentieth contains the Ten Commandments, a statement of the moral law which in succinctness, simplicity, and power has never been equaled. Man must be supremely loyal to God and never degrade his conception of the highest; he must take time for spiritual cultivation; he must honor the family relationship; he must not take away his neighbor's life, nor his property, nor his reputation: this reverence for God and respect for man must issue from a generous heart.

These laws governing human conduct are as inexorable as the laws of gravitation. A people ignorant of them, or forgetting them, will perish. The effectiveness of their statement is increased tenfold because they come as direct oracles of Deity and not as a formulation of ethical principles. The truths are enforced by amplification: 'Thou shalt not do any work, thou, nor thy son, nor thy daughter, thy man-servant, nor thy maid-servant, nor the stranger that is within thy gates.' Law for once hides its sternness and becomes almost poetry, singing its way into the memory.

In calling attention to memorable expressions of spiritual truth, one should not omit the wonderful description of God in chapter 34:5–7. It is unmatched in the Old Testament. The Lord descends in a cloud. In the Old Testament God is often conceived as hiding himself in darkness; in the New Testament light is his symbol.

> And the Lord passed by and proclaimed, The Lord, the Lord, a God full of compassion and gracious, slow to anger, and plenteous in mercy and truth; keeping mercy for thousands, forgiving iniquity and transgression and sin: and that will by no means clear the guilty: visiting the iniquity of the fathers upon the children, and upon the children's children, upon the third and upon the fourth generation.

What a noble conception of God! Merciful, forgiving, patient, yet maintaining the sanctity of the distinction between right and wrong. Observe especially the statement that good extends itself to thousands of generations (Deut. 7:9), while evil is self-destructive and the blood cleanses itself or perishes by the fourth generation.

This stern law of heredity made an equally profound impression on the minds of the earliest of the Greek dramatists. Æschylus in the 'Orestia,' the most powerful of his plays, has for his central theme the blood taint that descends through the house of Atreus, 'who breaks the close linked woe which heaven entaileth.'[1] God is not mocked—

[1] Agamemnon.

the deed unlawfully done is not trodden down nor forgot
When the sinner outstrippeth the law and heedeth the high God not;
But justice hath planted the anvil and destiny forgeth the sword
That shall smite in her chosen time.

The Greek of the fifth century had the same sense of an inexorable moral law which is announced in Exodus:

Blood for blood, and blow for blow —
Thou shalt reap as thou dost sow;
Age to age with hoary wisdom
Speaketh thou to man.

And Sophocles envisages the same august law in his dramas: God

never yet to human wrong
Left the unbalanc'd scale.

The truth is that all the greatest writers have an instinct for the moral law; its precision and majesty found clear expression in the supreme minds of antiquity, whether Greek, Babylonian, or Hebrew.

The book was written to preserve the memory and enforce the truths of God's providential government. He was not unmindful of his bondsmen, he raised up a deliverer, through very trivial events his purposes were carried out, the hard heart of Pharaoh is used to bring good out of evil. A morally earnest God will not clear the guilty nor abandon the faithful.

LEVITICUS: THE BOOK OF THE LAW

In Egypt religious ceremonials were constant and exceedingly elaborate. The temples were the social centers of the people and the most imposing buildings of their cities. Religious pageants and rituals were to the masses of that day what the drama and movies are to-day. Against this gorgeous ceremonialism the early simple religion of Israel was a protest. God, it insisted, was not confined to temples, nor acceptable sacrifices to the priesthood. A rude altar of unhewn stone could be built by anybody anywhere, and the offering made. So Saul sacrificed at Gilgal and Elijah on Carmel. As the nation increased in prosperity and social complexity, a priestly cult would develop as naturally as a military or commercial class. With the priestly order would come ritual, institutionalism, and ecclesiastical law. These are a help to many and would tend to become more elaborate until, established in custom and upheld by priestly authority, they would be considered a divine order. Such is the Levitical Code, the codification of the ecclesiastical customs which had grown up during some nine centuries of Jewish life. When practices became venerable through long habit, the priests would quite naturally claim that they had been used by the fathers at the divine command. Against this claim and its attendant evils the prophets vigorously protested. 'Did ye bring unto me sacrifices and offerings in the wilderness forty years, O house of Israel?' exclaims Amos (5:25). And still more emphatically Jeremiah (7: 21–23): 'I spoke not with your fathers, nor did I command them in respect to burnt offerings and sacrifices the day I brought them out of the land of Egypt, but this thing I commanded them: harken to my voice and I will be your God and ye shall be my people.' These unequivocal statements indicate quite clearly that the prophets did not believe in the Mosaic origin of the Levitical laws. In a volume of ritualistic regulations we do not expect to find literary charm, yet set in the heart of the book is an exceedingly interesting document called the Holiness Code,[1] a combination of the early teachings of the prophets and the priests, which in its original form is to be dated soon after the first captivity in 597 B.C., though supplemented by later editors. It is as different from what goes before and comes after as the call of a bugle differs from a judicial decision. The sentences are militant, resonant, peremptory. One feels the throb of passion in them after all these centuries, and they have permanent worth. The phrase, 'I am the Lord your God,' comes in like a constant refrain in great music.

The spiritual value of the book for us to-day is the motive presented for right human action. One is to be generous to the poor, not because generosity is humane and popular, but because 'I am the generous God'; you shall not steal, nor lie, because 'I am God' and these things are contrary to my righteousness. You shall not oppress the hireling, nor curse the deaf, nor cause the blind to stumble. Why? Because it will cause a strike, or make you unpopular? No, but because these things are contrary to the nature of God. We often appeal to men's lower motives; we charge them to do right because it is expedient, it is profitable, it is the best policy. Enlightened self-interest is perhaps the supreme motive with many.

[1] Chapters 17–26.

Now this magnificent code demands humaneness, not because it is popular or politic, but in the name of the Most High. Man must be like God, he must bring all his actions into harmony with the Eternal Order.

To appreciate the literary quality of this Code we may contrast it with our own legal forms. They begin, 'Be it enacted,' and then the law is stated in precise and formal terms. This is good law, but not good literature. Here the law is represented as being spoken directly by God himself. Here are his very words! They have the rhythm of deep emotion, they make clear a truth and incline the heart at the same time. Thus they have a vitality and a dramatic appeal which is alien to the law books of the nations.

NUMBERS: HISTORY WRITTEN AS HOMILY

The book receives its name from the fact that the people were numbered at Sinai and again at Moab. It is legendary history written with a didactic purpose by a priest who had a flair for miracles. The author had two very distinct purposes in mind: one was to teach the people that God is a jealous God who will surely punish sin, and the other was to show them that the priesthood existed by the divine will (chapters 16 and 17). Hebrew literature may contain no drama, but the Jews certainly knew how to tell a story dramatically, for history and law-giving are here conceived as intense interaction of person with person. God speaks, Moses pleads, the people murmur. The atmosphere is one of miracle; sin is immediately and theatrically punished. The conception of God here presented is much inferior to that given in Exodus. There he was long-suffering and gracious, slow to anger and of great mercy. Here his fierce anger is constantly flaming forth against this ignorant and childish body of recently released slaves. The author has a narrow and naïve mind, shaping history to enforce his moral lessons, and finding God in signs and wonders.

The literary gem of the book is the story of Balaam, a tale 'more elaborately told and more richly adorned with poetry than any other of the Biblical stories.' The tradition that the enemies of Israel, greatly fearing the abundant power of this people whose God is the Lord, sought out a famous seer to curse this people, and that his prophetic spirit could only bless, would be much cherished and often repeated. It became part of the folklore of the nation. It is indelibly marked with the seal of that type of literature. Balaam received a threefold warning as he set out, three times he smote the ass, three times he built seven altars and offered seven bullocks, and the oracles uttered were seven.[1] The much quoted protest of the ass is a fable — 'a brief story invented to embody a moral and introducing animal and even inanimate things as rational speakers or actors,' as the definition runs.

The delightful story of Balaam fits in well with the main purpose of the book, showing how futile are the enchantments of heathen seers to resist the intentions of the God of Israel. The priestly benediction is the most beautiful in the Scriptures (6:24–26).

[1] See Numbers 23:7–10, 18–24; 24:3–9, 15–19, 20, 21–22, 23–24.

DEUTERONOMY: LAW THAT IS LITERATURE

This is one of the most revolutionary books ever written. When its contents were discovered in 621 B.C., as we may read in II Kings 22 and 23, it produced a profound sensation and led to a thorough-going reformation. Its clear statement of spiritual truth, the rhythm of its deep emotion, have given it enduring influence. Our Lord quoted from it more than from any other book of the Old Testament. The name is taken from the Septuagint and means the second giving of the law. The author must have been a man of strong feeling, abundant imagination, and disciplined mind, for he has transformed law into literature and made legal statutes flame with spiritual passion.

The Literary Power of Deuteronomy

Laws are commonly dry enough reading, but this author has touched the dry bones with the magic of a vivid imagination. He has caught the essential spirit of the law and the passion which gave it birth and has put it into a form which brings it within the comprehension of the common people. In this book we have something unique: law flaming with personality, the spirit of the law speaking in the cadences of great music, statutes luminous with spiritual passion. Law has become literature, the literature of power.

Deuteronomy is melodious prose, and nowhere can the benefits and perils of rhythm, euphony, and harmony be more easily studied. Here the sentences flow on with the sweep, the majesty of a vast river. The thought is simple and upon the surface, but beneath it and carrying it forward is the swell of strong emotion. Now the rhythm of deep feeling is like music in its power, heightening the sensibility of the reader, making him susceptible of suggestion. There is an hypnotic effect which lulls the mind and opens it to receive the thought conveyed.

The perils of the sonorous style are obvious. It tempts the author to sacrifice precision of thought to the musical effects of language, and whenever accuracy is modified in the slightest degree to suit the requirements of harmony then decadence begins. Moreover, strong feeling can often flow on carrying very little freightage of thought and neither speaker nor hearer be immediately aware of the fact.

This Deuteronomic style also affects the alertness of the mind of the reader, the sentinel who guards the gates becomes drowsy and either permits error unchallenged to steal into the mind or fails to distinguish between resonance and reason.

The 28th chapter is an excellent illustration of the best qualities of the style of this book. Of this chapter John Milton declared that it should be read again and again by those in charge of political affairs. Like Edmund Burke, the speaker uses amplification to achieve his effects:

> Blessed shalt thou be in the city, and blessed shalt thou be in the field. Blessed shall be the fruit of thy body, and the fruit of thy ground, and the fruit of thy cattle, and the increase of thy kine. Blessed shall be thy basket and thy kneading trough. Blessed shalt thou be when thou comest in, and blessed shalt thou be when thou goest out.

These words have the beat of poetry, and being homely and familiar, are rich in emotional effects. The virtue of amplification is that it gives the central thought the value of time exposure while it is presenting its different aspects or component parts. It is like firing a rapid succession of shots at the same target. Note also the magnificent confidence of the statements, and the manly earnestness which keeps the melodious sentences from swinging into sing-song.

Spiritual Values

Exceedingly important is the fundamental assumption of the book that the nation is not a collection of independent individuals, but a moral person, having a conscience, a will, a unity of spirit which joins together the generations. A nation has a soul: it stands a spiritual entity before the judgment seat of the Almighty and chooses life or death. The supreme virtue insisted upon is obedience, and the motive to which appeal is made is enlightened self-interest. This is below the elevated standard of Leviticus, 'I am the Lord thy God,' but enlightened self-interest is after all the strongest appeal to a nation. Only in the excitement of a crisis do the people rise for a moment to loftier considerations. In this book we meet with the statement of the first great commandment, only the words 'with all thy mind' are omitted (6:4–6). In the same chapter, from the sixth to the ninth verses, there is an excellent declaration of the method and spirit of religious instruction, and in chapter 33:27 are the immortal words: 'The Eternal God is thy refuge, and underneath are the everlasting arms.'

JOSHUA: HISTORY SHAPED BY TRADITION

Joshua appears from this record to have been a prototype of the best commanders of history — a forthright, single-minded man, of sound judgment and resolute purpose. He thought of himself as but the servant of a cause, duty was his watchword, courageous obedience the virtue he most enjoined. A victorious soldier, he did not set up a military despotism, or found a dynasty, but was the last of all to receive his wages.

The book covers a period of about twenty-five years, and, as we know from Judges 1:19–21 and from many a story, the promised land was not conquered by a brilliant campaign. The Israelites confronted a civilization older and more advanced than their own, with greater wealth and living in walled towns. The conquest was a long process of assimilation. Jerusalem was not taken until the time of David, and it was centuries later before the inhabitants were throughly one people. The author wrote for edification and crowded the events of centuries into a short space. To set forth clearly God's providential purpose was more important to him than to ascertain what actually occurred. We have here history dramatically conceived and with a homiletical purpose. It is interesting to note that Joshua's vision of God is under the forms of his own experience and temperament. The God he sees is a captain with a drawn sword (5:13 ff.). In accord with the brave temper of the book is Caleb's heroic mood. At eighty-five, all he asks is an unconquered mountain for his inheritance. What he really cares for is a big task worth doing.

The ancient ballad about the sun and moon standing still over the Vale of Aijalon shows how soon poetic fancy touched the facts of history (10:12). As literature Joshua is inferior to the book of Judges which follows, for the latter, although like Joshua shaped by priestly minds, has for its substance more traditions as they were told in the tents of the people, and less of the material found in temple archives and in priestly predilections.

JUDGES: THE DARK AGES OF HEBREW HISTORY

After the death of Joshua there followed what has been aptly called the Dark Ages of Jewish history. The period was very critical, for there was no central government, the land was but partially conquered, and the people were subject to severe temptations to fall away from their religion. The Canaanites held the majority of the walled cities and the more fertile stretches of country; they were superior in numbers and civilization, and had the advantage of being agriculturists and of living a settled life. The Sons of Israel were compelled to pass through the dangerous process of changing all their habits; from nomads they must become farmers. Usually when invaders settle on conquered territory they are absorbed by the native inhabitants; they take the language, the customs, the religion of the land. Thus the Saxons of England assimilated the Normans, and conquered Rome gave her religion and laws to the barbarians.

By what means did Israel reverse the usual relation of victor and vanquished and give her religion and institutions to a more numerous and civilized people? The racial victory was partly due to the strong blood of the Hebrews, which has kept them a distinct people in many countries and through many generations. But the influence of race was supplemented by the work of Moses. This great leader had organized their sense of blood relationship into a national consciousness and strengthened it by the power of a congenial religion. Pride of blood, intense patriotism, faith in a jealous God, united to give them the predominance in the varying fortunes of the contest between two religions and two civilizations.

Yet Israel was seriously affected by the Baal-worship of the land and for over four centuries the issue hung in the balance. Such periods of anarchy are usually rich in adventurous heroes, and to later times an atmosphere of romance hangs over them. Ballads, war-songs, epic stories come from such days. Some genius did for Israel what Walter Scott did for the folklore of Scotland. He preserved their traditions, wove them together, touched them with the magic of his mind. Then later some earnest moralist, probably the author of Deuteronomy, for he has the same style and enforces the same lesson, looked over these stories of Israel's heroes and selected such as would illustrate the much needed lesson of loyalty to Jehovah. He begins his account at the second chapter, sixth verse, and continues through the sixteenth chapter. His purpose is to teach that national sins are visited by national calamities, but that repentance brings deliverance (2:11–19). The stories are all fitted into the same framework; the people forget God, who gives them into the hands of their enemies, their sufferings lead them to repentance, a deliverer is sent who holds the people loyal to their religion, but upon his death they again fall away. The general introduction (1:1 — 2:5) and the appendices (17–21) probably belong to the earliest documents.

Notable Literary Features

Exceedingly precious is Deborah's song, the earliest piece of Hebrew literature of whose date (about 1150 B.C.) we may be reasonably sure. It is a ballad — which according to definition is 'a short narrative poem, especially one adapted for singing; partly epic and partly lyrical.' The prominence given to Deborah, Jael, and the mother of Sisera suggests that it was written by a woman, and certainly the emphasis on the spoil of diverse colors of embroidery (5:30) represents a woman's point of view. The picture the reader must hold in his mind is of a dance accompanied by recitative singing, Deborah leading the women, and Barak the men. The ballad glows with passion and glitters with brilliant sentences: 'The stars in their courses fought against Sisera'; 'So let thine enemies perish, O Lord; but let them that love him be as the sun when he goeth forth in his might.' Also, the limp falling of Sisera, described in verse 27, is very effective. So full of lyric fire is this song that no serious critic doubts that it was composed contemporaneously with the victory over Sisera. William Watson is not exaggerating when he calls it 'the most superb expression of the intoxication of triumph.'

Gideon's test of the quality of soldiers is very subtle. He selected those who in the presence of duty drank like a hound, and not like an ox. Every farmer's boy can appreciate that distinction.

The fable of Jotham (9:7–15) is a classic expression of the sad fact that trivial men often control the affairs of state.

Samson is the humorist of the Old Testament. An uncouth country giant, he delights in tricks and horseplay; an athlete, he wastes his strength, yet he had his second chance and in the hour of his death accomplished more than in his life.

In our English Bible there is a fine touch of literary skill. In 16:28 our translator has so arranged the English words that, short, tense, they actually express the panting Samson straining at the pillars as he prays: 'O Lord God — remember me, I pray thee, and strengthen me, I pray thee, only this once, O God; that I may be, at once, avenged of the Philistines for my two eyes.'

Prominent Truths Taught

The most impressive lesson one gets from the Book of Judges is the fact that individual liberty leaves much to be desired. Self-determination is not the whole philosophy of life either for a nation or for an individual. To do what is right in one's own eyes has its satisfaction, but it often leaves one naked to his enemies. Coöperation and organization are essential to prosperity and safety. Liberty and union are forever one and inseparable. The individual has his largest freedom in a well organized society.

Emphasis is also laid on the redemptive power of one man. When the hero comes, the people take a step upward; when there is no open vision, the people cast off restraint. In the clan period of history everything depended on the hero; to-day literature preserves the inspiration and wisdom of the past, so that when the great men disappear the people are not left without guidance. As the world grows older, the accumulated experience of the race preserved in books makes less necessary the masterful man; the power of ideas is curtailing the power of persons. Pre-literary ages were dependent upon the sporadic appearance of superior men. One of the blessings of literature is that it preserves the standards and inspirations of the high epoch, it organizes the ideals and experiences of generations into a common body of knowledge, so that great memories sustain a people when there is no prophet or open vision.

I AND II SAMUEL: BIOGRAPHICAL HISTORY

In the Hebrew Bible these two books are one, and their division in our translation seems unfortunate. The whole is made up of three biographies — those of Samuel, Saul, and David.

Samuel was a stern, unbending puritan, absolutely loyal to duty, both as a child and as a man when he renounced his leadership to make way for a king. 'Obey' was the motto of his life. It is significant that when Saul was in trouble, it was the ghost of Samuel that he consulted.

Saul was a tragic figure. Every inch a king in appearance, his mind was not large enough for his task. Impulsive, subject to fits of deep melancholy, a gallant leader of a clan, he had little skill as a civil organizer and was too jealous to employ so useful a man as David. It is not improbable that justice has not been done his memory. The records were edited by the friends of Samuel, and the subsequent glory of David has dimmed whatever of greatness Saul had. Evidently he was thrust into a position too difficult for his powers. To rule a turbulent and undisciplined people, confronting a powerful enemy, was beyond his abilities.

Mistrustful of gigantic men, Samuel — when it was necessary to choose a successor to Saul — passed by the seven stalwart sons of Jesse and chose one whose distinction was in his mentality. David was a man of many talents and many passions, a warrior uniformly successful, an able administrator, a poet who left an enviable tradition, a hero for whom men periled their lives. He was a great saint and a great sinner. Yet his sins were largely those of his time and did not alienate his people. He extended his kingdom from the Red Sea to the river Orontes, and from the Mediterranean to the Euphrates. He unified the nation by giving it Jerusalem as a capital and consecrating the city with the Ark of the Covenant. He created a national consciousness and brought prosperity to extending trade.

Four streams of influence have come to us from

his times. First, by establishing the City of David he set in motion all that Jerusalem has meant in war and in song. Secondly, he founded a dynasty, and the sanctity, the authority, the splendor of the House of David have moulded the hopes of Israel and the forms of Christian faith through all subsequent generations. Thirdly, his reign was marked by a signal development of poetry and music; he is credited with the orchestration of wind, stringed, and percussion instruments; and with nobler music the psalms of worship became more numerous and significant. Fourthly, about this time public records were kept with systematic care; Samuel left written documents (I Samuel 10:25), David appointed court recorders and scribes, Nathan the prophet wrote history (I Chron. 29:29). Under David the harassed tribes became a conquering, self-conscious nation, and music, song, history, and prophetic dreams sprang to life.

It is interesting to note that no miracles are associated with David. He was admired for the bigness of his human nature, not for supernatural powers, and the historians wrote down his deeds before they were touched by the magic of tradition.

The reader, as he gives attention to these pages of I and II Samuel, has the feeling that he is dealing with material quite different from that of the Pentateuch. Scribes are now keeping records. These tales, put in writing soon after the event, have the marks of actuality.

The early chapters, which tell the story of the boy Samuel, are remarkable for their beauty. Only an artist of genuine dramatic instinct and a real gift of character portrayal could have sketched so powerfully the scene of Saul in the witch's cave. The early exploits of David are vivid story-telling. David's lament over Saul [1] is one of the most perfect elegies in any language, and it was written three thousand years ago by a young man just turned thirty. Men sitting at the gate of Jerusalem were fond of telling the story of the adroitness of the messengers who brought the news of the death of Absalom to that very gate and of the cry that came from the chamber over the gate; and thus the story became vital.

I AND II KINGS: RELIGION INTERFERING WITH TRUTH

First and Second Kings are to be considered as one book giving the history of the land from 970 to 586 B.C. It begins with the reign of Solomon and records the doings of the kings of Judah and of Israel until the fall of the Northern Kingdom, and then, confining attention to Judah, continues the narrative to the Babylonian captivity. The two books of Samuel cover about one hundred years and tell the story of three notable men, Samuel, Saul, and David; the two books of Kings cover a period of nearly four hundred years and throng the pages with many characters. The author, when he set himself to his task, had at his hand many sources for his history. There were the Acts of Solomon, the court records, the Chronicles of the Kings of Israel and Judah, the popular hero-tales of Elijah and Elisha, a biography of Isaiah, and a temple history. The main body of the

[1] II Samuel 1:17–27.

history is thrown into a curious framework having something of the rhythm and artificial structure of verse, and is pleasing to the ear. The time when the King began to reign is stated, the length of his reign, his mother's name, judgment is passed upon him, his acts are briefly summarized, and then the refrain, 'And the rest of the acts of —— are they not written in the book of the Chronicles of the Kings of Israel' — or 'Judah,' as the case may be.

The principal interest of the author who gave the book its character is not to preserve accurate records. He is citing history to illustrate a conviction passionately held. His thesis is that the proper worship of Jehovah is the basis of national prosperity: serve God in the right place and in a suitable manner, and the nation prospers; worship in the wrong place and manner, and the nation is in disfavor. Every king of Israel is condemned because he followed in the sin of Jeroboam, who erected sanctuaries at Dan and Bethel. Among the kings of Judah, only Josiah, who destroyed the shrines outside of Jerusalem and gave himself wholly to keeping the Law of Moses, is unreservedly commended.

But at this point the writer confronts a fact which confutes his theory that a proper worship of Jehovah insures divine favor and prosperity, for Josiah is defeated and killed in battle by the King of Egypt and the nation is soon carried into captivity and Jerusalem destroyed. He explains this tradition by asserting that Jehovah's anger, which had been provoked by the sins of Manasseh a hundred years before, was still hot and therefore Jerusalem and the temple were razed (II Kings 23:26, 27).

This writer of the Book of Kings is a conspicuous example of that fault, most subtle and plausible, which has caused inconceivable disaster to religion. He has allowed his religion to interfere with his morality. 'There is one proposition,' wrote Mr. Gladstone, 'which the experience of life burns into my soul; it is this; that a man should beware of letting his religion spoil his morality. In a thousand ways, some great, some small, but all subtle, we are daily tempted to that great sin.'[1] This statesman knew by sad experience that his very zeal for righteousness often tempted him away from charity and sympathetic judgment, tended to make him dictatorial and to use questionable means to attain worthy ends. This was the conspicuous sin of the Pharisees, it is the blot on the escutcheon of Calvin and the Puritans, it is the chief sin charged against the Jesuits. This writer's zeal for Jehovah and his temple leads him to read history in the light of his preconceptions. This makes him unjust to strong characters like Omri and Ahab, to overemphasize miracle, and to credit wonder stories. Seeking to honor God, he degrades the character of the Eternal. How vast a distance between the spirit of the author of the Book of Kings and of him who said: 'The hour cometh when ye shall neither in this mountain nor yet at Jerusalem worship the father.'

In reading the Old Testament, we must not mistake the superstition and narrow views of the writers for inerrant truth, nor fail to recall that revelation is progressive and that earlier actions and methods are

[1] John Morley: *Life of Gladstone.*

to be judgéd in the light of the best disclosures of truth which we have. In extenuation of the fault of this writer, we must remember that he gave shape to his material somewhere between 561 and 538 B.C. and that what we conceive the true historical spirit did not appear until over a hundred years later, and in Greece. Both Kings and Chronicles are unique as histories in putting the service of God above patriotism.

The period of Solomon's reign became an ever-increasing tradition because of its splendor. He was a despot, acting for his own glory and not for the welfare of the people. To supply money for his court expenses he divided the land into twelve districts, each of which taxed itself to meet the expenses of the court for a month. He engaged extensively in trade, collected toll from caravans, borrowed about $48,000,000 from Hiram, King of Tyre, and gave twenty cities as security. His court was the center of literary activity (I Kings 4:29–34), and his wisdom and prosperity were magnified by later generations (I Kings 10:28). His despotism, like that of Louis XIV, sowed the seeds of disruption. 'After us the deluge,' might well have been the proverb of the time.

Then follows the history of the Northern Kingdom with its nineteen kings and nine dynasties for a period of about two centuries, and of Judah with its twenty kings and the single dynasty of David.

Woven into this narrative of the doings of the kings we have a hero-tale — the dramatic story of Elijah. This is not taken from court records or histories, but is a popular tradition of a prophet who caught the people's imagination in a peculiar degree. As about one hundred years elapsed between Elijah and the record of Northern Israel contained in the 'E' manuscript, there was time for the deeds of the hero to gather about them the atmosphere of wonder and dramatic interest. The stories of Elijah have all the marks of folklore — three times he stretched himself on the body of the widow's boy; three times was a captain of fifty sent against him; three times he says to Elisha, 'Tarry, I beg you.' Twice the voice said, 'Arise and eat'; twice, 'What doest thou here, Elijah?' Moreover, ordered history is never quite so continuously dramatic as in this story.

Fire was the fitting symbol of Elijah, and in intensity of zeal, fearless courage, singleness of purpose, he became the personification to the Hebrew of the essential spirit of prophecy. There was sore need for a brave man exceedingly zealous for Jehovah's honor and for righteousness. Should Israel sink to the level of Baal-worship, and think of the Most High under the forms of nature-fertility, or should the people follow a God of righteous character and purpose? It is the most permanent religious issue of history pictured in its most dramatic form. Shall we interpret God through Nature and her processes, or through Man and his experiences? Is he Force or Person? Shall we search for him most eagerly in the laboratory, or in the aspirations of our spirit and in conscience? Never was the question more insistent than to-day, when the wonderful discoveries of science are leading us to think of the Eternal in terms of the material order and to neglect the noblest and truest symbol — the personal spirit of man.

In the scene on Horeb, Elijah's whole career is poetically conceived and dramatically told. He had felt all the physical wonder of the Deity, the famine, the rain, and his own work had been as the earthquake, wind, and fire. At last he learns that gentler methods are superior, for God is a spirit and men are permanently won only by persuasion. Long afterward our Lord in his temptation refused to use the spectacular and determined to rely on the persuasions of the truth.

A SECOND HISTORY: WRITTEN WITH AN ECCLESIASTICAL BIAS

Chronicles, Ezra, Nehemiah

After the Babylonian captivity, Israel was no longer a nation, for the Jews were dispersed throughout the known world. There were temples to Jehovah on Mount Gerizim, on the island of Elephantine, probably one in Babylonia. The priests in Jerusalem were jealous for the primacy of the temple on Mount Zion and their exclusive right to be considered the true priests of the Most High. Therefore world history was again rewritten to exalt Jerusalem, its laws, its liturgies, its priesthood. Beginning with Adam, the first chapters of Chronicles are occupied with genealogies; the narrative proper commences with David, for he prepared for the temple; his personal history and that of his successor are generally omitted, to insert in their place lists of Levites, priests, and singers. We have here ecclesiastical history concerned almost exclusively with the institutional religion of Judah.

This is followed by Ezra and Nehemiah, written in the same spirit and probably shaped by the same author. Only here we have not connected narrative, but a collection of what purport to be historical documents, personal memoirs of Ezra, and the diary of Nehemiah. The Book of Ezra relates to the rebuilding of the temple, and Nehemiah to the rebuilding of the walls of the city. Compared with the Greek historians, the chronicler who brought these four books to their present form makes a poor showing. Either he or his sources greatly exaggerate numbers, and he modifies the older accounts to give force to his argument. He is an interesting propagandist, whose zeal for his church interferes with his love of exact truth. Fortunately the chronicler lighted up his pages by incorporating large portions of the diary of Nehemiah. Here we have excellent autobiography. A strong man reveals his hopes and fears, his methods and his faith. 'I am doing a great work so that I cannot come down.' 'Should such a man as I flee? and who is there, that being such as I, would go into the temple to save his life?' (6:3, 11) are brave words. He carried his zeal to the extent of cursing his opponents and pulling out their hair, and then commends his good deeds to God for reward. This is very human and good reading.

CHAPTER X

BIBLICAL POETRY

If we should take all those Figures and Tropes which are collected out of secular Poets and Orators we may give higher and livelier examples of every one of those Figures out of the Scriptures than out of all the Greek and Latin Poets and Orators: and they mistake it much who think that the Holy Ghost hath rather chosen a low and barbarous and homely style than an eloquent and powerful manner of expressing himself.

JOHN DONNE

POETRY was the earliest, and still remains the noblest, form of speech and from the Hebrews one would naturally expect poetry abundant and noble. They spoke a musical language, they easily visualized experience in vivid imagery, and their feelings were powerful and elevated. But that this little people, standing at the beginning of the world's literary achievement, should have produced so large a body of religious lyrics, which have become the treasured possession of all sorts and conditions of men in subsequent centuries and are still living in an alien world and in a foreign tongue in undiminished vitality, is a cause of wonder.

When the Bible was translated by King James' men it was not suspected that much of the book was poetry. And the reason is evident, for in the manuscripts the words succeeded one another with little to indicate the length of a sentence, the meter was not that with which the translators were familiar in classic and English poetry, and they found no indication of rhyme. It was not until 1753 that Bishop Lowth published his 'Lectures on the Sacred Poetry of the Hebrews,' calling attention to the fact that this poetry was based on a rather elaborate system of parallelism. Whereas English poetry depends so largely for its effects upon the recurrence of sound, Hebrew poetry cultivates the recurrence of thought. Sometimes the second line is synonymous with the first; often it is antithetical. Sometimes it adds to the first line statement. This repetition is natural, for the mind is wont to delay on a thought and either say the same thing over again, or slightly modify it, or affirm the antithesis. These forms are seen in the very earliest snatches of poetry that have come down to us. The 'Song of the Sword' (Gen. 4:23) begins with two synonymous parallelisms:

> Adah and Zillah, hear my voice;
> Ye wives of Lamech, harken unto my speech;
> For I have slain a man for wounding me,
> And a young man for bruising me.

The song closes with a progressive parallel in which the second line adds to the meaning of the first:

> If Cain shall be avenged seven fold,
> Surely Lamech seventy and seven fold.

In the first oracle uttered by Balaam we have seven synonymous couplets, in the second oracle there are two progressive parallels, and the third oracle closes with an antithetical parallel:

> Blessed be every one that blesseth thee,
> And cursed be every one that curseth thee.[1]

From these simple forms many combinations and modifications were afterwards made.

The lines have also an accentual pattern, but — un-

[1] Numbers 24:9.

like the Greek and the English — the Hebrew poets considered only the syllables receiving the stress and permitted three or even four unaccented syllables to be inserted between the beats. The usual line has three beats. In the dirge the first line has three and the second two. In Lamentations the measure is 3×2. Readers will have noticed, I am sure, how in the 23d Psalm the lines gradually lengthen. In the original the first stanza has three beats, the second four, and when 'surely goodness and mercy' is reached we have a five-beat measure. Yet scholars have not completely solved the riddle of Hebrew poetry. No account has come down to us from the times when these poems were written, explaining the principles upon which they were constructed; the ancient texts are corrupt, and our knowledge of vowels incomplete. Even less than the Psalms are the oracles of the prophets amenable to known poetic forms. They are poetry because they possess the rhythm of impassioned speech rather than by virtue of strict adherence to the principle of parallelism.

The truth is that absolute symmetry is not in accord with Semitic genius; this is seen in their architecture and their rugs as well as in their poetry. Symmetry was the aspiration of the Greeks. The broken music of Hebrew poetry is a better medium for the expression of the sublimities of religion than would be more formal art. The mood which comes over you as you sit in a Gothic cathedral cannot be represented in a Greek temple.

Mr. R. H. Hutton,[1] in a richly informing essay on

[1] *Essays Theological and Literary*, vol. 2.

Hebrew poetry, affirms that the Psalms have the sublimity of the sea, the naturalness of the wind. To change this natural beauty and power into orderly time would destroy a thing of beauty for the uncanny, as though the sea should murmur sonatas, and the wind whistle a tune. Power goes from the elemental emotions when they are tamed and harnessed to the niceties of rhyme. The incongruity of imposing formal art on the burden of the mystery of the world is seen by comparing the natural rhythm of vast thoughts found in the 139th Psalm with Edgar Browning's careful paraphrase:

> Where from thy spirit shall I go, where from thy presence hide.
> Climb up to heaven, thou'rt there: or to hell, thou'rt by my side.
> If morning's wings I take, and dwell beside the farthest sea,
> E'en there thy hand shall lead me, and thy right hand shall succor me.

The glory of Hebrew poetry is its naturalness. Not that formal art was lacking — especially do we find it in the later poetry of Israel, as in the alphabetic Psalms — but in the best Psalms the ardor of the poet has made his art minister to his emotion, in the inferior ones we have artifice without inspiration. On the whole, the rules of art are not thrust between the soul of the writer and the soul of the reader. Our attention is not distracted from the thought to the form.

In our English Bible the natural nobility of the poetic parts of the Hebrew Scriptures has not been diminished but rather enhanced by the careful work of the translators. The disciplined taste and the infinite care of many devout men have given to ancient thought, in many instances, an inevitable and ultimate expression which has made them immortal. Because of the similarity of the English to the Hebrew, the readers of the Psalms in our standard versions get nearer the exact rhythms of the Hebrew poetry than did the readers of the Vulgate during the Middle Ages, or even the Jews of Alexandria through the Septuagint.

ANCIENT PSALMODY

Psalmody is not an invention of Israel. There were psalms in Babylon and in Egypt as well as in Palestine. Many of the Hebrew songs contain imagery which shows the influence of other peoples in the ancient East. The similarity between Psalm 104 and Ikhnaton's noble hymn has often been noticed. Not that there was conscious borrowing, but similar emotions found similar expression. 'Hide me under the shadow of thy wings' seems to be reminiscent of Egypt, for Jehovah had no wings, but the Egyptian Horus stretched his wings over the king. The Hebrew singer is bold to ask that the privilege of kings be extended to the common people. The following words are found in a hymn sung in honor of Amen-Rā in the temples of Egypt before the days of David: 'He heareth the cry of him that is oppressed. He is gracious of heart to him that appealeth to him. He delivereth the timid man from the man of violence. He regardeth the poor man and considereth his misery.'

A few Babylonian hymns reach a high level of thought, but the majority do not. They cannot free their prayers from magic. But in the Hebrew psalms there is no hymn to accompany spells or exorcism. Babylonian thought has left its traces in the hymns of Israel. In Psalm 139:15 we read these cryptic words:

> My frame was hidden from thee,
> When I was made in secret,
> And curiously wrought in the lowest parts of the earth.

This reflects the teaching of the 'Epic of Gilgamesh' that the souls of men were fashioned in Hades. And Psalm 74:13–14 suggests an old legend of a fight with sea monsters.

We have in our English literature poetry of the same nature as the Psalms and which was doubtless moulded by them. Such is Milton's noble sonnet beginning, 'Avenge, O Lord, thy slaughtered saints,' and Kipling's 'Recessional.' In American literature we have the 'Battle Hymn of the Republic,' Whittier's 'Eternal Goodness,' Van Dyke's 'God of the Open Air.' But on the whole our hymnology suffers because too much theology is unsubdued by the poetic imagination; our loftiest lyrics are predominantly individualistic in emotion and expressive too exclusively of the mystical temperament. Too often the slight intellectual substance is drowned in a gush of sentimentality, and morbidity is mistaken for piety.

The Psalter, as we have it, was the hymn-book of the Second Temple. It is composed of the sacred songs of some eight hundred years written or modified to meet the needs of temple and synagogue worship.

Both the Hebrew Psalter and the Standard English versions divide the Psalms into five distinct books or sections, each ending with a doxology to mark the division. The books are 1–41; 42–72; 73–89; 90–106;

107–150. The last psalm is a doxology in itself and thus fitly closes the whole. These divisions were probably introduced in imitation of the five books of the Pentateuch. The general divisions are divided into smaller groups, such as the Psalms of David, the most forceful of all; the Psalms of the Sons of Korah, of which 42–49 are supposed to be from the hymn-book of the temple of Dan, though modified to suit the needs of the temple at Jerusalem; there is a collection known as the Psalms of Ascent, 120–136, and the Psalms of Asaph. Some of the songs appear in two collections, as Psalms 14 and 53, and much liberty has been taken by editors in fitting ancient hymns into the changing needs of the temple.

All occasions and all moods seem here to find expression. There are national hymns of praise,[1] and many laments chanted on days of national humiliation and distress.[2] There are songs sung on the enthronement of the king, or upon some anniversary or birthday, when he went forth to war, or when he returned. They celebrate his glory with Oriental extravagance and thus easily lent themselves to Messianic [3] interpretation. Many relate to thank offerings, confessions of sin, and cleansing. As the synagogues multiplied, hymns of a more personal character, both of thanksgiving [4] and of lament,[5] would be introduced, and old songs would be changed and spiritualized.

The dramatic element in the Psalms arises from their antiphonal character. Many of them are liturgic. The chorus utters the petitions of the people, a soloist

[1] 145, 147, 148. [2] 44, 79, 80, 83. [3] 20, 21, 45, 72, 101.
[4] 30, 66. [5] 3, 13, 54, 88.

N

gives the divine answer, and thus in various forms the perpetual debate between man and God goes on.

SOURCES OF POWER

There are many reasons which may be mentioned why the Psalms have held their place in the admiration and affection of so many races and generations. They find people because they express in such worthy form the emotions which are both universal and elemental — thirst for God, the sense of unworthiness, the struggle with doubt, the confidence and peace which come from hiding in the shelter of the Most High. They place man directly before the Eternal and then utter the moods arising from this relationship.

The manner of the Psalms is simple and concrete. Emotions common to all men are expressed in imagery and diction which in lucidity and appropriateness place them above the limitations of race and nationality. It is because they are so universal that scholars have difficulty in dating them. Like all great art, the temporal is soon lost in the eternal. The occasion producing them is merged in the meaning and the emotion. The imagery of the Psalms is not only easily apprehensible because of its simplicity, it is usually flung out with a vigor and majesty of phrase which is very effective. It was a bold imagination which conceived of seizing the 'wings of the morning' and flying into the mystery beyond the Pillars of Hercules to find there the unescapable Presence. There is splendor in the figure, 'Thou coverest thyself with light as with a garment,' and comforting strength in the words, 'Thy righteousness standeth as the mountain of God.' A recent writer has compared the natural vigor of 'rejoiceth as a strong man to run a race' with Milton's paraphrase,

> jocund to run
> His longitude through Heaven's high road.[1]

Another element of power is the visualizing of emotions. Instead of using such a washed-out metaphor as, 'I was greatly relieved,' the psalmist says, 'Thou hast turned my mourning into dancing; thou hast loosed my sackcloth and girded me with gladness' (30:11). Job wishes to state that God has afflicted him. Notice with what vigorous imagination he pictures his emotions:

> I was at ease, and he brake me asunder;
> Yea, he hath taken me by the neck, and dashed me to pieces:
> He hath also set me up for his mark.
> His archers compass me round about,
> He cleaveth my reins asunder, and doth not spare;
> He poureth out my gall upon the ground.
> He breaketh me with breach upon breach;
> He runneth upon me like a giant.[2]

Even such an abstract subject as the attributes of the Most High are treated pictorially. In stately language the Shorter Catechism declares that 'God is a spirit, infinite, eternal, and unchangeable in his being, wisdom, power, holiness, justice, goodness and truth.' These are sublime and true words for the philosophic intellect, but their appeal is quite different from, and for religion inferior to, the metaphors of the Psalms. God is a sun and a shield, a rock, a fortress, a high tower, a dwelling place for all generations. We are

[1] *Paradise Lost*, II, 374. [2] Job 16:12–14.

dealing with a picture book; all of the thoughts are illustrated. Our emotions are stirred in proportion to the perspicuity and significance of the picture in the mind. Because these writers speak so habitually in vigorous imagery, not even hesitating to represent the Eternal in terms of human experience, they are masters of emotional effects.

There is an enthusiasm for God in the Psalms which lifts them into sublimity. The Hebrews did not flatter their God, and then, after a quite common practice in the Babylonian and Egyptian hymns, add a petition. They were obsessed with his glory and sang his praises with a joyful abandonment to their emotions. They did not enumerate his attributes in a dull, mechanical manner, but poured forth whole-heartedly their gladness of his majesty and splendor. This wonder at the majesty of our God, issuing in joy and breaking forth into spontaneous praise, is sadly lacking in modern hymnology. We have lost the glad objectivity of the Hebrew and have grown introspective, and introspection leads to sadness. Adoration is a lost art in our Protestant churches. A mild benevolence towards man has taken the place of enthusiasm for God.

We must not omit to mention the note of sincerity which is so conspicuous in all the great Psalms. Born in extreme crises, they came from the heart and are not the efflorescence of the imagination. Hebrew poetry in this respect is helped by being lyrical rather than dramatic.

Common experiences expressed in clear and natural imagery, with the simplicity of intense sincerity and with the pulsations of deep feeling, make for power in literature. And this power comes to the reader through our standard versions because the translators wisely refrained from trying to reproduce Semitic art in English form, and allowed the thoughts and emotions to be uttered in a manner having the freedom of prose and the natural rhythm of poetry. How excellently this is done, let a single illustration indicate. When one looks into the heavens on a clear starlit night the soul is lifted up in an emotion which is solemn, serene, awed to quietude. The standard translation of the 19th Psalm gives adequately our noblest thought in our meditations and conveys our feelings. The long music of the lines expresses the quiet of our mood. The cadence fits the high tide of the spirit.

> The heavens declare the glory of God;
> And the firmament showeth his handiwork.

The King James Version holds its place in popular esteem because the translators sought, not only to render the thought of the original writer, but to bring to the reader through the cadences of our speech the full force of the emotions that accompany the thought. They translated the feeling as well as the idea. The iambics and the anapæsts in the lines quoted above give the rhythm appropriate to the mood. To interpret an awed and serene mood by irregular beats, as a modern scholar does, brings in abrupt stresses to suggest quietness!

> The heavens proclaim God's splendor;
> The sky speaks of his handiwork.

Here the thought is conveyed, but the emotions of the writer fail to get through such staccato accents.

GREAT TRUTHS FORCIBLY STATED

To enumerate all such truths contained in the Psalter would be like describing the multitudinous beauties of autumn, but I wish to indicate a few. In the first Psalm there is graphic contrast between the wicked who are like chaff, controlled by their environment, without an inner principle of life, and the righteous who are like a tree, deeply rooted and drawing vitality both from the seen and the unseen. Nowhere in literature is the contrast between man and nature put more gloriously than in Psalm 8. The heavens are filled with glory, but the prattle of babes is a more powerful revelation of the divine greatness. Nowhere is God as a shepherd and God as a host so wonderfully expressed as in the 23d Psalm. The most spiritual conception of religion in the Psalter is found in the 51st Psalm. God requires above all else a clean heart, and something mightier than our own will must lay hold of us and wash us thoroughly. In the sun-drenched and storm-swept desert of life man needs shelter, but the rock must be higher than the traveler, and the only thing higher than a man is a divine personality — a personality too high for him to compass. (Ps. 61:2.) There is no more significant sentence in the Bible than the sentence in the 76th Psalm:

> Surely the wrath of man shall praise thee:
> The residue of wrath shalt thou gird upon thee.

The saints may affirm that God is good, but the reason we really believe their affirmation is because we find in actual experience that working through our individual lives and through the ages there is a Power that brings light out of darkness, wisdom from suffering, good from evil. And if there is anything so hopelessly evil that no good can be extracted from it, then the Eternal hangs it upon his belt as a trophy, conquered in war! This is a more powerful expression of a great truth than Shakespeare's utterance:

> There is some soul of goodness in things evil
> Would men observingly distil it out.[1]

The 90th Psalm closes with a prayer rich in meaning: 'Let thy work appear unto thy servant' — let me apprehend what God is doing in the world, in my generation, in my life, that I may coöperate with him. Then permit the glory of my faithful work to be manifest to the coming generations: may the beauty of the Lord God rest upon me — keep me from being deformed and crippled by my tasks, and may the work of my hands not be transitory, but so built into what is good and true that it shall be established.

The supreme problem in religion is, Does the Eternal Power care for me? The 139th Psalm gives the answer with a confidence and a majesty of utterance that goes deep. He besets us behind and before, his hand is always on us, he knows our thoughts and our actions. We cannot escape either in space or time. He is like the atmosphere, which we cannot elude and which penetrates us and all our works. Although written over two thousand years ago, this conviction of a besetting God has not been more acceptably expressed since that day by any writer. The words of Paul, 'for in him we live and move and have our being,' are less

[1] *Henry V*, Act IV, Sc. 1.

impressive. In this connection we think of Mrs. Browning's

And I smiled to think God's greatness flowed around our in-
completeness, —
Round our restlessness, his rest,[1]

and Francis Thompson's

Does the fish soar to find the ocean,
The eagle plunge to find the air,[2]

yet in these poems we have not the sustained grandeur of the psalm.

Because of this established confidence in God the dominant note of the Psalms is one of rejoicing. The dark problems of life are faced, but trust lifts the soul above them into singing joy:

Bless the Lord, O my soul,
And all that is within me
Bless his holy name.

LAMENTATIONS

The Hebrew has been too much given to lamentation; witness the age-long habit of weeping at the Wailing Wall in Jerusalem and the fierceness with which he has fought to maintain this privilege. It is to be expected, therefore, that a whole book would be given to a prolonged lament. We have here five poems in which sorrow is shaped in most delicate artistry. The first four are acrostics and the fifth is made up of twenty-two verses, the number of letters in the Hebrew alphabet. The third, the most highly finished of all, has sixty-six verses, three times twenty-

[1] *Rhyme of the Duchess May.* [2] In *No Strange Land.*

two, and accentuates the acrostic by repeating the letter at the beginning of each of the three successive lines of the stanza. In our translation the acrostic form of these poems could not be reproduced, but the cadence of the dirge, a long line followed by a shorter, is preserved. They are all concerned with the incidents and the emotions connected with the destruction of Jerusalem. The author's purpose was to write laments, in a form easy to remember, which might be used at feasts commemorating the desolation of the Holy City. It is interesting to note that the noblest elegies in every language — for example, those of Milton and Gray — are far from being effusions of emotions; they are the result of most painstaking art. One best expresses his individual sorrow spontaneously, but he conveys it to others by appealing to the imagination through artistic skill.

SONG OF SONGS

The perfect song, or the best collection of songs, is the meaning of the title. Probably we have here a group of wedding songs sung during a week's marriage festival, the couple being saluted as king and queen in language presumed to be of the court. The central theme is the delights of wedded love, yet nothing is said of the character of the marriage relation or of its spiritual aspect. The book was admitted into the canon because the Jews considered it to be an allegory of the love of the Divine King for his spouse Israel. The Church also took the poems in an allegorical sense, Christ being the bridegroom and the Church the bride. Its ecstatic language made an especial appeal to the mystics of the Middle Ages. Saint Bernard is said to have preached eighty-six sermons from this book and then only reached the third chapter.

The poems contain many delightful sentences, the most famous being the passage on love and jealousy which George Saintsbury has called perfect English prose. We quote it as it is found in the King James Version:

> Set me as a seal upon thine heart, as a seal upon thine arm: for love is strong as death; jealousy is cruel as the grave: the coals thereof are coals of fire, which hath a most vehement flame.
>
> Many waters cannot quench love, neither can the floods drown it: if a man would give all the substance of his house for love, it would utterly be contemned.[1]

Money cannot buy true love, neither can misfortune drown it or death destroy it, yet 'hell hath no fury like a woman scorned.'

[1] 8:6, 7.

CHAPTER XI

BIBLICAL POETRY (*continued*)

THE BOOK OF JOB

I call the Book of Job, apart from all theories about it, one of the grandest things ever written with a pen. One feels indeed as if it were not Hebrew; such a noble universality, so different from noble patriotism or sectarianism, reigns in it. A noble book; all men's book. It is our first, oldest statement of the never ending problem-man's destiny and God's way with him here in this earth. And all in such free, flowing outlines; grand in its sincerity, in its simplicity, in its epic melody and repose of reconcilement.... Such living likenesses were never since drawn. Sublime sorrow, sublime reconciliation; oldest choral melody as of the heart of mankind; so soft and great, as the summer midnight; as the world with its seas and stars. There is nothing I think, in the Bible or out of it, of equal literary merit.

THOMAS CARLYLE

THE two poets of superlative greatness in the ancient Hebrew writings are the Second Isaiah and the author of the Book of Job: one of soaring, radiant genius, whose temperamental hopefulness, sustained by disciplined faith, moved naturally towards the brighter aspects of the Divine Providence and the sure glories of the future; the other more somber, keeping close to humanity and its struggles, advancing steadily along a reasoned way, only achieving by flashes of intuition those glorious high confidences which the other sang so naturally. Both poets, by reason of the penetration of their spiritual insight, the sweep of their imagination, and their command of the resources of language, are entitled by merit to be numbered in the small group of the world's very greatest poets. The Second Isaiah is a prophet-singer and boldly interprets the ways of God to men; the writer of Job, like Dante, begins with man, rather than God, and fights his way through darkness and flame until he attains the vision splendid.

Both of these remarkable works are anonymous. Both suffer from numerous interpolations and from the modifying pens of other writers; but through each shines a distinctive and powerful personality which gives unity and splendor to the whole. The author of Job is both a sage and a poet. Scholars place the book in the collection of wisdom literature because Job is not arraigned, after the manner of the prophets, but reasoned with. He is condemned because he foolishly fails to understand the unsearchableness of God; he darkens counsel by words without knowledge. Such terms as instruction, wisdom, reproof constantly recur, and then there is that wonderful poem to wisdom in Chapter 28. But although his attitude and technique is that of the sage, the soul has in it the fire of a great poet. In popular thought, also, his work is ranked with the superlative products of the creative imagination; therefore we claim the privilege of considering him in this chapter on Hebrew poetry.

The question of the date of the book is of minor importance. Some critics put it in the sixth century before Christ, because in the period of the Babylonish captivity the problem of the suffering of the righteous was especially acute; others credit the prose section to the fifth century, the dialogues to the third, and the speech of Elihu to the second century before Christ. But as Carlyle so well says: it is a 'timeless book.' It deals with a universal problem in a manner that affixes no date. Although written in Hebrew its very structure suggests its universal breadth. The land of

Uz is an unknown region, the three friends are not Jewish, Job might be any Semite, for he sacrifices without the aid of a priest, and no mention is made of the temple or the law.

The problem discussed is also one common to all humanity: Why do the righteous suffer? This question has been put with passionate intensity by thinking men of every generation and race.

When we seek to classify the poem as literature we have difficulty, because, as we have said before, we derive our standards from the Greek, and Greek categories do not fit nicely the Hebrew genius. The work is more than a dialogue, for it is not without structure and unfolding plot. To call it a symposium, as Jastrow does, describes a characteristic of the form but gives no inkling of its emotional contents: neither is it a drama, for it lacks action. It comes closer to being an epic, as an epic tells a story of the adventures of a hero under supernatural guidance. Only here the adventure is not a conflict on sea or land, but a desperate struggle in the soul. It is the quest of a smitten and bewildered spirit for light and God, and as such it finds affinity with 'In Memoriam' and the 'Divine Comedy.' When Professor Genung called the piece 'An Epic of the Inner Life,' he came as near as possible in our English speech to describing the nature of the book.

As printed in the Revised version, the book is seen to be a combination of prose and poetry — the prose being as distinct from the poetry in teaching as in form. The prose gives prominence to the intrigues of Satan, whom the poem does not mention: it raises the question whether man serves God for naught and represents Job as patiently submissive — 'the Lord gave and the Lord hath taken away: blessed be the name of the Lord' — whereas the hero of the poem is a resisting and agonized spirit. Moreover, material prosperity is the climax of the prose portion, while the vision of God is the climax of the poem.

The best explanation of this composite structure and diverse treatment is this. Probably drifting through the East there was a prose tradition of a man both good and great who had suffered terrible and apparently unmerited afflictions, but who had afterward prospered. This tradition had been written down in prose for the purpose of teaching that suffering did not prove guilt, but might be a test of character and have a significance beyond our comprehension. Some great poet, reading this prose story with its happy ending, revolted both at the delineation of Job and at the facile termination. We can imagine him to have exclaimed: 'A strong man does not lie down so tamely under unprovoked disaster. I will show the promethean struggles of Job's spirit and the processes by which he became reconciled to his strange fate.' So he wrote his great poem to interpret in his own fashion how a brave man passed through the 'dark night of the soul' and, by keeping his integrity, found God.

The structure of the poem is very simple. Job, so submissive in the preceding prose version, opens the poem by terribly and magnificently anathematizing the day of his birth; the three friends answer, one after another, in accordance with the current theology, that suffering proves sin. And Job replies to each one.

This ends the first cycle, with Job confused, but resolved to maintain his integrity:

> Though he slay me, yet will I wait for him;
> Nevertheless I will maintain my ways before him. (13:15.)

And because he keeps his spiritual integrity, in the second cycle of the dialogue there surges up from the deeps of his nature the certainty so magnificently expressed in the immortal words: 'I know that my Redeemer liveth' (19:25).

In the third cycle, which begins with Chapter 22, Job has an intimation that his sufferings may be designed for his own good:

> He knoweth the way that I take:
> When he hath tried me I shall come forth as gold. (23:10.)

In the 28th chapter there is a brilliant poem in praise of Wisdom, containing a most interesting description of mining operations. Job now sums up his case with an oath of clearance, and a newcomer, Elihu, takes fifty-two lines to announce that he will speak, and then says little, his heart giving way as thunder-clouds blacken the sky and out of the whirlwind God speaks, setting forth in words of incomparable majesty and grace his wisdom and power as revealed in nature.

A lesser writer would have attempted an answer to Job's perplexity, explaining that his sufferings had convinced the sons of God that men did serve God for naught, and that having been tested and found true his woes had proved valuable to himself and to others.

But the author had too deep an insight into the

facts of experience to make this mistake. The Eternal does not answer our insistent questions. God does not explain, but he does give to the anguished spirit such a sense of the Divine greatness that questioning ceases in the peace of submission. He does not answer the interrogations of the mind, but does satisfy the profound yearnings of the spirit.

The closing words of the poem are its key and its culmination:

> I had heard of thee by the hearing of the ear;
> But now mine eye seeth thee,
> Wherefore I abhor myself and repent
> In dust and ashes. (42:5, 6.)

In all the greatest literature the hero struggles through tragic experience to peace and reconciliation. In no true drama does the curtain fall leaving the spectator confused and distraught. The mind must be at peace: there must be reconciliation of some sort. In 'Hamlet,' life's perplexities and passion culminate in the mystery of death and its suggestion that flights of angels sing the tortured soul to its rest. In 'Henry VIII,' Queen Katherine meets her misfortunes with such nobility of spirit that her sufferings are more than compensated by the glory revealed in her. Lear finds his reconciliation in that moment of insight into the love of Cordelia. The solemn quietude of death, the victory of the spirit over all disaster, the vision of God in some of his manifestations are the methods used by the great writers to reconcile spectators and sufferers with life's tragic experiences. Job caught a vision of the power and wisdom of God; Dante's long journey found its significance and final satisfaction in that beatific vision of Divine Love, penetrating and binding together all human experience. Through shadows to reality, through the temporal to the eternal — this is the meaning of all life greatly lived and the theme of all literature greatly written.

To end the book with the prose epilogue describing the temporal prosperity of Job in after years is an anti-climax. One who has looked into the fires of hell, and experienced a vivid realization of God, is not much concerned thereafter about the number of his camels.

The 'Prometheus Bound' of Æschylus is often compared with the Book of Job, and there are points of similarity. Yet Prometheus is a god, and he meets the cruelty of Zeus with undaunted fortitude. He is a more heroic figure than Job, who is after all a frail man, inclined to yield to self-pity and to give full vent to his complaints. In Æschylus there is a sense of atmosphere, of the out-of-doors, which is lacking, not only in Job, but in most of the narratives of Scripture.

But the Greek dramatist has not the subtle insight into the workings of the mind that is displayed by the author of Job, neither has he the same wide sweep of thought or wealth of imagery; nor are his pages so rich in glorious sentences: 'I know that my redeemer liveth'; 'Lo! these are the outskirts of his ways; and how small a whisper do we hear of him! But the thunder of his power who can understand.' 'Man that is born of woman is of few days and full of trouble.' Then there is the incomparable grandeur of the 38th chapter. To appreciate the superior literary beauty of the standard translation, we have only to make a few contrasts. Compare

> Where wast thou when I laid the foundations of the earth?
> Declare, if thou hast understanding

with

> When I founded the earth, where were you then?
> Answer me that, if you have wit to know.

This last has the tone of a woman shaking a naughty boy.

Of the light which is thrown upon the problem of human suffering, a word may fitly be said. Job's friends held the conventional view that suffering is punishment for sin. The prologue declares that often it is a test of character and may have a significance which does not end with the sufferer. Job has the further insight that pain is disciplinary — 'When he hath tried me I shall come forth as gold' (23:10)—and Elihu's long speech argues that suffering comes of God's goodness rather than of his wrath. The teaching of the whole poem is that calamities faithfully borne issue in the vision of God.

It is instructive to remember that the Greeks emphasized an aspect of this problem which the Hebrew ignored, that is, the glory of heroism. Homer's heroes endure for the glory that will enshrine their names. Euripides puts these glowing words into the mouth of Hecuba to console the Trojan women in the hour of their utmost extremity:

> ... All is well.
> Had he not turned us in his hand, and thrust
> Our high things low and shook our hills as dust,

> We had not been the splendor, and our wrong
> An everlasting music for a song
> Of earth and heaven.[1]

Not resplendent fame, but an inner spiritual beauty is the Biblical promise to the much-enduring spirit. Our light afflictions 'are working out an exceeding weight of glory' — glory of soul, not of renown. The vicarious nature of the suffering of the innocent, glimpsed in the prologue, finds its classic expression in Isaiah 53, and is the power of the Cross. Beyond this the Bible is silent, and human experience since that day has added nothing except the idea that suffering is involved in a developing universe.

AN APPRAISAL OF VALUES

It is never sufficient to state truth clearly to insure its permanence in human thought; the form and clothing are quite as important as the substance, if it is to be held in the memory. Poetry at its highest expresses thought and feeling by using 'the best words in the best order.' Great poetry is not understood by being submitted to a process of analysis, and by displaying the skill of its technique. We cannot weigh beauty, and have no precise line to plumb the depths of enchantment. How can we best experience, and awaken in another, an appreciation of the true values of poetic expression?

Matthew Arnold in his memorable essay on 'The Study of Poetry' affirms that 'there can be no more useful help for discovering what poetry belongs to the class of the truly excellent, and can therefore do us

[1] *Trojan Women*, translated by Gilbert Murray.

most good, than to have always in one's mind lines and expressions of the great masters, and apply them as a touchstone to other poetry.' I know of no better way of appraising the true value of the poetry of the English Bible than by comparing it with the expression of similar ideas in other books. Much of the Hebrew poetry is not of the highest order — it ranges from the commonplace and artificial to the very best. What I shall attempt to do is to compare the best with the best.

Every people has looked out upon nature and beheld in it the glory of God, and their poets have endeavored to express this universal feeling. Here is the best that has come out of Egypt. It is from the mind of Ikhnaton, the philosopher-king, and is thus translated by Breasted:

> O loving Aton, beginning of life!
> When thou riseth in the Eastern horizon,
> Thou fillest every land with thy beauty,
> All cattle rest upon their pasturage,
> The trees and the plants flourish,
> The birds flutter in their marshes,
> Their wings uplifted in adoration to the sun,
> All the sheep dance upon their feet,
> All winged things fly,
> They live when thou hast shone upon them.

The whole hymn is often compared by scholars with Psalm 104, beginning:

> Bless the Lord, O my soul.
> O Lord my God, thou art very great:
> Thou art clothed with honour and majesty.
> Who coverest thyself with light as with a garment;
> Who stretchest out the heavens like a curtain:

> Who layeth the beams of his chambers in the waters;
> Who maketh the clouds his chariot;
> Who walketh upon the wings of the wind:
> Who maketh the winds his messengers;
> His ministers a flaming fire:
> Who laid the foundations of the earth,
> That it should not be moved forever.

Both are beautiful, but the former grows out of a fancy which delights in the glory and the joy of physical things; the latter passes through the shining creation to contemplate the Creator. It shows profounder thought and a vaster range of the imagination. This was unapproached until Wordsworth wrote the lines above Tintern Abbey. 'Who coverest thyself with light as with a garment' is equaled by 'A presence... whose dwelling is the light of setting suns.' The Hebrew poets have not been excelled in their ascription of praise to God. They were first in the field and used all the symbols of earth and heaven to ascribe honor to the Most High. In two thousand years only one anthem of praise that is at all comparable with the psalms has established itself in the love of the Church, and that is the *Te Deum*.

The eternity of God and the transitoriness of life have impressed the mind of man powerfully in every age and country. The thought is too vast adequately to be put into human speech. At best it can only be suggested, and for this purpose a line is better than a page. We are all familiar with the noble statement in the 90th Psalm, where the ephemeral nature of man is set against the everlasting eternity of God.

> Before the mountains were brought forth,
> Or ever thou hadst formed the earth and the world,

Even from everlasting to everlasting, thou art God.
. . . .

For a thousand years in thy sight
Are but as yesterday when it is past,
And as a watch in the night.
. . . .

We bring our years to an end as a tale that is told.

This contrast of the shadowy life of man is as impressive to the modern man as to the ancient, and has been the theme of many of our poets. Perhaps Shelley has formulated this awe as well as any:

The One remains, the many change and pass;
Heaven's light forever shines, Earth's shadows fly;
Life, like a dome of many-colored glass,
Stains the white radiance of Eternity,
Until death tramples it to fragments.[1]

It is unjust to compare poems so unlike. The former conceives the Deity more personally, and in terms nearer to common experience; the imagination of Shelley soars into more ethereal air, and speaks to our imagination with a splendor of utterance quite unlike the comforting appeal to the heart which has caused the words of the Psalm to be incorporated into the funeral service of the Prayer Book. The Psalm is firmer in expression, more natural, and simpler. The mountains, the years, the watch, are nearer to common experience than the dome of many-colored glass and eternity's white radiance.

The insistent yearning of the soul for God finds classic expression in the 42d Psalm: 'As the hart panteth after the water-brooks, so panteth my soul after

[1] *Adonais.*

thee, O God.' The English equivalent to these immortal words is the hymn, 'Nearer, my God, to thee.' The Psalm is the more direct, wholesome utterance of the soul's ceaseless craving. The thought is more weighty and the measure more stately. The hymn is more lyrical, but the substance is thinner, and the author borrows her imagery from the experience of another. Intense thirst is a truer simile of the soul's craving than an exultant flight beyond the stars.

God has been a refuge to his people in all generations. This sense of safety is communicated in words strong and calm in the 91st Psalm — 'He that dwelleth in the secret place of the Most High shall abide under the shadow of the Almighty' — and more excellently in Psalm 46:

> God is our refuge and strength,
> A very present help in trouble.

Whittier's 'Eternal Goodness' —

> I know not where his islands lift
> Their fronded palms in air;
> I only know I cannot drift
> Beyond his love and care...

has its own appealing beauty, but it has not the accent of greatness found in the two psalms. Lanier's 'The Marshes of Glynn' —

> As the marsh-hen secretly builds in the watery sod,
> Behold I will build me a nest in the greatness of God;
> I will fly to the greatness of God as the marsh-hen flies
> In the freedom that fills all the space and the skies;
> By so many roots as the marsh grass sends in the sod,
> I will heartily lay me a-hold of the greatness of God...

has more fluent beauty than the Psalms, but lacks their robust vigor of phrase.

Habakkuk's ringing words,

For though the fig tree shall not blossom,
Neither shall fruit be in the vines;
The labor of the olives shall fail,
And the fields shall yield no meat;
The flock shall be cut off from the fold,
And there shall be no herd in the stalls:
Yet I will rejoice in the Lord,
I will joy in the God of my salvation.
Jehovah, the Lord, is my strength,
And he maketh my feet like hinds' feet,
And will make me to walk upon my high places...

express the triumph of faith over temporal losses, but Watts' noble hymn,

When I survey the wondrous cross
On which the Prince of glory died,
My richest gain I count but loss,
And pour contempt on all my pride

has a serenity of mood more lasting than the prophet's exultant cry, for it is based on meditation of a single act of God, something definite and concrete, rather than on the general character of Jehovah.

Churton Collins points out the sublime simplicity of the Psalmist's description of the greatness and littleness of man as contrasted with Shakespeare's more resounding lines. The Psalmist exclaims:

When I consider thy heavens, the work of thy fingers,
The moon and the stars, which thou hast ordained;
What is man, that thou art mindful of him?
And the son of man, that thou visitest him?

For thou hast made him but little lower than God,
And crownest him with glory and honor.[1]

Shakespeare puts similar sentiments in the mouth of Hamlet. Mark the difference.

This most excellent canopy, the air, look you, this brave overhanging firmament, this majestical roof fretted with golden fire — why it appears no other thing to me than a foul and pestilential congregation of vapors. What a piece of work is man! How noble in reason! How infinite in faculties! In apprehension how like a god! The beauty of the world! The paragon of animals! And yet to me, what is this quintessence of dust? [2]

In the Psalm there is a simplicity and consequent power in the statement of contrast between the majesty of the heavens and the insignificance yet glory of man which are lacking in Hamlet's somewhat bombastic words. In the Psalm one's attention is not distracted from the objects of contemplation; in 'Hamlet' the multiplying of exclamations draws attention away from the sky and man to the intellectual brilliancy of the speaker.

Contrast the idea of the omnipresence of God as contained in Psalm 139,

Lord, thou hast searched me and known me.
Thou knowest my downsitting and mine uprising,
  Thou understandest my thought afar off...

with Tennyson's

Speak to him then for He hears, and Spirit with Spirit can meet —
Closer is He than breathing, and nearer than hands and feet...[3]

[1] Psalm 8:3–5. [2] *Hamlet*, Act II, Scene 2.
[3] *The Higher Pantheism*.

or the bold sweep of the imagination in

> If I ascend into heaven, thou art there;
> If I make my bed in Sheol, behold, thou art there.
> If I take the wings of the morning,
> And dwell in the uttermost parts of the sea;
> Even there shall thy hand lead me,
> And thy right hand shall hold me...

with Emerson's 'Wood-Notes,' or, better, with these lines of Derzhavin:

> O thou eternal one! whose presence bright
> All space doth occupy, all motion guide;
> Unchanged through time's all-devastating flight;
> Thou only God! There is no God beside!
> Being of all beings! Mighty One!
> Whom none can comprehend and none explore;
> Who fill'st existence with thyself alone:
> Embracing all, supporting, ruling o'er, –
> Being whom we call God, and know no more.

Concerning the brevity of human life, Shakespeare's

> We are such stuff
> As dreams are made of; and our little life
> Is rounded with a sleep...[1]

is not inferior to

> My days are like a shadow that declineth;
> And I am withered like grass.[2]

Neither have the Hebrew poets surpassed Macbeth's fine statement of the monotony and vanity of life:

> To-morrow, and to-morrow, and to-morrow,
> Creeps in this petty pace from day to day
> To the last syllable of recorded time,

[1] *The Tempest*, Act IV, Scene 1. [2] Psalm 102:11.

And all our yesterdays have lighted fools
The way to dusty death. Out, out, brief candle!
Life's but a walking shadow, a poor player
That struts and frets his hour upon the stage
And then is heard no more: it is a tale
Told by an idiot, full of sound and fury,
Signifying nothing.[1]

It is interesting, also, to compare Wordsworth's

The world is too much with us; late and soon
Getting and spending, we lay waste our powers;
Little we see in Nature that is ours;
We have given our hearts away, a sordid boon!

with Isaiah's singing challenge,

Wherefore do you spend your money for that which is not bread,
And your labor for that which satisfieth not?[2]

There is a marked directness in the best Hebrew poetry; the fact, the thought, the emotion are put in a small compass. English poets are wont to philosophize, to construct an argument. This may be equally great, but it is of a different kind and can never have an appeal so universal. As English poetry introduces recurrence of sound, that is rhyme, it gains in singing quality and tends away from brevity. It is inclined to carry the thought through four lines rather than to condense it into one or two. Yet the stream of song flows wider with us.

I know of nothing in the Old Testament to be put by the side of Wordsworth's 'Ode to Duty,' for the idea is too abstract to awaken the Hebrew mind. The vague, mystical note, which is so pronounced in

[1] *Macbeth*, Act V, Scene 5. [2] Isaiah 55:2.

modern poetry, is lacking in the ancient writings. The Hebrew mind was too clear and definite: it was incapable of producing an effect such as we receive in reading Francis Thompson's 'The Hound of Heaven.' Neither do we find in Biblical poetry the constant expression of evangelical fervor so characteristic of our gospel hymns.

Old age comes with the frosts to every generation. How humanity feels toward this inevitable decay is revealed by the fact that the poets leave it severely alone. Browning, indeed, defied it in the well-known words,

> Grow old along with me,
> The best is yet to be.

But it has remained for a Hebrew, with the racial talent for clothing thought in figures, to make immortal poetry out of the body's decay.

> In the day when the keepers of the house shall tremble,
> And the strong men shall bow themselves,
> And the grinders shall cease because they are few,
> And those that look out of the windows be darkened,
> And the doors shall be shut in the street;
> When the sound of the grinding is low,
> And one shall rise up at the voice of the bird,
> And all the daughters of music shall be brought low.[1]

The English equivalent to the 23d Psalm is 'Lead, Kindly Light.' The theme is the same, the wandering spirit of man under divine protection. How typical they are of the two civilizations! One is an affirmation, the other a prayer. The Hebrew keeps close to familiar experience. Everything in the picture is definite,

[1] Eccl. 12:1–7.

solid, of the earth: the seen reveals the Unseen. The Englishman begins with his feelings and clothes them in imagery. The connecting thread is an unfolding aspiration, not the sequence of a journey. The reader feels that he is away from earth in the realm of emotions.

The power of Hebrew religion and of Hebrew literature is the same. The word becomes flesh and dwells among us and we behold its glory. English religious poetry quickly leaves the earth for the sky — 'sun, moon and stars forgot,' 'in the morn those angel faces smile.'

Regarding the two greatest themes which occupy the human mind, love and immortality, no literature, ancient or modern, has anything comparable in weight of thought, conformity to experience, and surge of inspiration, to Paul's magnificent ode in First Corinthians, the thirteenth chapter; no glorious rhapsody of confidence in the soul's victory over death matches the fifteenth chapter of First Corinthians. And surely there is no picture of the redeemed, written in any country or by any person, that can hold equal rank in power of comfort, vividness of conception, and cadence of genuine emotion, with those sentences beginning, 'These are they which come out of great tribulation.' [1]

[1] Revelation 7:14–17.

CHAPTER XII

THE PROPHETS

The Sublime consists of a certain loftiness and consummateness of language, and it is by this and this only that the greatest poets and prose writers have won preëminence and lasting fame.

LONGINUS

For a work of genius does not aim at persuasion, but ecstasy — or lifting the reader out of himself. The wonder of it wherever and whenever it appears, startles us; it prevails where the persuasive or the agreeable may fail; for persuasion depends mainly upon ourselves, but there is no fighting against the sovereignty of genius. It imposes its irresistible will upon us all.

LONGINUS

THE quality and genius of a people are seen in the kind of men whom they permanently honor. Greece paid homage to poets, orators, sculptors, philosophers, athletes, but who knows the name of a pythoness of Delphi or her interpreters? Rome gave sovereign regard to emperors, generals, poets. But Israel stands unique among the nations of ancient and modern times in producing, selecting, and revering prophets as her most memorable men. Nowhere is there to be found a succession of men like them in character, in vision, in eloquence. They were a composite of dervish, oracle, reformer, poet, and statesman. They uttered truth in ecstasy: the soberest judgments of a statesman were spoken with the passion of a reformer and with the lyrical cadence of poetry. Our reformers pour forth their intense moral passion in forms of stinging and superb rhetoric; and the glowing ardor of our didactic poets, like Whittier and Lowell, is never elevated to the rapture of the

Hebrews. No other nation, either before or since, has a literature quite like this — page following page representing the Most High as speaking directly to the people, arguing, pleading, exhorting; the Everlasting earnestly concerned in the welfare of a feeble and shifting people. In the Hebrew seers we have a unique group of men and a unique literature.

POLITICAL CONDITIONS PRODUCING THE PROPHETS

But it was not by chance that prophets arose among the Hebrews and that they came when they did. This phenomenal succession had a cause, exigent, continuous, and powerful enough to produce the amazing result. The cause was the imminent peril to which this little people was exposed by an overwhelming, irresistible enemy. The tortured soul of the nation insistently demanded to know why the Almighty permitted his chosen people to be the sport of ungodly barbarians, and men of vision and emotion endeavored to justify the ways of God to men. Whenever the peril was acute, there was lifted the voice of a prophet, either in denunciation or in hope. The oracles they uttered were patriotic because the country was threatened; they were religious because deliverance depended on the favor and intervention of God.

Let us glance for a moment at the world conditions which produced this succession of prophets. Call to mind that this small nation lived on a strip of land between Egypt and the vast and greedy empires whose seat was in the Tigris-Euphrates valleys. In the eighth century, Assyria, in the flush of vigor, was training its immense armies for conquest. This black cloud to the northeast sent terror to the small nations dwelling on the road leading from Assyria to the Nile. The profoundest minds among the Hebrews pondered deeply on the meaning of this Assyrian portent. Why did God permit it? What did the future hold in store? What could be done to avert the threatening peril? The heart-searchings produced by imminent danger called forth the latent energies of four of the greatest prophets of Israel — Amos, Hosea, Isaiah, and Micah. Again in the seventh century, Nineveh, that great city which had terrified the world, was tottering to a fall and Nahum chanted his solemn dirge, Zephaniah predicted a day of wrath, and Habakkuk sent his challenge to Jehovah. In the sixth century, Babylon was conquering the nations, and out of agony was born the supreme insights of Jeremiah, the oracles of the Great Unknown, and the ecclesiastical statesmanship of Ezekiel. The period of the greater prophets coincided with the years of Assyrian aggression, Assyrian decline, and the domination of Babylon. Great emergencies called forth great men who interpreted faith in the terms of current events, and vehemently pressed home upon the people the meaning of the tremendous upheavals amid which they lived.

COMMON BELIEF IN GOD POSSESSED MEN

The notion that God completely possesses certain men and utters his voice through them was not peculiar to the Hebrews. A recently discovered Egyptian papyrus records the marvelous adventure of Wenamon about 1113 B.C., in which a royal page fell into a frenzy lasting all the evening and through his mouth there came what purported to be a message from Baal. This is the first recorded instance of that religious frenzy which reveals possession by the divine spirit.[1] In Greece, Homer in the first book of the 'Iliad' introduces Calchas as one who knew the secrets of Apollo. In the time of Saul in Palestine, we read of groups of men who were susceptible to this possession and who wandered about Israel arousing patriotic sentiment and doing valuable service in unifying a scattered people and in enkindling a common purpose.

Of the oracles of the classic world, Delphi was the most famous and may serve as an illustration of all. The priestess — at first a young girl, later a mature woman — sat on a tripod directly above an aperture in the floor of the temple of Apollo, through which issued vapor from the stream of the Cassotis. Intoxicated by the vapors, the pythoness gave utterance to frenzied words; these, commonly incoherent, were written down by scribes and given to the priests representing the five leading families of Delphi to interpret. They reduced the oracles to an intelligible form, usually metrical and enigmatic. As people from all parts of the world came to Delphi to interrogate the oracle, these priests were in a better position than most to know the trend of events and to give excellent advice. But after the year 400 B.C. Delphi began to lose its influence and by A.D. 300 all the oracles were dumb.

[1] Baikie: *Egyptian Papyri*, p. 128.

Israel's prophets spoke for God in oracular form, but generally their meaning was perfectly clear. For the most part, they spoke or wrote under strong emotional stress, yet the spirit of the prophets was subject to the prophets. So sure were they of their inspiration that they did not, like the oracles of the nations, conceal the uncertainty of their minds in ambiguous pronouncements. In their affirmations there was a clarity born of perfect confidence that their message was of divine authority. It was God who was speaking, and he spoke to reveal his will, not to conceal it. Whence came that certainty which enabled them to use so freely that tremendous sentence, 'Thus saith the Lord,' or, more powerfully still, to assume that the Most High was using their lips in direct speech to the people. No sane man could speak to-day so confidently in the name of the Eternal. Yet if the prophets had toned down that 'Thus saith the Lord,' they would have been shorn of their authority.

THE PROPHETIC CONSCIOUSNESS

Let us examine for a moment this prophetic consciousness which made these men so sure, so clear, so persuasive of speech.

In men of genius, the connection between the conscious and the subconscious mind is very close. A thought dropped into the 'Deep Well' seems to be taken up subconsciously, analyzed, arranged, clothed, and then projected, vivid and complete, into consciousness. The genius is unaware of any volition on his part. The vision, the word, has come without his seeking. There is a vast gulf separating Nietzsche from Isaiah, yet the experience of the former throws light on the experience of the latter. 'If one had the smallest vestige of superstition left in one, it would hardly be possible completely to set aside the idea that one is the mere incarnation, mouthpiece, or medium of an almighty power. The idea of revelation in the sense that something which profoundly convulses and upsets one becomes suddenly visible and audible with indescribable certainty and accuracy describes the simple fact. One hears — one does not seek; one takes — one does not ask who gives; a thought suddenly flashes up like lightning, it comes with necessity, without faltering. I have never had any choice in the matter.' One might quote at great length similar experiences, in which the truth flashes upon the mind in an instant, complete, resplendent, indubitable. To the religious mind these spontaneous thoughts are revelations of the Most High. Because the prophets were unhampered by any consideration of mental processes or second causes, they could speak unhesitatingly in the name of God and wield a literary weapon of unsurpassed power. And God did, indeed, speak through them, for the Eternal utters his most authentic voice when lofty minds in their great moments express their knowledge of the Everlasting Righteousness and Beauty which dwells behind all the shadowy forms of time.

The Greeks and the Romans might read the will of God in entrails of animals: the prophets heard his voice in what was best in their own souls. They interpreted the Most High through the most exalted organ they knew — their own exalted moral sense. Surely man gets his clearest insight into the Ultimate Reality when his own highest nature is at its best.

The use of this method had a literary result which helps to explain the conditions in which the prophetic oracles have come down to us. If the Word was not the word of the prophet, but of God, then any authentic words of God could be grouped, without giving credit to the human instrument. Therefore, the sayings of different prophets on diverse occasions were brought together if they threw light on a certain truth or event, and this without wrong to the one who wrote them, for God was the author of all. This practice has given the Old Testament scholars their occupation.

Because the predictive sayings of the prophets have led Bible readers into such excesses of fanciful interpretation of history, it has become quite common for modern scholars to ignore this element almost entirely, yet prediction was certainly very prominent in the prophetic message. The prophet's face was always toward the future. Gunkel says there never arose a prophet in Israel whose first word was not prediction. It was by his ability to foretell the future that the people knew him to be a prophet.[1] Many of these vaticinations failed, as we shall see later, so that to us the permanent importance of these men lies in the pictures they give us of their own times and in their moral teachings. Their writings are valuable as historical documents, and they themselves

[1] Deuteronomy 18:21, 22.

have never been surpassed in their power to make men realize the moral framework of the world.

With excessive brevity we shall touch on the individual characteristics of the leading prophets, estimate the particular contribution of each to his own time and to the world. We shall close the chapter with an appraisal of the group as a whole.

AMOS, PROPHET OF JUSTICE

This herdsman of Tekoa was the first of the prophets who became famous for what he wrote rather than for what he did. He was the initiator and purest type of a new school of prophecy, and in vividness, vigor, and simplicity of speech he was not surpassed by any of his successors. It is instructive to note the similarity between the outbreaking of the prophetic spirit in Greece and Israel. Æschylus and Amos are names to be remembered together. Each was a stern, unbending puritan; each was a consummate artist, owing his effects to natural ability rather than to rich culture; each was an uncompromising oracle of the divine justice; each was the pioneer of a movement which marked a notable advance in the spiritual progress of mankind.

The story of the bitter experience which forced Amos to write down his warnings is too familiar to need rehearsal here.[1] The event which aroused him in his wilderness home and made him a world figure was the menace of an Assyrian invasion. He sought for a reason why the Almighty permitted this vast heathen power to lay waste the earth, and he found it

[1] Amos 7–10 ff.

in the iniquity of the nations. He denounced the foreign peoples for their barbarism and their wanton wars, and Israel for social wrongs and moral impurity. God is not mocked, neither is he propitiated by feasts and offerings, 'but let judgment roll down as waters, and righteousness as a mighty stream.'[1] He rested the truth of his affirmation neither on miracles nor on a book, but on conscience and history. He was one of the first to discover that God's favor means discipline for service, not prosperous ease: 'You only have I known among all the nations of the earth, therefore will I visit upon you all your iniquities.'[2] He also glimpses the truth of a universal providence: 'Are ye not as the children of the Ethiopians unto me, O children of Israel? saith the Lord. Have not I brought up Israel out of the land of Egypt, and the Philistines from Caphtor and the Syrians from Kir?'[3]

The book consists of a series of oracles (1:3 — 2:16), a series of sermons (3:1 — 6:14), and a series of visions (7:1 — 9:10).

The more one reads this remarkable collection, the more one wonders that this herdsman, living in a country so barren, with a literary tradition upon which to form his taste so pitifully meager, could by the vigor and originality of his genius set a standard of literary expression which has been equaled by few in the succeeding civilizations.

His imagination was one of extraordinary vividness. The opening sentence reveals this: 'The words

[1] Amos 5:24. [2] Amos 3:2.
[3] Amos 9:7.

of Amos... which he saw'; 'the Lord showed me'; 'I saw the Lord standing by the altar.'

His writings are vital because he drew directly from his own experience. Having few established standards to imitate, he kept close to fact and reality. He uttered himself with the full force of unconscious sincerity; hence his thrust and tone. The words and the imagery which he uses are his by right, for they are drawn from the observations of his daily life — the bird in the nest, two men meeting in the desert, a shepherd snatching from the mouth of a lion two legs and the piece of an ear. He had seen these things, therefore he makes us see them. Nothing is vague or florid or borrowed. He keeps close to earth and within the circle of his own observations; he writes of what he sees; he preserves the originality of his mind: consequently, no prophet has written in a purer, more virile style.

Seeing clearly, he felt deeply, and the natural rhythms of his emotions fell easily into the parallelisms of poetry, which his poetic taste combined into strophes, composed now of four, now of six, never exceeding ten periods. In his first oracle he employs a curious literary device, 'For three transgressions, yea for four,' and then he proceeds to point out one. It has been suggested that three represents completeness, and four abundance. Four and three equal seven, the mystic number, and this formula is repeated seven times before he denounces the sin of Israel.

Much as we may admire the ability and heroism of Amos, we should not fail to note his limitations.

He saw the evil of his day and the consequences which were sure to follow, but he did not see through evil to the transforming good. He discerned no gleam of the light behind the cloud.[1]

Neither can we accept his strong affirmations that famine, mildew, and drought are direct evidences of the wrath of God. Neither was the overthrow of Israel clearly a punishment of her own sin. She was like a house standing in the path of a flood, humanly helpless before the oncoming waters. The sin which caused the present danger was the world lust of the Assyrians. History does not bear out the implication of the prophet that a little people will be protected by their righteousness from the greed of unscrupulous dynasties.

HOSEA: PROPHET OF PITY

Some twenty years after Amos came Hosea, the first of the prophets to preach a gospel. Out of his own sad experience he had learned the divine nature of pity. His wife proved unfaithful to him and became a common wanton of the street, yet his love followed her in her degradation until he brought her back to his home, and then he reasoned: If I, a frail human, could follow my wife in tender solicitude into her sin and pay the price of her redemption, would not the Divine Love cling to Ephraim?

As a writer he lacks the fire, the vivid, concrete imagination, the rhythm of strong emotion which

[1] Amos 9:11 ff. seems to contradict this statement. But scholars are quite generally agreed that, as this vision contains no ethical element, it is not from his pen.

characterized his predecessor. As a stylist he fails to develop his thoughts consecutively. He flashes forth brilliant sentences, but writes no great chapters. Yet he sees more deeply than Amos. Religion to him is more than just dealing: it is a knowledge of God, growing into loving, spiritual intercourse with him.

It is significant that the Hosea *motif* is not common in literature. There are many stories deriving their interest from the loyalty of a pure woman to an unfaithful husband. But to represent a vigorous man following an unfaithful wife patiently with his solicitude through years, and finally redeeming her to respectability through his magnanimity, seems too high and godlike for credibility. Tennyson, in his treatment of Arthur's forgiveness of Guinevere, follows the line of Hosea's thought. The prophet, having recovered Gomer from a life of defilement, could not restore her to the full relationship of wife. She was too stained with shame, too closely associated with disquieting memories. Therefore he said: 'For many days shalt thou abide for me alone: thou shalt not play the harlot, thou shalt not be for thy husband; and I for my part also shall be so towards thee.' Arthur could say to Guinevere:

> Lo! I forgive thee, as Eternal God
> Forgives: do thou for thine own soul the rest.

Not until the Queen had lived down her sin could she be reunited to the King in perfect union.

ISAIAH: THE ELOQUENT

Isaiah is by general consent one of the greatest of the prophets in splendor of intellectual endowments and in the weight and balance of his character. He is the first prophet whose message came to him through a sense of personal sin and forgiveness. In the sixth chapter it is all expressed in the glowing light of a transcendent vision. In the temple, at a time of spiritual distress, during a period of profound meditation, the vision came of a God enthroned above all, yet whose glory filled all things. That God is high, that God is near, that God is holy — this is hereafter his message. This vivid sense of God revealed his own personal unworthiness. Being forgiven, he completely dedicated his life to service, and by sad experience learned that although the multitudes should fall away, yet through a faithful remnant the divine purpose would be accomplished.

The political policy which Isaiah advocated was very sagacious and very simple: it was for Judah to take advantage of its isolation, and to trust in God's purpose and character rather than in political intrigue and expediency for safety. Northern Israel, he declared, would be destroyed, and Jerusalem punished and purged by Assyria, who was unconsciously a weapon in the hand of God. Yet this cruel nation should be punished for its pride and wantonness. Ultimately a remnant of the faithful shall return from all quarters of the earth and Zion shall be the center of a universal religious dominion in which there shall be peace between man and animals; innocence shall dwell in safety by the side of force; the wolf shall not become a lamb — it will continue to be a wolf, yet with a better disposition.

Isaiah takes an unchallenged place among the very

great writers whom humanity has produced. His prophecies are almost without exception either poems or fragments of poems. The longest (9:8 — 10:4 with 5:25–30) does not exceed three hundred Hebrew words and could be delivered in a very short time. They were either composed to be sung or recited, or else were speeches afterwards reduced to poetical form. In some cases they are sayings which Isaiah's disciples remembered and wrote down.

The first characteristic of Isaiah as a writer which attracts attention is the superlative energy and splendor of his imagination. Truth came to him in visual form, it was a vision which he 'saw.' Sin was not an abstract conception: it was scarlet, forgiveness washed one white; 'wickedness burneth like the fire';[1] 'righteousness is a girdle';[2] even the penal judgments of God are the 'eyes of his glory';[3] a great man is 'the shadow of a rock.'[4] What more forcible statement of the helplessness of nations could be made than this: 'As one gathereth eggs that are forsaken, have I gathered all the earth, and there was none that moved the wing, or that opened the mouth, or that chirped.'[5] In four verses he describes the swift movements of an invading army more concisely and vividly than any other poet has done.[6]

He had easy control of the resources of language: metaphor, simile, personification, apostrophe came pouring forth in exhaustless abundance. He not only makes us see the truth, he glorifies it; his thought is clothed in splendor. This power of vivid, luminous

[1] Isaiah 9:18. [2] Isaiah 11:5. [3] Isaiah 3:8.
[4] Isaiah 32:2. [5] Isaiah 10:14. [6] Isaiah 5:26–30.

visualization of truth was matched in Isaiah with an extraordinary depth of emotion. He saw gloriously, he felt profoundly, and his sentences rolled forth with the majesty of sublime music. He is equally distinguished for intensity and for majesty of utterance: 'Wash you, make you clean; put away the evil of your doings,' is from the same pen which wrote the stately harmonies of the sixth chapter. Not so lucid a writer as Amos, he has a statelier surge of emotion. His writings are unequal. None of the oracles against foreign nations are of the highest order of merit, but his imagination catches fire when he contemplates the majesty of God and the glorious future of his people. His supreme chapters, therefore, are those, like chapters 1, 6, 11, in which intellect, heart, and imagination are raised to their utmost elevation and work together to show the dramatic contrast between the present sad condition of the people and God's glorious purpose.

He was a very great writer because he was a very great man; yet he had distinct limitations. He could not conceive of the redemption of the world except through the political sovereignty of Mount Zion. Neither could the era of universal peace dawn until Jerusalem had repaid her enemies in their own coin.[1]

Neither was he infallible in his prophecies, as in 19:23 ff., in which he predicts that Egypt, Assyria, and Israel shall be joined in league to worship Jehovah. He foresaw events in greatly foreshortened perspective. His Immanuel did not come for some seven hundred years, and the golden age when a vile

[1] Isaiah 11:11 ff.

person shall not be called noble is still on the far horizon.

MICAH: THE VILLAGE PROPHET

A contemporary of Isaiah was Micah, a man of the people, who dwelt in an obscure village; yet his influence was felt in the court, for Jeremiah tells us that Hezekiah repented when he heard that Micah had threatened that Mount Zion should be plowed as a field.[1] Being himself from a small village, he believed that the hope of the nation was to come from the country town, not from Jerusalem. Bethlehem had given David to be king and deliverer, and out of Bethlehem should come one who would be great unto the ends of the earth.[2]

The style of this book is rapid, bold, and vivid. The classic passage of the book is in Chapter 6:8. Of this, Huxley wrote: 'In the eighth century before Christ, in the heart of a world of idolatrous polytheists, the Hebrew prophet put forth a conception of religion which appears to me as wonderful an inspiration of genius as the art of Phidias or the science of Aristotle. "He hath showed thee, O man, what is good: and what doth the Lord require of thee, but to do justly, and to love mercy, and to walk humbly with thy God?" If any so-called religion takes away from this great saying of Micah, I think it wantonly mutilates, while if it adds thereto, I think it obscures, the perfect ideal of religion.'[3] Whether written by Micah or some later poet, it is an ultimate statement which can never be forgotten.

[1] Micah 26:18. [2] Micah 5:2–4.

[3] *Nineteenth Century*, December, 1885.

NAHUM: SINGER OF DOOM

Now the scene changes. Assyria, that dread power, is tottering to its fall. Nineveh, its capital, is besieged by both the Medes and the Babylonians, when out of Judah comes the exultant cry of Nahum. Why should he not rejoice, for lo, Jehovah is taking vengeance on the enemies of his country. 'Behold upon the mountains the feet of him that bringeth good tidings, that publisheth peace! Keep thy feasts, O Judah, perform thy vows; for the wicked one shall no more pass through thee: he is utterly cut off.'[1] This prophet is a very vivid writer, his description of battle in Chapter 3:2, 3 is brilliant and spirited; his joy in seeing the foes of his country in trouble so elevates his emotions that he strikes off some unforgettable sentences: 'The Lord hath his way in the whirlwind and the storm, and the clouds are the dust of his feet';[2] 'The Lord is good, a stronghold in the day of trouble; and he knoweth them that put their trust in him.'[3] Unlike the eighth-century prophets, he has no word of condemnation for his people.

ZEPHANIAH

Zephaniah, a contemporary of Jeremiah, is much inferior as a writer to Nahum. To him the confusion of the times appears as the wrath of God visiting punishment upon all the nations. His imagination is neither powerful nor original, yet, as he piles woe upon woe which are to come in the great day of vengeance, he suggested to a greater poet of the Middle

[1] Nahum 1:15. [2] Nahum 1:3. [3] Nahum 1:7.

Ages the well-known hymn *Dies Iræ*, which is the Vulgate translation of the prophet's denunciation.[1]

HABAKKUK: A VOICE FROM THE CROWD

In him emerges a quality which is very precious to the believer: he claims the right to question and to investigate in the field of religion. Other prophets speak from God to the people; he addresses God in behalf of the people. Others denounce the sins of the nations and declare impending punishment; he sends up from humanity a challenge to the Almighty and interrogates his providential government. In this he is the predecessor of Job. He is the forerunner of a long line of poets and philosophers, who since his day are supremely interested in the meaning of life. With him religious speculation begins in Israel. He does not go far, but he states the perennial problem of why a good God permits the evil man to prosper. 'Thou that art of purer eyes than to behold evil,' he says, 'and that canst not look upon perverseness, wherefore lookest thou upon them that deal treacherously, and holdest thy peace when the wicked swalloweth up the man that is more righteous than he?'[2] Then he stands upon his watch-tower to receive what God will speak to him.[3] The answer comes in double form: the wicked will ultimately be punished, the righteous man has an inner assurance and experience which make him independent of prosperity. In the sentence, 'The just shall live by his faith,' or, more properly, by his faithfulness, there crept into the currents of history one of the most revolutionary truths ever

[1] Zephaniah 1:14–18. [2] Habakkuk 1:13. [3] Habakkuk 2:1.

proclaimed. It was the heart of Paul's theology and of the German Reformation. Christ put the same truth in another form when he said, 'A man's life consisteth not in the abundance of the things which he possesseth,' and Socrates in another when he declared, 'No harm can come to a good man.'

The third chapter is a psalm taken from the temple hymnal and here inserted because its thought is similar to the rest of this book. The favor of God consists in an inward grace, not in outward prosperity. The kingdom of heaven is within. 'Though the fig tree shall not blossom... yet I will rejoice in the Lord.' In spiritual insight and in memorable sentences this book is one of the noblest in the Old Testament.

JEREMIAH

Jeremiah is the first of the prophets to recognize the place of the individual in religion. Heretofore religion had been closely identified with the tribe or the nation; even in Isaiah it was a matter of the group.[1] But Jeremiah, living in a time when the state was unstable, realized that religion must find a base more permanent than nation or temple or church, so he boldly declared that there was to be a new covenant when the law should be written on the heart.[2]

He was a man of deep and tender spirit, who grieved over the sins of his people and courageously pleaded with them. Essentially a man of prayer, much of his book is a record of his meditations before

[1] Isaiah 8:16 ff. [2] Jeremiah 31:31–34.

God.[1] Strongly emotional, he often is on the verge of hysteria.[2] In his earlier days he thought of God as a being of loving-kindness, judgment, and righteousness,[3] but in accordance with prevalent conceptions he saw God's avenging purpose in the droughts that afflicted the country [4] and in the political turmoil of the time. A God whose immediate action is seen in the horrors of war must be a God of terrible vengeance. This false notion — so it seems to us — reacted on his character and he grew embittered and vengeful, so that at the end of his life he is not the sane and sympathetic man he was at the beginning. There are reformers who so meet overwhelming adversity as to grow in the graces of patience and charity: Jeremiah was not one of them.

As a writer he lacks the range, the dignity, the splendor of Isaiah; his speech is simple, direct, and homely, rising at times to genuine eloquence. Many of his writings are in the form of a dirge, the five-beat measure; that is, the three-beat line followed by a line with two beats.

EZEKIEL: THE HIGH CHURCHMAN

Ezekiel was a priest-prophet, an ecclesiastical statesman, after the order of Hildebrand or Calvin. In 597 B.C., when Nebuchadnezzar carried the flower of Judah to Babylon, among them was this young priest. For five years he meditated on the strange ways of God before he began to prophesy. Then he coöperated with Jeremiah in predicting the destruc-

[1] Jeremiah, chapters 14 and 15.
[2] Jeremiah 9:1, 2, and 23:9.
[3] Jeremiah 9:23, 24.
[4] Jeremiah 3:3 and 5:24, 25.

tion of Jerusalem for her sins of idolatry. After the city fell in 586 B.C., his problem was to conserve religion and hold the people together that they might carry out the plans of the Most High. To this end he with others prepared a code known as the Holiness Code (Lev. 17–26) to be used in the restored temple, and encouraged the exiles by promises of return. This strong emphasis on ritualistic righteousness shows Ezekiel to have been possessed of a very different temper from the great prophets of the eighth century. With him the priestly element in religion became dominant. He based religion upon a book: indeed, his own inspiration came to him in the form of a book.[1] With Jeremiah he shares the honor of making the first clear statement in Hebrew history of individual responsibility.[2]

As a man, he was austere, fearless, giving with impassioned earnestness all he had for the glory of God. He felt that the hand of God was on him and the roll of lamentations tasted sweet as honey in his mouth, yet he was very tender toward the remnant of Israel who remained faithful. More self-restrained than Jeremiah, under personal affliction his calmness is phenomenal. Nowhere does he, like Isaiah or Jeremiah, express a sense of personal unworthiness.

As a writer, he is inferior both in matter and in manner to the great prophets of the eighth century. His imagination is not of the first order, as can be readily perceived by comparing his description of the vision of his call [3] with that of Isaiah.[4] It is fantasti-

[1] Ezekiel 2:8—3:3.
[2] Ezekiel, chapter 18.
[3] Ezekiel 1—3:15.
[4] Isaiah, chapter 6.

cal, mechanical, not glowing with inspiration. His visions are literary devices, not born of his intuition. His style is prolix, painstaking, formal, yet at times it is so exceedingly forceful that his description of the spirit within the wheels,[1] the valley of dry bones,[2] the elders in the dark,[3] are indelibly stamped on the memory. He was the first to use the apocalyptic style, and the author of Revelation was much influenced by him.

As a religious leader he had distinct limitations. His severe and vengeful God is far from being the God of the New Testament; the individualism which he taught was extreme, and his prophecies of what should happen after the return — the establishment of Ephraim-Judah, which he united under one ruler of the house of David — were not fulfilled.[4]

SECOND ISAIAH

The prophetic genius of Israel reaches its flood tide in the chapters included in Isaiah, chapters 40–66. These chapters take their place easily in the very great literature of the world. Scholars are divided in their opinions regarding the date of their composition and the author. The majority hold that most of chapters 40–55 issued from a great unknown prophet about 540 B.C., who consoled the exiles in Babylon with predictions of the deliverance about to come through Cyrus the Great. Regarding chapters 56–66, many believe them to have been written in Palestine about 450 B.C. Professor C. C. Torrey,

[1] Ezekiel 1:20. [2] Ezekiel 37:1–14. [3] Ezekiel 8:12.
[4] Ezekiel 37:22.

however, has just published an able volume claiming that chapters 34–66, excepting 36–39, were all written by one poet who lived in Palestine about 400 B.C.; that there are twenty-seven poems, all written in strict metrical form and addressed to the Jews of the Dispersion. To reach this conclusion he is forced to consider the passages containing the name of Cyrus to be interpolations.

These questions are exceedingly interesting, but are outside our present purpose. As poems these oracles are a precious literary heritage; a radiant and powerful soul shines through their glowing sentences. The poet was a seer who, more than any of the remarkable succession of poets. and prophets, saw through the tragic experiences of life to the overruling good. Where others were preoccupied with the penal sufferings of Israel, this man was obsessed with the glorious purposes of the Most High. So dazzling was his vision of God that he could not refrain his lips from speaking comfort, nor his heart from songs of rhapsody. His message is a glowing philosophy of history: Jehovah is God of all the earth; Israel has been chosen as his servant for the salvation of mankind; in the fulfillment of this mission Israel conquers by vicarious suffering, not by self-assertive might; and through it all God knows, he helps, he suffers, he conquers.

The greatness of the Second Isaiah consists in this: more than any prophet in Israel, or any mind of the ancient world, so far as we have knowledge, he discerned a governing purpose working through individuals and nations for a vast consummation in redemption; he apprehended the unfolding purpose and he perceived the method by which it works, a method so strange that he exclaimed: 'Who hath believed our report, or to whom hath the arm of the Lord been revealed?' The poet reaches his highest inspiration in four songs known as the Songs of the Servant of Jehovah. Scholars differ in delimiting these poems, but all agree that a description and interpretation of the true servant of Jehovah appear in chapters 42:1–4; 49:1–6; 50:1–9; 52:13 — 53:12. In the first, God speaks; in the second and third, the servant speaks; in the fourth, his story is told by an onlooker. In Chapter 42:1–4 there is a vivid description of the servant in the fewest possible words: his equipment — 'I have put my spirit upon him'; his purpose — 'he shall bring forth judgment to the Gentiles'; his method — 'He shall not cry, nor lift up, nor cause his voice to be heard in the street. A bruised reed shall he not break, and the smoking flax shall he not quench; he shall bring forth judgment in truth.' He shall not be hysterical, nor self-advertising; compassionate, he will not compromise the truth.

In Chapter 49:1–3 the servant declares his call and the stern discipline by which he has been made a polished shaft, a sharp sword, yet is kept waiting until the moment of opportunity. The last two songs predict that only through suffering can he fulfill his mission.

Let any reader try to describe in a few words the character, the purpose, the method of a true servant of Jehovah, and he will then begin to appreciate the achievement of this poet in putting so much truth in such arrestive imagery, with such restrained depth of emotion. The 53d chapter of Isaiah shares with the 13th chapter of First Corinthians the distinction of expressing an ultimate truth in ultimate form.

This author had the ability not only to tell the truth; he sang it; he made it glorious. Beholding his subject in range and majesty, he enforced it by repetition in such a variety of forms and assertions that richness of vocabulary became opulence, and opulence became, not intoxication, but power, ennobling, not surfeiting, the mind of the reader. His glowing imagery, his elevated and contagious emotion, his energy, range, and splendor of diction have challenged the emulation of superlative writers ever since his day.

It has been affirmed that, brilliant as this prophet is, in him prophecy begins to decline. Gardiner[1] thinks he breaks away from fact and gives himself to rhapsody which in later prophets degenerates into apocalypse. We must go, he says, to Herodotus for knowledge of the times, while in Amos and Isaiah we are given the data of history. But it must be remembered that this prophet was not a statesman charged with responsibility for meeting an immediate crisis, but a seer unfolding a philosophy of history. He was dealing with principles and ideals rather than with contemporary facts. It is true that in him imagination and emotion are strained to the utmost, but his thought is never obscured, neither is the effect weakened by any touch of hysteria.

Cornhill[2] thinks that this prophet falls below Jere-

[1] *The Bible as English Literature*, p. 241 ff.

[2] *The Prophets of Israel*, p. 143 ff.

miah in that the latter universalized religion by making it an affair of the individual conscience, while the former identified religion with a restored Jerusalem. This criticism is not without force, yet the Jerusalem of the prophet was not the actual city of stone and brick; it was an ideal whose foundations were sapphires, and whose pinnacles were rubies. His language has created that golden city of God whose gleaming towers still encourage humanity on its pilgrimage.

PROPHECY AT A LOWER LEVEL

Haggai, Zechariah, Malachi, Joel, Obadiah

With the capture of Babylon the political power of the Semitic race was broken, for in Cyrus the Aryan civilization became supreme, and has remained so until this day. The exiles were now permitted to return, but few of them availed themselves of the opportunity. And as they went back over the intervening miles, did the mountains and the hills break forth before them into singing?

Seventeen years of poverty and disillusionment followed. Then arose two prophets, Haggai and Zechariah, to demand the rebuilding of the temple and to encourage the people in the attempt. Haggai's four oracles were all about the rebuilding of the temple, and were so effective that he had the people at work in less than a month. The tone of this prophet is that of 'a secretary raising a budget.' He is a layman, and his style is plain, direct prose.

Zechariah also wrote in prose, dictated by an artificial fancy rather than creative passion. His is the familiar sentence: 'Not by might, nor by power, but by my spirit, saith the Lord of hosts.' [1]

Fifty years after Zechariah, the people had again become discouraged, and the oracles given the title of 'Malachi' were issued. The writer lived in the days of Socrates and used the same method of question and answer to enforce truth. The work is in prose with some strong passages; especially precious are the closing words of the third chapter, concerning the book of remembrance.

Probably later than Malachi, Joel, clear and fluent in style yet narrow in vision, calls upon the people to repent and promises them prosperity. Censure is not so prominent in him as in the older prophets; his God is gracious and full of compassion. But Joel's interest is centered in Zion, and in his zeal for vengeance he reverses the famous dictum of Isaiah, saying to the people: 'Beat your plowshares into swords, and your pruning hooks into spears.' [2] One memorable sentence has come from him: 'Your old men shall dream dreams, your young men shall see visions.' [3]

Brevity is not always the soul of wit, for Obadiah was the briefest of the prophets, yet he uttered no sentence which is cherished.

THE PERMANENT CONTRIBUTION OF THE PROPHETS TO RELIGION

Having stated thus briefly and imperfectly the characteristics and leading thought of the individual prophets, it is pertinent to ask concerning the fundamental truths upon which they were agreed and which

[1] Zechariah 4:6. [2] Joel 3:10. [3] Joel 2:28.

constitute their lasting contribution to religious thought and life.

They clearly perceived and got into the currents of history three ideas of superlative importance. One was the universality, the justice, the compassion of the One God; another was that this Supreme Spirit was working out in history the ethical redemption of mankind; from these the third logically followed, namely, that man's highest interest is to be like God in character and to do his will.

The conviction of the sovereignty of One God was domesticated in the spiritual life of the Western world, not by the teachings of Greek philosophy, but as a heritage from the Hebrews. This belief has had great reënforcement from other sources, yet historically this stream had its rise in the mountains of Judah. That the Supreme is loving and righteous has been taught by many faiths, yet none has held it with the passionate intensity of the Hebrews or proclaimed it with equal effect.

In the wonderful sixth century before Christ the foundations of the great world religions were being laid. Gautama in India proclaimed the eightfold path to peace, but he neither affirmed nor denied the reality of the many gods of India. Confucius in the same century sought to establish the social stability of China through the channel of good manners. He, too, neither spoke for nor against the worship of the gods. Consequently, both in China and in India the way was clear for all kinds of superstitious practices.

What one believes and lays to heart regarding the nature of the Supreme Power working through and constraining one's life is of the utmost importance. It determines character and the chief concerns of endeavor. The fatal weakness both of Confucianism and of Buddhism is that they are centered upon no ennobling conception of the Eternal Being. The stone which these builders rejected is the head of the corner of Hebraism. Men are saved, not by manners, nor by self-discipline, but by looking unto God. 'Look unto me and be ye saved all the ends of the earth,' is their proclamation. 'Thou shalt love the Lord thy God with all thy heart.' All well-being was centered on likeness to a God of righteousness and mercy. The prophets laid no stress on miracles, but on ethical conduct before God.

Other religions and literatures have glimpses of all these truths, but nowhere else are they held with such intensity. It is interesting to contrast the Greek with the Hebrew conception of God. Æschylus in the 'Suppliants' makes the chorus declare:

> All godlike power is calm; and high
> On thrones of glory seated,
> Jove looks from heaven with tranquil eye
> And sees his will completed.

How different this from the Hebrew idea of Jehovah's intense concern with the affairs of men! Listen to the Second Isaiah's descriptions of his God: 'The Lord shall go forth as a mighty man; he shall stir up jealousy like a man of war; he shall cry, yea, he shall shout aloud; he shall do mightily against his enemies. I have long holden my peace... now will I cry like a travailing woman: I will gasp and pant together.' [1]

[1] Isaiah 42:13, 14.

The prophets thrust into the courses of history an inexpugnable hope. They taught that their holy God, jealous of his honor, was working out in history an ethical redemption through Israel for the world. Human affairs are not a purposeless swirl and agitation; a strong tide moves toward a definite end. Tennyson can sing of 'a far-off divine event toward which the whole creation moves' because of the Hebrew strain in his faith. This firm conviction of something better further on was woven into the tissue of the mind of the race by the prophets. This glorious hope of a divine future for mankind did not come historically from Egypt or Babylon, it did not arise in India or China, neither was it an intuition of Greek genius. The Greek dramatists, indeed, represent Zeus as weaving his web of destiny. Æschylus expressly says:

> O would that Jove might show to men
> His counsel as he planned it;
> But ah! he darkly weaves the scheme,
> No mortal eye hath scanned it....
> Firm to the goal his purpose treads,
> His will knows no frustration.[1]

But this plan is the destiny of families, the issue of a battle, not a vast world progress toward a glorious goal.

The prophets of Israel impressed indelibly on the religious mind of Europe and America the conviction of one universal, holy, and compassionate God, who inspires an inextinguishable hope because he is carrying out a benign purpose through the ages, and

[1] *Suppliants.*

who demands of his worshipers an obedience which redeems character and induces loyal coöperation. They gave to the world a tremendous sense of God and of man's responsibility to do his will and be conformed to his likeness.

THEIR LITERARY POWER

Their success in launching their conviction was the result in a large measure of their eminent literary ability. Religion, by its very nature, is productive of literature, for it deals with superlative themes and creates elevated emotions. The prophets wrote enduring literature because in their pages moral truth glows with moral passion, and shapes itself in the natural rhythms of sincerity. Their intuitive minds saw clearly and spoke without equivocation. Their method of speaking directly in the name of Jehovah gives to their words immense effectiveness. When a message seems authentic through its appeal to our deepest instincts, no other device has such power.

Their utter sincerity, the tremendous importance of the truths they spoke, their vivid realistic imagination shaping these truths into impressive imagery, profoundly stirred their emotions, so that their language issued in the beat and beauty of poetry.

The attractiveness of the original form, of course, escapes us in our English version. It cannot be successfully imitated. It was native to them, and is as yet imperfectly understood by our scholars. Some writers lament that the English Bible presents the oracles of the prophets in prose, and many commentators and translators have endeavored to convey to the English reader the form and flavor of the original. This is praiseworthy and enlightening, yet it is fortunate that the authorized versions have refrained from such experiments, for the ordinary reader comes much nearer the inner spirit and passion of the prophets through the lucidity and natural rhythms of prose than he would through poetic measures which are unfamiliar.

THEIR LIMITATIONS

With all their unique greatness, the prophets had some very distinct limitations — limitations common to their time, and limitations growing out of their peculiar temperaments.

We wince under their fierce assertions that famine, droughts, the horrors of war came directly from God in punishment for the sins of the nation. Where the prophets were confident, our Lord was reticent. When the tower of Siloam fell, he refrained from attributing it directly to the divine wrath against those who were destroyed: he predicted what would befall Jerusalem as the result of the fierce intolerance and spiritual blindness of the people, but he did not state that the Romans were the instruments of the divine anger. And when he was rejected, he showed a pity for the people which was not characteristic of most of the prophets.

This error of ascribing pestilence and invasion to the wrath of God was common to men everywhere in those days. It was not until the fifth century before Christ that Hippocrates (460–377 B.C.) stated, for the first time in history of which we have record, that maladies have natural causes. It is significant that this discovery was made by a Greek and not by a Hebrew.

But a more serious limitation was a certain lack of generous humaneness. Their zeal for God stifled their love for man. Against other nations they were very fierce and very intolerant. They were apparently incapable of putting themselves in the place of others. In this they contrasted with the Greeks. Æschylus, whose conception of the divine justice was as august as that of Amos, wrote 'The Persians,' a drama in which the scene is laid in Susa and Xerxes is represented returning from his ill-starred expedition against the Greeks. The situation is so handled that the Greek audience, instead of exulting against their late foes, are made to understand them and even to feel a pity for them. So in 'The Trojan Woman' Euripides enters sympathetically into the tragic sufferings of the victims. Only in the writings Jonah and Ruth do we find something of a broad humanitarian spirit toward the outsider. There are glimmerings of it in the Law, but it is not a prominent characteristic of the prophets. On the contrary, there is a conspicuous lack of it. They conceived tremendous principles, but in a provincial and intensely partisan manner. It seems never to have occurred to them that other nations were groping after God through their religions: they were idolaters and should be given to the sword.

From our point of view, they erred in their philosophy of the activity of God in nature and in history; they certainly erred in their teachings of the central glory of Israel and its capital in the future history of the world. They were thunder and lightning and knew little of the persuasive power lying in charity and loving-kindness. They were also lacking in moderation: 'Naught in excess' was certainly not their motto. The methods of Jeremiah would gain few adherents at any time or in any place.

Wendell Phillips used to say that each generation should have one agitator who would fearlessly expose the evil of his day without fear or favor. Such men do serve a most useful function, but God in his mercy limits the species. Indeed, as a distinct type the prophets are as extinct as the mastodon. In the future we shall have historians, poets who will write noble psalms, authors of proverbs and short stories, but the prophet who can declare, with unclouded conscience, 'Thus saith the Lord,' and think of himself as a privileged mouthpiece of the Almighty, has passed. His insights, his spiritual elevation, his utter courage and consecration, his gift of powerful expression, will appear for the saving of the nations in a noble succession, but his peculiar type has gone forever with the world view which made him possible.

CHAPTER XIII

THE HUMANISTS OF ISRAEL

The words 'And God said, Let there be light: and there was light,' still sound as sublime to us as they sounded to Longinus, who first quoted them as an example of sublimity. In the Song of Solomon all the passion of the East is naturalized among us. There are the Proverbs to be quoted, like Horace, for their worldly wisdom. There is Ecclesiastes, full of the ancient weariness of life which still comes to those who are sated with pleasure and see nothing beyond it.

Clutton-Brock

We have discussed poets and prophets; now we are confronted by another type of mind, another kind of literature. Jeremiah recognized the diversity of gifts and the permanent value of writings less impassioned than his own. 'The law,' he says, 'shall not perish from the priest, nor counsel from the wise, nor the word from the prophet.' [1] The books of the wise men as we have them in the Old Testament are Job, Proverbs, and Ecclesiastes, and are called the wisdom literature. Although Job bears many of the marks of this kind of expression, the author is so essentially a poet that we have treated him as such, and shall consider the Hebrew wisdom in its two most characteristic productions — Proverbs and Ecclesiastes. The sage has a cooler temper and less fervid imagination than the prophet and is quite incapable of experiencing the rapture of the poet. A more familiar name for the wise man is the humanist, for he is concerned with man rather than with God, and with human problems rather than with national politics. The humanist has

[1] Jeremiah 18:18.

adorned the letters of every great people. Ptah-hotep, a king of the fifth Egyptian dynasty, living some two thousand years before Solomon, gave initial honor to the proverb. When the Assyrian Ashurbanipal collected books for his library in Nineveh, he sent copyists to the old temples of Babylon to copy hymns, epics, and wise sayings. The practical mind endowed with the gift of sententious speech gave form to the writings of Epictetus in Greece, Marcus Aurelius in Rome, Alexander Pope in England, and Benjamin Franklin in America. In the Old Testament the distinctive writings of the sages are Proverbs and Ecclesiastes; in the New, this same method of thinking appears in the Epistles of James, in the parables of our Lord, and in part of the Sermon on the Mount.

The prophet thought of sin as disobedience, the priest as defilement, but the wise man said, 'It is foolish.' The priest said of righteousness, 'It is commanded'; the sage, 'It is prudent.' The prophet would justify the ways of God to man; the humanist accepted his ways as unsearchable. That wisdom literature should flourish in Israel is not strange. The Hebrew was eager to make the best of life, and his intuitive, practical mind would delight in 'the wisdom of many framed in the wit of one.' So well does Proverbs interpret human interests that Bartlett has sixty-nine quotations from this book — this is more than from any other Scripture, excepting the Psalms.

PROVERBS

Like the Psalms, the book is divided into five sections. The oldest collection is named the Proverbs of

Solomon, and from Chapter 10 to 15 antithetic couplets prevail, from Chapter 16 onward to 22:17, the synthetic couplet expresses a complete thought, afterwards there is more freedom, until we come to a poem on wine (23:29–35), where the thought is carried through seventeen lines. The men of Hezekiah returned to the couplet (25–29). The lines of Agur (30) are as shrewd as they are fine in workmanship. The book culminates in the famous description of the virtuous woman comprising twenty-one lines in our English Bible. It is an acrostic poem, the severest form of Hebrew versification.

Writing in the form of proverbs has the advantage of stating truth so briefly that it is easily remembered; hiding it in a figure of speech excites the mind

> To understand a proverb and a figure;
> The words of the wise, and their dark sayings.[1]

The literary power of this aphoristic method of presenting truth has been forcibly stated by an English writer who is unexcelled in its use, Francis Bacon:

> The writing of aphorisms hath many excellent virtues, whereto the writing in method does not approach, for first it trieth the writer, whether he be superficial or solid, for aphorisms, except they be ridiculous, cannot be made but of the pith and heart of science; for discourse of illustration is cut off. So there remains nothing to fill the aphorisms but some good quantity of observation; and therefore no man can suffice, nor in reason will attempt to write aphorisms, but that he is sound and grounded.

[1] Proverbs 1:6.

It is significant of changing times to note that the qualities which we lay greatest stress upon to-day — courage, moderation in thought, self-sacrifice for the common good — these are not mentioned. Prudence, sobriety, chastity are placed in the foreground.

Jesus had in mind the words in Chapter 25:6, 7 when he said it was better to take the lowest seat at the feast, and Paul found his forcible metaphor about heaping coals of fire upon the head of an enemy in the 21st and 22d verses of the same chapter.

ECCLESIASTES: 'MOCKING THE RUNNER'S HEAT'

This book is quite outside the circle of Old Testament thought, yet there would have been a real gap in the Scriptures had it not been inserted. If literature is an interpretation of life, surely the pessimist must be represented. Having seen the experience which men of ardent faith have had with God, it is profitable to learn the fortunes of a disillusioned mind. The book is a quest for the *summum bonum*, and in this respect is like Goethe's 'Faust,' but in style and temper it is more like Omar Khayyám, and finds a spiritual ancestor in the 'Song of the Harper,' found in Egyptian Antuf's tomb of the third century before Christ.[1]

The author is a man of intellect and culture who is thinking his way through life's experiences to life's meaning. Touched with cynicism, he is not bitter, but disillusioned. He may have been a Sadducee, disbelieving in revelation, yet resolved to face the facts of life. The great writers of the Scriptures had lived in the ages of faith, when imagination was confident and

[1] Budge: *The Literature of the Egyptians*, p. 242.

enthusiasm natural. This man lived at a time of downward drift from the imagination to the understanding, from faith to incredulity. Babylon and Assyria had profoundly stirred the genius of Israel; now Greece exerts her influence. Athenian culture from the time of Euripides had grown skeptical and its temper was overspreading the world. This book shows its effect. Putting his thoughts in the mouth of Solomon for literary effectiveness, the author, after concluding that life is a dreary round, sets himself to search for something that is worth while, and finds that wisdom is sadness, mirth is vanity, and pomp a wind. Through some eleven chapters he moves, testing all experience and finding only futility and dreariness, yet in spite of the encircling gloom his constant refrain is 'Be glad.' 'Truly the light is sweet, and a pleasant thing it is for the eyes to behold the sun.' [1] 'Behold that which I have seen to be good and to be comely is for one to eat or to drink, and to enjoy good in all his labor.' [2]

From a literary point of view the book reaches its culmination in the noble description of old age and death, beginning: 'Rejoice, O young man, in thy youth.' [3] There is an originality, boldness, and precision of metaphor which holds the attention, and a solemn harmony of verse which induces a noble mood in the mind of the reader. No one has ever written on the same subject quite so well.

The quest for satisfaction ends with the sane conclusion, 'Fear God, and keep his commandments: for this is the whole duty of man.' The word 'duty' is in

[1] Ecclesiastes 11:7. [2] Ecclesiastes 5:18.
[3] Ecclesiastes 11:9 ff.

italics and therefore is not in the text. It was the prophets who stressed obligation; the wise men looked for what is valuable. The meaning seems to be that the one permanent satisfaction is to accept the universe in a spirit of trust.

As literature, Ecclesiastes ranks very high. The Preacher may profess that all things are vanity, but the pains he took to perfect his diction bear eloquent testimony to the fact that he thought literary excellencies to be eminently worth while. The sentences are smooth and balanced, the emotional element, although subordinated to the intellectual, is sufficient for sustained rhythmic beauty. Mr. Stedman gives the book this tribute: 'Whether prose or verse, I know nothing grander than Ecclesiastes in its impassioned survey of mortal pain and pleasure, its estimate of failure and success; none of more noble sadness; no poem working more indomitably for spiritual illumination.' [1]

The cause of this 'noble sadness' should not be overlooked. If one would rejoice in life, let him live intensely for high ends. Then the question, 'What is it all worth?' will never occur to him. This author sat on the side-lines and watched the game; he did not understand it, and he felt no thrill. Life yields its secrets more easily to the doer than to the thinker.

Yet the book is very comforting. We all have our cynical moods and moments of disillusionment. In these dark hours what advice carries its own evidence and gives cheer? What better than this: 'Be glad in common things, and obey the laws of Nature.'

[1] E. C. Stedman: *Nature and Elements of Poetry*, p. 212.

CHAPTER XIV

PROSE FICTION

There are not many means among us now of producing the beauty of holiness; but the Bible remains the chief of them, because it connects holiness with beauty more directly and more closely than any other work of man.... It says what is best worth saying in the best possible words.

CLUTTON-BROCK

IT has been said that fiction began in this wise. Once upon a time a man told a story about another man; later, some one spun a yarn with a woman for the principal character; finally, some genius devised a tale about a man and a woman, and the novel was launched on its amazing career. But a career means fashions, and fashions change. Few are the stories that interest more than one generation. Still fewer are the tales of one people that can be transplanted into another soil and climate. Stories are so interwoven with the thoughts and habits of their time and country that when they are separated from their background, they have no vitality. Those that do live often suffer a curious fate. 'Gulliver's Travels' flamed out of the fierce soul of Swift as withering satire; to-day boys and girls read it as a delightful narrative. As some one has happily remarked: the glare of a volcano now lights a child to bed. Often a story survives because of qualities, and for purposes, which were not at all in the author's mind: it contains something which is not peculiar to any time or place, but awakens feeling common to all humanity. When, therefore, a tale is told from generation to generation, and even passes beyond the borders of nation and race in undiminished vitality, it is for two reasons: something universal shines through the local incidents, and over all plays the flame of beauty. Let us not forget our formula: truth plus beauty equals immortality.

RUTH

The Book of Ruth is one of the best short stories ever written. Originally propaganda, the purpose is so concealed in the perfection of its art and the art is so exquisite that it survives for quite other reasons than the one which caused it to be written. It is a plea for tolerance. Ezra and Nehemiah had been pressing their drastic reforms, driving out all foreign wives lest the blood of the alien pollute the stream of the nation's life. Much cruelty was doubtless inflicted, much inhumanity was exhibited. While the hundred per cent Jews were pursuing their fanatical way, some broad-minded humanist wrote this story of a woman of Moab whose loyalty had become a bright tradition and whose blood flowed in the veins of their most famous king. From Ruth and Boaz came Obed, Obed begat Jesse, who was the father of David. Here is the Old Testament parallel to the parable of the Good Samaritan, breathing the same spirit of broad humanitarianism. Was ever social bigotry more gently or more effectively rebuked? The story is what Goethe called it, 'the daintiest of love idyls,' but the love is not between a man and a woman, but between a mother-in-law and her daughter-in-law! — a theme which has certainly not been overworked in fiction. Notice its further peculiarities: it is a story without a villain, there is no analysis of character, no description of scenery, and the moral teaching is brought out by the whole action of the narrative and not appended. The atmosphere is golden and serene, yet dramatic situations are not wanting. Only an artist of elevated spirit could have handled the scene of Ruth's midnight talk with Boaz so delicately. How suggestively and through how many chapters would one of our sex-drenched novels have treated the situation! There is one passage in the tale that is immortal through its sheer perfection of phrase:

> Intreat me not to leave thee, and to return from following after thee; for whither thou goest, I will go; and where thou lodgest, I will lodge; thy people shall be my people, and thy God my God; where thou diest will I die, and there will I be buried; the Lord do so to me, and more also, if aught but death part thee and me.[1]

Here prose certainly has the flame and the form of poetry. It has been suggested that this is a quotation from an ancient folk-song. But if so, the author was a true poet. It is not necessary to make the assumption, for the fine mind that wrote the prose narrative was quite capable of attaining this level of expression. We have the parallelism of poetry, also its rhythmic movement. The translators have not only preserved these, but they have perfected the balance of the sentences. Notice in the first half the two 'I will's,' changed in the last half to 'will I,' thus perfecting the form to fit the nobility of the thought. The bright ring of the words becomes discord when a recent translator beats them out on his anvil:

[1] Ruth 1:16, 17.

Wherever you die, there will I die, and I will be buried beside you. May the Eternal kill me and worse, if anything but death part you and me.

One of the best of our American critics has this to say: 'Ruth and Esther, written in the poetic Hebrew, though not in verse, fulfill every requisition of the prose idyl; the one a pure pastoral, the other a civic and royal idyl of the court of a mighty king. There is not a phrase, an image, an incident, too much or too little in either; not a false note of atmosphere or feeling. These works, so naïvely exquisite, are deathless. Their charm is even greater as time goes on... that idyllic perfection came from a really advanced art. However spontaneous of impulse, it was not perpetuated through the uncertain process of oral transmission, but by a polished Scripture text.' [1]

ESTHER

Ruth and Esther are the only books in the Bible bearing the name of a woman; but how different their spirit! The one written to condemn racial intolerance, the other to exalt it. Esther is a brilliant historical romance, although the author is far from being accurate in his historical data. His purpose was twofold — to explain the origin of the feast of Purim, and to show that a special Providence guarded the Jew. Into his story he poured all the passionate hatred of his people for the enemies who had oppressed them. The plot has all the elements for arousing and retaining interest: the ways of the mighty, the heroism of a beautiful woman in the midst of her enemies, a great villain caught in

[1] E. C. Stedman: *The Nature and Elements of Poetry*, p. 175.

his own trap, divine Providence protecting the right. The name of God is not mentioned and no miracle is suggested, yet the faith in a providence caring for the Jew is the basis upon which the whole story rests. 'For if,' says Mordecai to Esther, 'thou altogether holdest thy peace at this time, then shall relief and deliverance arise to the Jews from another place, but thou and thy father's house shall perish; and who knoweth whether thou art not come to the kingdom for such a time as this?'[1]

The heathen might trust to the lot; Jehovah used the lot as a mockery. He worked through the disobedience of Vashti, the sleepless night of the king, the trickery of Mordecai, to carry out his purpose. If one instrument should fail, then another would be chosen, but woe to the one who was faithless. Nothing could thwart the plans of the God of Israel.

JONAH

In this much-abused book the religious spirit of the Old Testament reaches its purest and amplest expression. It is placed in our Bibles with the prophetic books because it bears the name of an ancient prophet,[2] although not written by him, but by a gifted humanist of the third century before Christ to rebuke by proclaiming the wideness of God's mercy, the very spirit we find in the Book of Esther. This tale cannot well be history, for it would be humanly impossible for one speaking a foreign tongue to enter the capital of a great nation and by a single proclamation convert king and city to obedience to the true God. If such an

[1] Esther 4:14. [2] II Kings, 14:25.

astounding event had occurred, some reference would have been made to it in the Old Testament and in contemporary records. Neither could one compose a psalm with the seaweed wrapped around his head and his body washed in the digestive juices of a fish's belly. Christ, indeed, referred to an experience of Jonah to illustrate his own resurrection, as one today might refer to William Tell without raising the question of historicity.

We have here evidently a satire, in the form of an allegory, on the narrowness of the Jewish sympathies. It is an epitome of the nation's history. Jeremiah had written: 'Nebuchadnezzar the king of Babylon hath devoured me... he hath swallowed me up like a dragon, he hath filled his belly with my delicates, he hath cast me out.'[1] This figure of a nation being swallowed by a dragon and afterward belched forth gave the writer his suggestion, and he put the history of Israel into this short story. Israel, like Jonah, had once thought that Jehovah was only the God of Palestine; by fleeing this land they escaped his authority, but, lo, he is God of the sea also. Jonah found the heathen sailors to be more merciful than he; Israel, like Jonah, was swallowed up, and in the Babylonish captivity they indeed learned to sing the songs of God in a strange place; then they were cast forth, but their subsequent history showed them to be more devoted to their personal comfort than to their prophetic mission to the world. Continually they were complaining to the liberal God for his patience to the Gentiles. How difficult it was for them to learn that the divine plans were broader than their little systems!

[1] Jeremiah 51:34.

The English novelist, Charles Reade, thus appraises the literary qualities of this satire: 'Jonah is the most beautiful story ever written in so small a compass. It contains 48 verses and 1328 English words. One does not get far in an English novel in 1328 words. There is growth of character, a distinct plot worked out without haste or crudity. Only a great artist could have hit on a perfect proportion between dialogue and narrative.' [1]

[1] *Bible Characters.*

PART III

THE LITERARY QUALITIES OF THE NEW TESTAMENT

CHAPTER XV

THE GOSPELS

Who among His disciples or among their proselytes was capable of inventing the sayings ascribed to Jesus or of imagining the life and character revealed in the Gospels? Certainly not the fishermen of Galilee; as certainly not Saint Paul, whose character and idiosyncrasies were of a totally different sort; still less the early Christian writers in whom nothing is more evident than that the good which was in them was all derived, as they always professed that it was derived, from the higher source.

J. S. Mill

The New Testament is the Magna Charta of the Christian religion, yet it is the smallest in size of any of the chief books of the world's great religions. Smallest in size, it contains the largest variety of literary forms and presents the best arrangement of its contents. The qualities which make the Old Testament most notable literature are present here also. Here is the intuitional mind which feels deeply, thinks concretely, reasons by analogy, and utters itself with the austere simplicity of high seriousness, and the rhythm of strong emotion. Here, too, facts and truth are set forth in many ways, thus entering the mind by many channels. Here are legend and narrative, history and poetry, story, epistle, and vision. But in the New Testament the shining center of interest is a Man, not a nation, and the wonder of hope fulfilled heightens the note of joy and expectation. The New Testament is great literature because it grew out of a great love and centers around humanity's divinest figure. Its sublime truths are made flesh and blood, and are expressed for the most part in forms easily mirrored in the mind and in words of beautiful simplicity. Born of mighty love and intense hope, it speaks to the heart — deep calleth unto deep.

The writers of the New Testament were not literary craftsmen, nor were they masters of technique. With the exception of Paul, they had no inner fires of genius which would have burst forth into powerful affirmation whatever their lot. What effectiveness they had they all owed to one and the same source: all had come within the circle of the splendor of a tremendous personality. From him had shone a light which had kindled their spirits in the depths and heights. The stupendous truth they were possessed of broke through all their inhibitions of training and limitations of capacity, and their weakness became their strength. The downright sincerity of their convictions compelled them to restraint and simplicity of utterance. He who is convinced that he has something momentous to assert will go far in effectiveness of speech.

On opening the book, we find ourselves confronted by four writings that are so unique that a new classification has been invented for them. They are not biography, for the events in the life of Jesus have not been collected and arranged to set forth his figure and career in its entirety. Neither are they strictly reminiscences or memoirs. The dominant purpose is not the complete delineation of a person, but the establishment of a belief; therefore they are called Gospels, a new name to denote a new kind of literature. The material is arranged to publish and make persuasive the news.

To understand the style of the New Testament we

must remember that each of the Gospels, like the Old Testament history, is the work of many minds passing at last through the mind of one. Collections of sayings, oral traditions, reminiscences of eye-witnesses, some in Aramaic, some in Greek, were incorporated into the final text in substantially their original shape, yet were brought into unity and final form by the selective ability of one author. These books at last were translated into our English speech. The work of the translators would naturally tend to obliterate many peculiarities of individual modes of expression, and introduce a general uniformity of style. Nevertheless some characteristics were too pronounced to be thus planed away.

J. Middleton Murry, in his 'Problems of Style,' makes some interesting and rather sweeping statements regarding the literary achievements of the Evangelists. He says:

> When we consider style in the larger sense, it seems to me scarcely an exaggeration to say that the style of one half of the English Bible is atrocious. A great part of the historical books of the Old Testament, the Gospels in the New, are examples of all that writing should not be; and nothing the translators might have done would have altered this. The 'Life of Jesus' by Ernest Renan is, as a whole, infinitely superior in point of style to the narrative of the Authorized Version of the Gospels.... There are four styles, if there is a style at all, and the same varnish of propriety with which the good taste of the English translators has covered them all cannot change this substance. If we examine this, we discover only two elements that can possibly lay claim to be considered

creative literature: the actual words of Christ, such as 'Come unto me all ye that labor...' and 'My God, my God! why hast thou forsaken me!' and the dramatic effects, such as, 'Then all his disciples forsook him and fled.' The first do not belong to the Gospels, but to their author, and the second are not really the effects of style at all. It is not the authors of the Gospels who have given us the imaginative realization of the character of Jesus on which these dramatic effects depend. Take away the words of Jesus which they reproduce and nothing of that character remains. The written evidence of an honest policeman would give us as much. The most elementary conditions of the presence of style are lacking.[1]

This is certainly a thought-provoking passage, even if it is not quite true. What does Mr. Murry mean by 'style in the larger sense'? I think this is his meaning: He quotes with approval in another part of this same book [2] the saying of Stendhal: 'Style is this: to add to a given thought all the circumstances fitted to produce the whole effect that the thought can produce,' and then he proceeds to interpret the word 'thought' as signifying 'intuition, conviction, perceptions, and their accompanying emotions.' Applying this definition — which I cannot think is a complete one — to the first Gospel, I surmise Mr. Murry's criticism would be that the author did not conceive imaginatively the character of Jesus and set it in its historic background. The essential words in Mr. Murry's criticism are 'imaginative realization.' Jesus and his times have not been realized and presented vividly and

[1] Pages 135, 136. [2] Page 79.

with artistic unity. The whole power would thus lie in the words of the Master, which the author inserted into a mere skeleton framework. Renan, on the contrary, after collecting his information regarding Jesus, fused it by his creating and shaping imagination into a consistent whole, and with fine artistry so told his story that the reader would vividly perceive the circumstances which called forth the word or the deed and would feel the full force of its emotional content.

How fortunate that the writers of the synoptics were not professional literary artists! They are excellent examples of the assertion that out of the mouths of babes strength is established, and that fools in their foolishness reveal the wisdom of God better than the wise with their craft. That honest policeman will make a first-class witness if he has imagination enough to distinguish the significant facts, and his blunt sincerity will be more effective than the skill of a ready writer. It is because the evangelists were so sincere and unambitious to obtrude themselves that they let the splendor of their Lord shine through their very weaknesses. They accomplished their purpose: the great Figure stands forth in its essential glory.

Before considering the individual characteristics of the evangelists, let us glance at a few features which make the Gospels effectual. In the first place, these stories were an oral tradition before they were written down. Thus that was preserved which in substance and form made the strongest appeal. Again, the story is told from four different points of view, influenced by diverse temperaments. The Book of Matthew is concerned with the fulfillment of prophecy; Mark with the miraculous power of the Messiah; Luke with his humaneness; John with his cosmic significance. They all had the wisdom to refrain from attempting to describe the appearance of the God-man. In this they used the artistic method of Homer and Dante. Homer was not so foolish as to try to picture the most beautiful woman in the world. Instead, he describes the effect she produced on the old men of Troy as she walked along the walls of the beleaguered city. They said she was glorious as a goddess and it was small wonder that the young men were willing to die for her. Likewise Dante, in his 'Vita Nuova,' dwells on the effect Beatrice produced upon others — she seemed an angel of God, she enkindled their finer emotions; but of her appearance he writes nothing, except that her eyes were lucent and her smile of exceeding sweetness. The evangelists are equally wise in their restraint. They tell of the wonder their Lord excited among the multitude; the spell he cast upon harlots, publicans, and wise leaders in Israel; but of his form and lineaments not a word. Only Mark anticipates Dante's method and repeatedly hints at the power of Jesus' look. We catch Christ's spirit, his purpose, his attitude toward God and man, but each reader is left to imagine the face through which shone the splendor of God.

Let me mention another virtue: their skill in selecting the significant. An author is tested by what he leaves out as well as by what he puts into his narrative. It is said that Shakespeare never blotted a line. 'Would that he had blotted a thousand!' declared Ben Jonson. With what few lines the career which changed the world is sketched — the emerging consciousness of the boy when he is twelve, the baptism, the temptation, a sermon, a group of parables, a short paragraph glimpsing the awful agony of Gethsemane. Mark tells of the crucifixion in twenty short verses, and even John does not go beyond thirty. Instead of attempting to portray what was impossible of description, they gave the effect upon the different observers — what the two robbers said, the mocking of the crowd, the testimony of the centurion, the weeping women, a convulsed earth and a black sky. This, with a few lines describing what was done, and a few words from the cross, paints the world's supreme tragedy. Note how noble is the restraint of the writers. There is no outburst of wrath against Judas, no condemnation of Herod, of Pilate, of the priests. The world's mightiest figure is set forth with no word of eulogy, with no attempt at heroics, no analysis of the feeling of the actors in events charged with emotion.

Consider more in detail the unconscious art of the crucifixion scene. The writers have a tremendous task: they are to portray what they believe to be the most tragic and significant event in human history. To prepare for the intensity of the final act, Matthew, Mark, and Luke use well the principle of suspense. They linger on the way to Golgotha. They show Simon carrying the cross; they delay the narrative to recount the words of Jesus to the women of Jerusalem. The final tragedy is related in few words and with the utmost calmness of spirit. Such writing is born only of serene faith. Horrible as were the deed and the suffering, good had come out of it, and the emotions are now remembered in tranquillity. That the story is told with true art is proved by the fact that the mind of the reader is not horrified but ennobled. It produces upon us the purifying effect of all great art.

There is another test of art which this story will endure. One can come back to it again and again and find his emotions undiminished. The feelings that are aroused are legitimate, for they rest on valid grounds. The facts are related simply with the utmost sincerity, without sentimentality or theatrical devices.

How masterly, also, is the employment of the principle of contrast — the Holy One between two thieves, the darkness while the Light of the World suffers, infinite forgiveness confronting human malignity. The subsequent attitude of the world toward Christ is depicted in the different groups gathered about the cross: the soldiers 'sat and looked at him there,' unimaginative, indifferent; the centurion of finer clay recognizes a supernatural glory; the crowd rails and the women weep.

The evangelists may not have been men of trained artistic abilities. They could not weave sentences as delicate silk into exquisite patterns, but they did possess the cardinal virtues of effective writing — sincerity and simplicity. They obliterated themselves and let the Splendor shine through. Mr. Murry, were you not speaking a little hastily when you said that 'the Gospels are examples of all that writing should not be'? When you made that quick generalization, were you all that a critic should be?

If one having the genius of the Second Isaiah, or of the author of Job, had been in the early Church and had written a gospel, we should have had radiant diction, a rush of emotion, a luminous figure glowing through a golden haze, yet Mark has told the story better. The white light shines with less stain and distortion through his simplicity than if it had come through the shaping and coloring imagination of the greatest of the Old Testament poets.

The different Gospels have their individual peculiarities of style, and although recognizing them as composite works, it is legitimate to consider the outstanding characteristics of each. The Gospel of Matthew is thoroughly Hebraic and belongs to the school of the wisdom writers. The vocabulary is limited, but has the Homeric virtues of rapidity of movement and simplicity of expression. Above all, the author lets his hero speak for himself, supplying just enough narrative to break up the monotony of a monologue or of a collection of 'sayings.' For the most part he keeps himself in the background, but his chief defect comes from the fact that he is so full of the thought that Jesus is the fulfillment of prophecy that fourteen times he uses the expression 'that it might be fulfilled,' and makes the Master interpret his acts in the light of these foretellings.

He has no feeling for sentence structure, clause after clause being connected by a tiresome 'and.' Yet the story of the wise men is well told, a few words give us a vivid impression of John the Baptist, and the account of the temptation marvelously visualizes a prolonged mental struggle; a sentence from Satan and an answering one from Jesus reveal the issue and the method of victory. The sketch is made complete by the psychological touch — 'and angels came and ministered unto him.' When we come to the sayings of Christ, we have great style, but this is considered in another chapter.

The Gospel is supposed to be based on the Apostle Matthew's collection of the sayings of Jesus. Matthew, being a tax collector, would be accustomed to keeping records, and it is entirely credible that he wrote down many of his Lord's words soon after they were uttered. Familiar with money, what Christ said about spiritual values would especially attract him. It is Matthew who gives us the Buried Treasure, the Pearl of Price, the Unmerciful Servant, the Laborer and the Vineyard. As the end draws near, the imagination and the emotions of the author are touched, the writing grows in power, and we have in our version such revealing sentences as, 'Then all the disciples forsook him and fled,' 'and they sat and watched him there.'

Papias, living in the early part of the second century, says: 'Mark, having become an interpreter of Peter, wrote down accurately whatever he remembered... not in exact order.' The Gospel as we have it is substantially the teaching of Peter written by his follower. Mark's style is direct, brief, a little rough, yet he knows how to state most disturbing facts without comment. He it is who has preserved the tradition that the eyes of Jesus glowed with a compelling light.

Luke is the only writer of Scripture, as far as we have knowledge, who was a Gentile. Having the Greek belief that history should be artistic, he arranges his facts in order and weaves his sentences together with real literary ability. The stories of the birth of Christ are told with genuine skill. In him we find the Gloria, the Benedictus, the Magnificat. A humanist, he had little sympathy with social prejudice, but much with the poor and outcast. To this sympathy and his fondness for the short story we owe the preservation of some twenty parables, such as the Prodigal Son and the Good Samaritan, showing our Lord's broad humanity. He produces many of his impressions by the use of striking contrasts; e.g., the Pharisee and the Publican, Dives and Lazarus, Simon and the Sinner, the Elder Son and the Prodigal, Martha and Mary, the Penitent and the Impenitent Thief. With what ability he has described the walk to Emmaus! Luke has a sense of form and of sentence-structure, and his vocabulary is more extensive than that of the other evangelists. Because he recounts events so vividly, painters have turned to Luke for their subjects more than to any other of the Gospels.

The fourth Gospel differs in a marked degree from the first three, both in purpose and in manner. They essayed to relate the facts of the life of Jesus, but John declares 'these are written that ye might believe that Jesus is the Christ, the Son of God, and believing ye might have life in his name.' This purpose affects both the material he selects and his arrangement, for he is presenting an idea and is adjusting his facts to enforce his argument. He is a Hebrew, but he is writing after the manner of the Greeks. Instead of the Jewish Messiah, he is presenting the Eternal Christ. Jesus no longer speaks in sharp, epigrammatic sentences, but engages in prolonged argument; his thoughts are expanded and interpreted. The Hebrew method of thinking with which we have become so familiar — the intuitive mind, the straight, simple sentence — has disappeared, and we have argumentation, philosophical reasoning, dialogue and debate.

The author was an emotional mystic possessed of a strong, profound mind. The generation before his own had taught that Jesus was the Christ. A deeply satisfying spiritual experience had convinced him that he knew the Redeemer as well as the first disciples. Mingling his knowledge of the historical Jesus with his reflections on his personal experiences, he was persuaded that Jesus, the Christ, was the Son of God, the Eternal Word. His mystical mind saw the Eternal in the temporal. He thought of Jesus as a Supernal Light shining in darkness, the Light communicates Life, and is thus known intimately, and to know is eternal life. Thus he shows the perpetual significance of Christ and the possibility of continuance of vital union with him.

The author has a most dramatic imagination, and conceives the plan of redemption dramatically. The Eternal Light shines in the world's darkness — it divides men into the children of light and of darkness; the many love the darkness, but those who receive the light become the Sons of God. The imaginative and philosophical grasp of his mind is seen in the wonderful prologue which, patterned after the great hymn of creation in the first chapter of Genesis, is not inferior to it in sublimity of thought and in condensed energy of expression. Indeed, so majestic is its diction, so informed is it with the penetrative music of noble passion, that Burney affirms that this prologue is a hymn written in eleven parallel couplets, with here and there a comment introduced.

The author makes his narrative vivid by supplying details to his story. It was Peter who drew the sword, Malchus who was struck, Judas who objected to the waste of ointment, and Thomas who doubted. He also brings out the dramatic element in situations. The Eternal Life stands before the tomb of his dead friend. How can an artist tell the story to show its full significance? John does it in two words, which are translated, 'Jesus wept.' Again, when Judas left the upper room to betray his Master, the standard version says: 'He then having received the cup went out straightway: and it was night.' The author seems to see the black soul of the traitor meeting the night. Some modern translators ignored this effect by making a separate sentence, 'It was then night.' The darkness thus indicates the time, rather than the setting of the deed. Again, it is John who catches these memorable words of Pilate: 'Behold the man!' 'What is truth?'

In his treatment of both dialogue and miracle he follows a uniform method. Jesus makes a remark which his hearers misinterpret; he repeats it, and then amplifies and explains it. The same is true of the miracles. There is the deed, criticism, and then interpretation.

There is also a number pattern running through the whole. Jesus goes three times to Jerusalem and three times to Galilee; there are three Passovers and three other feasts; the Baptist makes three appearances as a witness; Jesus is three times condemned; he speaks three times from the cross, appears three times after his resurrection. There are seven miracles; seven references to the 'hour'; seven times Jesus says 'I am,' introducing a metaphor descriptive of himself; seven times he says 'these things have I spoken unto you.'

One cannot read this Gospel without a sense of wonder at the insight of the writer and the heights of power he attained. He is an early and conspicuous example of how Christ releases the latent energies of the soul and lifts men to greatness. The first chapter could only have been written by a powerful mind greatly exalted by vision and emotion. But the most perplexing chapters are the fourteenth to the seventeenth, inclusive, in which we have the Great Discourse and the Prayer for the Disciples. Unless we hold to a strict theory of verbal inspiration, we cannot maintain that we have here the precise words of Jesus. The style is that of John, not that of Jesus as he is represented in the first three Gospels. We know that it was the custom both of Greek and of Hebrew historians to put speeches in the mouths of their characters. But we cannot think of this author daring to enter the holy of holies of the Eternal Word and constructing out of his own imagination, however sympathetic, a lengthy address filled with most precious promises, ending in a prayer in which tenderest solicitude becomes divine sublimity. It is all too holy, too evidently the utterance of the eternal in man, to be the invention of the author; it is too sincere to be an artistic device, however pious. It has the note of reality; it appeals to the deep soul of man. A mind audacious enough to have invented these addresses could not have written so well. There would have been a hollow sound somewhere.

The most plausible explanation, to my mind, is as follows. The Last Supper was finished. Judas had gone out. Our Lord, relieved of the traitor's presence, poured out his innermost heart to his faithful disciples. They felt the solemnity, the importance, the power of it all. Their open, receptive minds would retain those keen, pregnant sentences, so characteristic of Christ — such as, 'Let not your heart be troubled,' 'I am the Way, the Truth, and the Life,' 'Peace I leave with you,' 'I am the Vine, ye are the branches.' These and others like them, together with the main petition of the prayer which followed, would certainly have made a profound impression. In all likelihood, some one wrote them down. They were too precious not to be preserved. Later, the author of this Gospel used these writings with confidence, for he wrote:'This is the disciple which testifieth of these things, and wrote these things; and we know that his testimony is true.' But he explained them after the fashion of his own mind and according to his own literary methods. Thus we have here the truth and passion of Jesus passing through the mind of John. Like everything else, in the Bible and out of it, we have the Eternal manifested through the temporal.

Inspiring and profound as John is, he has some weaknesses as a writer. The first three Gospels represent Jesus self-possessed, with a certain majestic self-restraint even in his indignation. John in the middle chapters of the book represents Jesus as overstrained, almost fierce in debate. His speech, instead of showing the old Hebraic control, becomes repetitious and monotonous through uniformity of rhythm and set formula of criticism and explanation.

Matthew Arnold [1] asserts that the writer does much loose work in the joining of his material. In Chapter 4:35–38 there are two *motifs*; 35–36 give us the ripe harvest and the reward; 37–38, the disciples reap where they have not sown. In Chapter 10 two ideas, 'I am the door' and 'I am the good shepherd,' are confusedly mingled. 'Arise, let us go hence,' shows the end of one set of notes, but the author left them in the heart of the discourse. As this stands in our Bible, it does seem out of place; but if, as Professor Torrey suggests, the Aramaic original read 'I will arise and go hence,' then the objection is removed.

The author of this book had the brain and outlook of a Hebrew whose thought was moulded by Greek forms. Writing in a language of which he was not the master, his vocabulary is meager, the same expressions constantly recurring. His favorite words are *light*, *glory*, *life*, *know*, *truth*. Few in number, they stand for luminous spiritual realities. John is a mystic presenting an argument; consequently he reasons, not analytically, using precise terms, but emotionally, clothing his thought in symbols which suggest the truth.

This book has no analogue either in ancient or in modern times. A drama, cosmic in its range, written by a Hebrew in the Greek manner, of lucid profund-

[1] *God and the Bible.*

ity, the most disturbing, the most comforting of all books, filled with sadness, filled with hope, love pervading it as an atmosphere, it is the Church's most precious spiritual document.

CHAPTER XVI

THE SAYINGS OF JESUS AS LITERATURE[1]

Jesus Christ said grand things so simply that it seems as though he had not thought about them, and yet so clearly that one sees that he must have reflected upon them. This clearness joined with this simplicity is wonderful.

PASCAL

My words shall not pass away. MARK 13:31.

WE think of Jesus as teacher, example, redeemer, but we are not accustomed to consider his marvelous power of literary expression. He came not to destroy, but to fulfill the literary genius of Israel, as he fulfilled the law and the prophets. In him all fullness dwelt — fullness of the prophetic spirit, fullness of wisdom, fullness of poetic utterance; supreme in spiritual glory, supreme in glory of speech. In him the wonderful gift of expression belonging to his race found its

[1] Modern scholarship has quite clearly established the existence in the church at Jerusalem of a document containing the sayings of Jesus, and commonly called the Logia of Matthew. Matthew was, according to tradition, a tax collector, and as such would be accustomed to the use of the pen, and it is not improbable that he wrote down the striking words which came from Jesus' lips. Others of the early disciples would remember different sayings, they that loved the Lord spake often one with another, and thus the collection grew until some one brought them into a whole.

That we have the authentic statements of Jesus in much the form that they came from his lips, we can easily believe. They radiate their own light; they express a unique personality; like sharply etched pictures they would abide in the memory of hearers, not vaguely, but usually in the very fashion in which they were spoken. Even in translation the spirit of the author shines through them, so that we may feel his power and learn his method.

culminating power. The characteristic Hebrew mind was intuitional in its processes, thought in figures, reasoned by analogy, was vividly concrete in utterance made rhythmical by deep emotion. We call Jesus the Son of Man, humanity's 'realized ideal,' but in his mental processes he was a Hebrew of the Hebrews. He thought with a Hebrew brain and spoke after the best manner of his people. He did not, like Socrates, reason toward a conclusion. He saw a truth and uttered it in clear, authoritative affirmations. Socrates in his last hours reasoned about immortality; Jesus pursued no argument; he simply said: 'In my Father's house are many mansions... I go to prepare a place for you.' His sentences inevitably fall into the natural cadence of deep emotion. He spoke in metaphors and reasoned in parables. He was a subject of Rome and was surrounded by Hellenistic culture, but no gloom or glory from the classic world fell upon his mind. Paul and John were Hebrews thinking like Greeks; Luke and the writer of Hebrews show the influence of their surroundings. Jesus was a Hebrew genius blossoming in a Greco-Roman world; in it, yet entirely apart from it. If he had the mentality and fire of the prophets, he used the method of the wisdom writers. His sentences were clear, short, balanced. They were jewels lying side by side, not a cloth of gold finely woven. The Sermon on the Mount is in the style of Proverbs — 'No man can serve two masters'; 'Cast not your pearls before swine' — and the distinction he draws is between the wise and the foolish man. He fulfilled the prophetic genius of Israel, yet he was the wisest of the sages; his aphorisms surpass in power and beauty all the sayings of the sons of Solomon. Equally was he the consummation of the poetic genius of Israel. For Jesus was essentially a poet. In common things — the seed, the bird, the flower — he saw the hidden beauty and spiritual significance. He spoke in metaphors: 'Ye are the salt of the earth... ye are the light of the world.' In the Sermon on the Mount there are fifty-six metaphors. According to a definition given in earlier pages, the poet conceives facts imaginatively and employs language more exquisite and heightened than that of prose. Jesus had the rare gift of so using common language that it glowed and became music; the hearers marveled at 'the words of grace that proceeded out of his mouth'; in them there was the ripe fruition of culture: 'How knoweth this man letters'; and Jesus himself could say of them: 'The words that I speak unto you they are spirit and they are life.'

His words were on a level with his claims. He made assertions regarding his essential nature, his position in the course of the world's affairs, the responsibilities resting upon his shoulders, perfectly staggering in their audacity. They are the assumptions of the insane. Now a single word will betray the unbalanced mind, or the pretender to an unpossessed greatness. Whether one says 'shibboleth' or 'sibboleth' indicates his lineage and culture. 'Thy speech betrayeth thee,' said the maid to Peter. The words of Jesus did not belie his claims. There is in them no hollow ring of pretense, no bombast, no fustian. What impresses one reading the records is the ease and naturalness with which his words, weighty with truth and lustrous with beauty, fell from his lips. His words were as divine as his character. 'Never man spake like this man.'

The poets, in order to produce an atmosphere of enchantment, use exquisite, lambent, musical words in their writings, but these same heightened, magical words would seem quite out of place in everyday intercourse. When one sees a ghost, he does not exclaim, 'Angels and ministers of grace defend us!' Nor does he ask prayers in language so fine as this:

> Sweet maid, in thy orisons, be all my sins remembered.

The poet elevates familiar thoughts into the domain of art by expressing them in the music and glory of selected words. The distinction of this Galilean poet is that in common life he spoke naturally the language of highest art. Here is the incarnation in the domain of letters. Celestial beauty clothes itself in common words about familiar things.

In the words found in Matthew 11:28–30 we have a most interesting example of the ability of Jesus, whose mind was steeped in the literature of his country, to express a great thought in the fewest and most forcible words. In the last chapter of the Book of Ecclesiasticus, Jesus, the son of Sirach, closes a prayer with this invitation concerning Wisdom:

> Draw near unto me, ye unlearned,
> And lodge in the house of instruction.
> Say, wherefore are ye lacking in these things,
> And your souls are very thirsty?
> I opened my mouth and spake,
> Get her for yourselves without money,

Put your neck under the yoke,
And let your soul receive instruction;
She is hard at hand to find.
Behold with your eyes,
How that I labored but a little,
And found for myself much rest.

The heart of this plea Jesus, the Divine Wisdom, applies to himself and then utters his invitation in those most precious words: 'Come unto me, all ye that labor and are heavy laden, and I will give you rest. Take my yoke upon you, and learn of me; for I am meek and lowly in heart, and ye shall find rest unto your souls. For my yoke is easy, and my burden is light.' Leaving out of mind the deep religious significance of the words, we have here an example of how a transcendant mind gives to a thought radiancy and power.

Being a poet and not a philosopher, he used picturesque, concrete words. He said: 'your Father,' not 'the Eternal'; 'your brethren,' not 'humanity'; not 'the processes of nature,' but 'the lilies, how they grow.' He thought in images; faith was like a grain of mustard seed, the Spirit was like the wind, the kingdom of heaven a pearl, leaven, a net; the temptation was a debate with Satan; his destiny was a cup held to his lips.

Being a poet he used language not precisely as a mathematician or a law-giver, but artistically to produce the greatest possible effect. He was not seeking to establish a new system of laws and regulations; he would quicken devotion, he would make ideals glow like a pillar of fire. Therefore he spoke in hyperbole.[1]

[1] W. G. Ballantine: *Understanding the Bible*. Chapter, 'The Letter or Spirit.'

When Emerson said, 'Hitch your wagon to a star,' he spoke as a poet to ardent youth, not as a stable-keeper to teamsters. He was advising men in the most powerful manner possible to follow the ideal. So Jesus said: 'If you have faith as a grain of mustard seed, you shall say to this mountain, Remove hence to yonder place; and it shall remove.' [1] Yet no construction engineer, finding a mountain impeding his way, searches for a man with a grain of genuine faith to pray for the removal of the mountain. In such sentences as, 'When thou makest a dinner or a supper, call not thy friends, nor thy brethren...bid the poor, the maimed, the lame, the blind'; 'Give to him that asketh of thee'; 'It is easier for a camel to go through a needle's eye, than for a rich man to enter into the kingdom of God'; 'If your right eye offend you, pluck it out' — Jesus is using language as a great poet uses it: artistically, to produce effects. Literalists make sad work of these high utterances. Those who try to follow Jesus literally usually wander far from the best experience of the race. His words are spirit and life, not precise formulas. The spirit maketh alive: the letter killeth.

Our Lord was a poet, he was also a street preacher. It was his purpose to proclaim his truth in words which his hearers would not forget. Profound thought and steady discipline lie back of those wondrous sentences. The experience of many generations of wise men in Israel had demonstrated that the parallel couplet, stating a complete thought in brief and balanced words, is the best method of arousing and im-

[1] Matt. 17:20.

pressing the memory. Therefore Jesus used this method of statement often. The distinguishing types of parallelism used by the Hebrew poets all appear in his teachings. Here is one of the many instances of the synonymous couplet:[1]

Be not anxious for your life, what ye shall eat,
Nor yet for your body, what ye shall put on.
For the life is more than food,
And the body than the raiment.[2]

Antithetical parallelism is a favorite method:

He that findeth his life shall lose it:
And he that loseth his life for my sake shall find it.[3]

So the last shall be first,
And the first last.[4]

He emphasizes a thought by the use of the step parallelism:

Be not anxious *for the morrow;*
For the morrow will be anxious for itself.[5]

Think not that *I came to send peace on the earth;*
I came not to send peace, but a sword.[6]

The synthetic couplet is constantly recurring:

The foxes have holes, and the birds of the heavens have nests;
But the Son of man hath not where to lay his head.[7]

He that receiveth a prophet in the name of a prophet shall receive a prophet's reward;
And he that receiveth a righteous man in the name of a righteous man shall receive a righteous man's reward.[8]

[1] I have taken most of the illustrations which follow from Burney's *The Poetry of Our Lord.*

[2] Luke 12:22, 23. [3] Matt. 10:39. [4] Matt. 20:16.
[5] Matt. 6:34. [6] Matt. 10:34. [7] Matt. 8:20.
[8] Matt. 10:41.

We do not mean to imply that Jesus forged with care and hid in the quiver of memory these polished shafts of speech to be taken out as occasion required, but being a poet, he instinctively used balanced and rhythmical sentences. This gift he cultivated, for it fitted his purpose and was the tradition of the best teachers of his people. The ages have proved his wisdom.

How great an artist our Lord was is further attested in his parables. They have been called the most perfect short stories in the world. Where can they be equaled? When has truth so significant ever been packed into a space so small! The characters are sketched, and even their development traced, by a word or a sentence, yet weight of truth and swiftness of movement do not mar the perfect beauty. They are taken from daily life and are therefore true to life and nature. None of them is bizarre or forced.

It is interesting to inquire how these apparently spontaneous, casual sayings could have such flawless beauty. Mr. Deane, in his valuable little book entitled 'How to Enjoy the Bible,' surmises that Jesus perfected them during his hours of retirement. He calls attention to the perfect form of the story of the Prodigal Son. The boy in the far country had carefully planned his penitent speech; this he repeated faithfully, but in the presence of his father he omitted 'Make me as one of thy hired servants'; it would have sounded false in that kindly atmosphere. Notice, also, the deep significance of 'this thy son' (not my brother), and the rebuke in the reply, 'this thy brother is come.' An equally fine touch is in the contrast of thought and perfect balance of cadence in the triumphal conclusion, for

> This thy brother was dead, and is alive again;
> And was lost, and is found.

Six syllables balance six syllables in the first line, and in the second three correspond to three. Note further that in these five hundred words three characters are portrayed and by their own words. No moral is attached, or explanation, for like true art it is its own interpretation. The parable was spoken in Aramaic, and preserved for us by Luke, whose prominent characteristic as a writer was his love of contrast: dead — alive, lost — found. The exquisite balance and cadence of the closing sentence is the master craftsmanship of William Tyndale. In the Greek the syllables are twelve to four in the first line and five to four in the second. The cadence there suggested is made perfect in the English. What a definite, resounding word 'found' is, with its single syllable and falling accent, to close the story! It is probable that the story came from the lips of Jesus perfect in thought and form. So compact of truth and shaped in beauty was it that its delicate organization was little modified by oral tradition. Passing from Aramaic to Greek and from Greek to English, each translator has held it a precious possession and has used the refinements of his native speech in a manner not to obscure the original art.

Jesus had the passion of the prophets, the soul of a poet, and the method of the sages. What most impresses us as we read the Gospels is the perfect balance in which he possessed his marvelous and varied powers. He was a unified personality. His intellectual, emotional, and volitional faculties were held in perfect equipoise. Heart, mind, and will worked harmoniously together.

While writing nothing himself, he has created writers of high merit. He has given to his disciples literary ability as well as righteousness. Beginning with Paul, Luke, and John, there has been a noble succession of gifted men and women who, quickened by his spirit, have caught something of his power of utterance. A great love gives liberty, vision, and persuasive speech.

CHAPTER XVII
PAUL AS A WRITER

For worthy deeds are not often destitute of worthy relaters, as by a certain Fate great Acts and great Eloquence have most commonly gone hand in hand, equaling and honoring each other in the same ages.

JOHN MILTON

PAUL was evidently built upon a large plan, for he has moved profoundly some of the mightiest spirits of our race. His casual letters have caused more than one world revolution; yet he affirmed that his physical appearance was contemptible. Some infirmity which he called a 'thorn in the flesh' afflicted him at times with much humiliation. Nevertheless he seems to have had most extraordinary endurance. Stoned one day in Lystra and dragged outside the city as dead, on the morrow he proceeded to Derbe, over thirty miles distant. 'Five times,' he writes, 'received I forty stripes, save one. Thrice was I beaten with rods, once was I stoned, thrice I suffered shipwreck, a night and a day have I been in the deep.' [1]

His oratorical power was notable. At Lystra he was honored as Mercury, god of eloquence,[2] he controlled the mob at Jerusalem, and Felix trembled [3] before his impetuous reasoning. All his natural powers, however, were strengthened and elevated by his tremendous religious experience. His conversion was something far more than a change in the direction of his thoughts and activities. Christ had been formed within him as a vital, spiritual energy, organizing and

[1] II Cor. 11:24, 25. [2] Acts 14:12. [3] Acts 24:25.

dominating his life. 'It is no longer I that live; but Christ that liveth in me.' Whatever heights Paul afterwards attained as a writer were due to this revolutionary experience. He proclaimed the doctrine of justification by faith because he himself had been liberated through possessing Christ by faith; the cross, from being a stumbling-block, became the key to the mysteries of love in Christ Jesus.

In attempting to form a just opinion of Paul as a writer, we must constantly bear in mind that his writings are all letters, but letters not written after the manner of those of Cicero, Pliny, or the author of the Epistle to the Hebrews — the leisurely and perfected production of men composing according to an artistic model. Many of his epistles were written in haste, to meet a specific need; they were dictated to an amanuensis, and much which is obscure to us was perfectly plain to those who received them, for they knew the situation which was being met. In the rush of his emotions he was guilty of all the faults which Sabatier notes as occurring in the Galatian letter: 'Unfinished phrases, daring omissions, parentheses which leave us out of sight and out of breath, rabbinical subtleties, audacious paradoxes, vehement apostrophes pour out like surging billows.' And Renan says of his letters as a whole: 'His writings, though works of highest originality, are without charm, their form is harsh and usually without grace.' It is true that he often fails in directness and simplicity, his long sentences are loosely bound together, he skips from one subject to another according to mood, or the needs of his readers whom he desires to influence. One finds in Cicero's letters restraint, elegance, perfect form, every virtue which the Apostle lacked, but a comparison reveals how the immense passion of Paul carried him triumphantly through all limitations to power.

Paul had a complex and richly varied nature: intense, yet tolerant; inflexible, yet kind; having an intuitive mind, yet given to argumentation; strongly emotional, yet of good judgment; a propagandist, yet considerate of the consciences of others; seer and metaphysician, saint and warrior, he kept the peace among his naturally discordant faculties only by bringing them all into subjection to the love of Christ.

Of his reasoning abilities John Locke, the English philosopher, who was certainly an excellent judge of the human understanding, asserts: 'I think there is not anywhere to be found a more pertinent, close arguer, who has his eye always on the mark he drives at.' But 'the mark he drives at' is not the complete and logical development of his thought, it is to carry the minds and hearts of his readers; therefore he frequently breaks his argument to insert personal reflections, and uses rabbinical reasonings which accorded with the habits of those days, but which seem specious to us.

He had a rare power of condensing much wisdom in a sentence — this is why preachers find him so rich in texts. 'The letter killeth, the spirit giveth life,' [1] 'Jews ask for signs, and Greeks seek after wisdom'; [2] 'Be not deceived: God is not mocked; for whatsoever a man soweth, that shall he also reap.' [3]

His mind was far from being a precise logic-chopping machine, it was urged on by the strong pressure

[1] II Cor. 3:6. [2] I Cor. 1:22. [3] Gal. 6:7.

of ardent emotion. Paul never wrote well when his understanding only was engaged. Then his sentences are involved and unmusical. But when his heart speaks, his words have a peculiar beauty, pathos, and simplicity, as in II Cor. 4:7–18, 5:20—6:10.

His memorable passages are those in which intellect, imagination, and heart are fused in one utterance; then his sentences are luminous and fall into persuasive cadences. In Romans, after the intense concentration of the mind on the profound doctrine of justification by faith, his heart catches fire in the noble chant of spiritual freedom found in the eighth chapter. Twice in First Corinthians he bursts into deathless speech when his heart sings of love and victory over death. He is never satisfied with merely stating a truth: he glorifies it, he sings it, he makes it visible in a metaphor.

The figures of speech which he uses all show a powerful imagination. He not only apprehended truth in a large manner, he felt it. He not only felt it, he saw it. The call to Macedonia came in the shape of a man speaking to him. He heard Creation groaning, he saw her standing on tiptoe scanning the horizon waiting for the revealing of sons of God to free her from her shackles. He saw the Church as a temple, as a body of Christ, death as a serpent with a sting, swallowed up by victory, love as a shining person, suffering, and kind.

In all Paul's greatest passages intellect, heart, and imagination work in unison. In I Cor. 15 the Apostle is conducting an argument on the resurrection. In the first thirty-four verses thought and emotion rise and fall, there are sandy spots, succeeded by oases rich in truth and beauty. With verse 35 his whole being catches fire: he sees truth visualized, he speaks in figures, and his emotions rise to full height and break forth into splendid utterance. The power of this chapter is not the clearness of its thought nor its logical coherence; it rests in the emotional significance of facts. The chapter is of enduring beauty because Paul is reasoning like a poet, he is talking in parables of seed and star, and Death swallowed up of Victory. Were ever words put into more triumphal music than these?

So when this corruptible shall have put on incorruption, and this mortal shall have put on immortality, then shall be brought to pass the saying that is written, Death is swallowed up in victory.

O death, where is thy sting? O grave, where is thy victory?

The sting of death is sin; and the strength of sin is the law.

But thanks be to God, which giveth us the victory through our Lord Jesus Christ.

Therefore, my beloved brethren, be ye stedfast, unmovable, always abounding in the work of the Lord, forasmuch as ye know that your labour is not in vain in the Lord.

Paul's manner of writing is powerful, despite its numerous defects, because of its utter sincerity. A great soul is speaking directly to us. No rhetorical artifice weakens the strong rush of his eloquence. We feel in all his letters the spontaneity and naturalness of an earnest mind, which make his words terse, incisive, smiting; they are not merely energetic and vital, they glow with passion. In the high moments they come pouring out with a fullness of utterance which sweeps away all resistance. His feelings 'break through language and escape': 'to the end that ye be strong to apprehend with all the saints what is the breadth and length and height and depth, and to know the love of Christ which passeth knowledge, that ye may be filled with all the fullness of God' (Eph. 3:18–20).

We come now to an interesting problem. By what mystery of genius or grace of divine plan did this naturally proud, self-assertive, intolerant man write the world's greatest ode to love? Love is a theme more written about than any other since the world began. The poets of all languages and all generations have sung its praises. Yet it was reserved for this persecuted Jew, with a mind trained in rabbinical subtleties, in a casual letter, written in haste to meet a pressing condition, to sing the song of love which surpasses anything in truth, in comprehensiveness, in beauty, composed by any poet of the ancient or modern world. The secret of it all is that a great, experienced soul uttered itself with the full force of unconscious sincerity. Thought long pondered over, an attitude of spirit won after desperate battle, a passion purified by many a trial, found unified and immortal expression that day. The very core of Paul's being was his sense of the unspeakable glory of the love of Christ; this kindled his whole nature, it was the strong urge which had driven him over land and sea; this he sought with all the ardor of his intense passion to reproduce in himself. Thus, without premeditation, without attempting to write greatly, in absolute self-forgetfulness, he uttered *himself* — the self living in Christ. Losing his life, he found it. Thus it came to pass that the most eager champion of faith wrote the world's supreme hymn to love; a man of action surpassed the poets in their own field.

Let the reader begin with Homer and follow the stream of poetry down through subsequent ages to our own day and find, if he can, any poet or philosopher who has spoken of the central theme of all literature in a way comparable with this outburst of the Apostle's heart. The rhapsody begins with an accurate assessment of the value of love. Paul, gifted with eloquence, a seer, champion of faith, devoted to martyrdom, knew that these things were all off center as compared to love, which he proceeds, not to analyze like a philosopher, but to describe in the good old Hebrew manner, objectively and in short sentences, what it did in practical life, and then in single lines which no poet has ever equaled he put love in its proper place, the capstone of the spiritual temple. Yet even Paul could not have evolved this wonder out of his inner consciousness: he was describing a model, the grace of his Master.

If we use now our accepted definition of literature, 'Moral truth and human passion, touched with a certain largeness, sanity, and attraction of form,' we must conclude that, while the letters have the defects of their occasion and author, they nevertheless contain great writing.

CHAPTER XVIII

NEW TESTAMENT HISTORY AND LETTERS

What then did they see, those godlike ones who set their hands to what was greatest in literature and thought little of meticulous scholarship? Besides much else, this: that it was no mean or low-born creature which Nature chose when she brought man into the mighty assemblage of life and all the order of the Universe, and ordained us to be spectators of the cosmic show and most eager competitors; from the first she poured into our souls a deathless longing for all that is great and diviner than ourselves.

And so, when in thought and contemplation we range over the field of human endeavor, the whole world is not enough, but often our thoughts transcend the borders that hem us in; and any man who will look at life in all its wide orbit, and consider how in all things it abounds exceedingly in what is great and beautiful, will know straightway to what end we were born.

LONGINUS.

THE Book of Acts is history and has many of the characteristics of the historical books of the Old Testament. Like them it is history written, not for accurate information, but artistically and for a purpose. The purpose was to trace the advance of the new religion from Jerusalem to the capital of the world, and also to convince Theophilus, perhaps a Roman official, and the Roman world in general, that Christianity is not hostile to the State and should not be persecuted. Therefore, the author shows how the great Apostle was a Roman citizen, was treated with consideration by Roman officials, and even in the Eternal City itself he was not hindered from preaching.

As in the Old Testament, the material is treated artistically to produce the greatest effect. It is grouped into six general divisions, marking the spread of the faith from the Holy City, through Palestine, to Antioch, through Asia Minor to Greece and then to Rome. The writer seems purposely to indicate the different stages by a vision, like the man of Macedonia, or by a miraculous revelation of the will of God, such as Pentecost. The narrative is not continuous: the author, a true artist, seizes a dramatic event to tell the whole story.

Like the Greek and Old Testament historians, he makes his narrative live by constructing speeches for his characters to deliver. In this his excellence is of a high order. Paul's addresses before Agrippa and at Athens are models of construction and of rhetoric fused by passion into true eloquence. He knows human nature, too, for Demetrius, inciting the mob at Ephesus, put the whole emphasis of his speech on the danger of the new religion to their trade, only at the end touching upon its effect on worship.

Like the Old Testament historians he writes graphically, but unlike them he does not strike out immortal sentences from time to time; neither is there in the movement of his thought the rhythmic beat which is so prominent in the older history. He is a Greek, the only Gentile, as far as we have knowledge, who has entered, through the Gospel and this history, into the Scriptures. Like the Greeks, and unlike the Hebrews, he is a lover of the sea, lingering upon the details of Paul's voyages and making us feel the storm. But, although a Greek, he follows the habit of the Old Testament historians of embodying his source material in his narrative in much its original form, leaving many discrepancies of statement unreconciled. For example, Paul is represented as saying in his speech before the Jewish mob [1] that during his vision outside of Damascus his companions 'heard not the voice,' and before Agrippa [2] he states that they all fell down, yet the author in his own account of the scene declares that they 'stood, speechless, hearing the voice.' [3] Moreover, part of the narrative is in the third person and part in the first person plural. The latter, the so-called 'we' sections,[4] have especial literary excellence. In vividness, movement, and stirring effect they have an epic quality. Evidently we have here extracts from a diary, and the writing has the brevity, the picturesqueness, the unconscious force of one who recounts his own experiences.

GENERAL EPISTLES

Every type of literature seems to have a period when it is peculiarly in vogue. Literature in the form of letters was a fashion in the fourth and third centuries before Christ. Men had written letters for purposes of personal communication since the invention of writing, but to make of them works of conscious art was the device of the centuries named. It is said that rhetoricians, giving much attention to the rules of epistolography, devised forty-one different kinds of letters. The Romans especially cultivated this art. Therefore, the early New Testament teachers were using no strange form when they wrote epistles to the early Church. Notice the advantages which letters have over the medium employed by prophets, sages, and law-givers in the Old Testament. They were

[1] Acts 22:9. [2] Acts 26:12–14. [3] Acts 9:7.

[4] Acts 16:10–17; 20:5–15; 21:1–18; 27:1—28:16.

oracular, they spoke down to the people: the letter makes intercourse personal, intimate, friendly. In the letter one speaks as man to man, not as the mouthpiece of the Most High.

The Epistle to the Hebrews is a treatise rather than a letter, and has come into the New Testament canon, not under the authority of a great name, but for its intrinsic worth. The fiction that Paul was the author was not accepted until the Middle Ages. The mind from which the epistle issued was very different from that of the Apostle, not impassioned and personal, but deliberate, balanced, formal. The author was a cultivated Hebrew whose thought and method were profoundly influenced by Hellenistic culture. His words read like those of a trained speaker addressing an audience; he carries his thought through his argument from beginning to end and moves forward in proper manner. Writing at a time when Rome was mingling all the faiths of the world, he wished to show that Christianity is the absolute religion: Christ, in his person and work, prefigured by tabernacle and temple service, does for man all that religion aims to do. The treatise opens with a statement so condensed that it puts the central thought of the Scriptures in three verses, so noble that it is an imperishable possession. The eleventh chapter is the classic definition and illustration of faith, culminating in those words of persistent suggestiveness, 'that apart from us they should not be made perfect.'

The Epistle of James comes from a plain, matter-of-fact man, who hates pretense, believes that religion consists in doing practical deeds and in keeping one's self unspotted from the world, and who writes in this general letter many common-sense suggestions for a working piety. He is a lesser sage, stating truth by analogy, fond of interrogation, and placing his solid sentences side by side without much organization.

The Epistle of Peter is like the letter of an old man to his children. It is simple, practical, without imagination, yet the author knows the difference between good and bad Greek, and uses his vocabulary easily.

The Epistles of John also have a distinct paternal note. He is not a master of words, and his vocabulary is limited. But he has a few tremendous truths to emphasize: God is love, we are the children of God and should love one another. These truths he forces home by reiteration. He is a mystic, thinking in terms of light and darkness, who speaks in straight sentences and clearly distinguishes between the essential and non-essential in Christianity.

CHAPTER XIX

APOCALYPTICAL WRITINGS

The majestic image of a high and stately tragedy, shutting up and intermingling her solemn scenes and acts with a sevenfold chorus of hallelujahs and harping symphonies.

JOHN MILTON

THERE are fashions in literature as well as in dress; the vogue of one period seems very strange to another. We shall discuss in this chapter a kind of writing which is as unlike the manner of our day as the dress of an Arab is unlike that of a modern American. Apocalyptic writing was a popular mode of expression in Jewish and Christian circles for about three hundred years — approximately from 168 B.C. to A.D. 150. Then it was abandoned. Those three hundred years covered a period of bitter persecution and of peculiar distress. It was a time of martyrdom, and books were written to encourage the faithful to endure. Of the large number of Apocalyptical writings appearing in these three centuries, the Book of Daniel in the Old Testament and the Book of Revelation in the New came into the canon of the Scriptures because of their exceptional merit.

Mark how pronounced the difference between the matter of these books and the writings of the earlier prophets. Righteousness was the burden of Amos, Isaiah, Micah: revelation is the constant theme of Apocalypse. The word itself is from the Greek, meaning revelation. The prophets had asked, What does

God require of man? Here we have an interpretation of what man expects from God.

This change of tone and of emphasis came from changed conditions. The prophets from Amos to Ezekiel were living in an independent state under their own monarch. They proclaimed that national stability and prosperity depended on national righteousness. Their God was mighty and was using Israel for the accomplishment of a world-wide purpose. Their monarchs would be glorious and universal in authority, the nation would become supreme in the earth, and all their wrongs avenged by the destruction of their oppressors. Then came the exile and the people passed permanently under the yoke of foreign dominion. Believing firmly in the predictions of their great prophets, the community which dwelt in Jerusalem and obeyed the law found nothing in contemporary events to substantiate their national hopes. They were too powerless to believe that anything they could do would hasten the fulfillment of their glorious prophecies. Their hope was in God only: that in some astonishing and irresistible way he would avenge his elect. Therefore, the post-exilic prophets were more concerned with divine revelation than with human righteousness. The writings of Ezekiel mark the turning-point. Before him the prophets had kept close to historic facts: they stood so solidly on the ground that we consider them as authorities on contemporary history. But Ezekiel leaves the earth for the clouds, he turns from the present to the future, and crowds his pages with angels and archangels, with visions and fantastic imagery. After him, the recurrent note in prophecy is the Great Day of the Lord, when Jehovah shall vindicate himself in the eyes of all nations.

Then suddenly a change in world conditions brings this helpless people, dreaming of a day of judgment, into acute distress, and their agony in a strange crisis utters itself in a strange literature.

In 333 B.C., Alexander the Great conquered Persia and Greek culture began its conquest of the East. On his death, Alexander's generals divided his empire between them, and Egypt, with Palestine as a province, passed under the control of the Ptolemies. In 198 B.C., the Syrian monarch, Antiochus the Great, wrested Judah from the hand of Egypt, and his son, known in history as Antiochus Epiphanes, determined to force the Greek language and customs upon its inhabitants. Judah was accustomed to invading armies; now she is confronted by a different danger, an invading culture. The more worldly-minded welcomed the freer life and the more comfortable philosophy of the Greeks, but to those loyal to the ancestral traditions it was a period of dire calamity. Antiochus ruthlessly carried out his purpose of completely Hellenizing the Jews. He erected an altar to Zeus on the great altar in the temple, compelled the priests to sacrifice swine thereon, and to eat the detested flesh. No one could keep the Sabbath or read the law without being in danger of the death penalty. This was too much. The slumbering fires in the hearts of this fierce and faithful people burst forth in a fury of rebellion. Led by the Maccabees, the Jews fought desperately, drove back army after army, and maintained the integrity of their faith and institutions.

It was during this period of relentless persecution and deep distress that the Book of Daniel was written. Its purpose was to strengthen the Jews in their loyalty to the faith of their fathers and to confirm in fortitude the martyr. The author accomplishes his purpose by appealing to the instinctive conviction that although for a moment overwhelmed the right will ultimately triumph; and the method he employs is the powerful one of impressing the mind through vividly presented pictures.

The first six chapters are to be classed as historical fiction. They belong with Scott's 'Ivanhoe,' or Bulwer-Lytton's 'The Last of the Barons,' for a nucleus of historical fact is moulded by the processes of constructive art to convey a truth to the mind through the imagination. The last six chapters consist of visions of the fall of Antiochus and predictions of the coming of the kingdom of God. They are valuable to the student of history, but have nu perpetual appeal.

The permanent spiritual value of the book lies in the stories of the first part and in a few verses of the last chapter. Truth in this first section is forcibly expressed in a series of tales. The Jews were commanded to eat food which was to them ceremonially unclean. This author encourages them to resist by telling the story of Daniel refusing to defile himself with the king's meat — which had been offered to idols — and of the reward which came from his adherence to principle. Another important teaching is the certainty of the divine protection in times of trial. Isaiah had proclaimed the comforting truth in language of glowing rhetoric: 'When thou walkest through the fire, thou shalt not be burned, neither shall the flame kindle upon thee.'[1] Our author does not state the truth, he paints it. To his countrymen, who are passing through a fiery furnace of affliction, he portrays three youths cast for their faith into a furnace seven times heated, yet they came forth without the scent of fire on their garments. They were cast in bound; they came out loosed, for affliction always sets free the good man from the shackles of the flesh. Notice also how forcibly is expressed the sense of divine companionship which is the reward of those who bravely endure suffering, for with the three there walked a fourth 'like a son of the gods.'

Socrates had comforted himself and his companions in the darkest hour of his life by these words, 'No harm shall come to a good man in this world or the world to come.' And a Hebrew poet, surrounded by his enemies, had written, 'My soul is among lions.'[2] This comfort and this metaphor are here put into the familiar story of Daniel in the lions' den. Paul changes the story back into a metaphor when he writes, 'I was delivered out of the mouth of the lion.'[3]

Soon the thought passes beyond the divine protection of the individual to the sure judgments of God. Belshazzar is having a drunken orgy in the royal palace. The cup of the divine wrath overflows when he profanes the sacred vessels taken from the

[1] Isaiah 43:2. [2] Psalms 57:4. [3] II Timothy 4:17.

temple at Jerusalem; a fiery finger darts through the air and writes the doom of an empire that was light in the scales of Eternal Justice. Really, if less dramatically, our own generation has seen that same writing on the wall. We have seen fall the dynasty of the Manchus, the Hohenzollerns, the Romanoffs, the Hapsburgs, the Ottoman, because they did not rest firmly on humanity and justice. Ever the scales of the Eternal are set, and man and institutions are constantly being weighed. Then 'the moving finger writes, and having writ moves on.'

The final triumph of spiritual forces is taught in a most unique and impressive figure. The ruling powers of the world — Babylonian, Median, Persian, Greek — are imaged in a figure with a head of gold and feet of iron mingled with clay. Out of the mountain comes a stone, hewn without hands, which expands until it fills the whole earth. Thus will the kingdom of God smite the apparently strong, but really weak, kingdoms of the earth, and, growing miraculously, fill the whole world.

We have in this book a clear intuition of a glorious life beyond the grave. The early Hebrews had no consoling hope of immortality. But the fierce stress of the days of persecution, when saints were being martyred and time-servers were prospered, pressed home the truth that this life is too short to express the full purposes of God. Therefore, the darkness of their despair was suddenly lighted by a conviction of a life beyond the grave, where virtue should receive its just fulfillment of joy, and evil its just recompense. Was ever this assurance expressed more beautifully? —

'And many of them that sleep in the dust of the earth shall awake, some to everlasting life, and some to everlasting contempt. And they that be wise shall shine as the brightness of the firmament; and they that turn many to righteousness as the stars forever and ever.'[1]

THE BOOK OF REVELATION

In the second section of Daniel there is a prediction of the coming of a divine deliverer.[2] Well, the deliverer came, but the people cast him out. His followers were convinced that he had risen from the dead and would come again with power and with great glory. Believing him to be the world's supreme king, they came into conflict with Rome. First Nero put them to the sword, afterward under Domitian the persecution was intensified and more extensive. During these periods of extreme distress the Book of Revelation was written, some of it before the destruction of Jerusalem, but the collection and revision of the whole belongs in the time of Domitian, about A.D. 93. Rome, which was tolerant of all religions, sensed danger in this faith, for the Christian refused to worship Cæsar and willingly died to attest the supreme sovereignty of Christ. To encourage the bleeding Church to be faithful to her Lord, this Book of Revelation was written. It strengthened Christians by describing the struggle of the Church with Rome, and by revealing the decreed victory of the saints and their blessedness in the glory beyond the grave. This strange writing has been called the

[1] Daniel 12:2, 3. [2] Daniel 7:13, 14.

'sphinx of literature,' but it is for the most part intelligible if we abandon the idea that it is a disclosure of the future history of the world and consider it as a history of the times in which it was written, thrown into the form of prophecy.

To minutely analyze the book is not necessary for our present purpose, but the reader will be most benefited by holding in mind a general outline. The first chapter is introductory; the second and third describe the universal Church, its strength and weakness, about to be caught in the desperate conflict with Rome. Before the strife begins, the courage of the reader is strengthened by a glimpse into heaven and a revelation of the divine resources. This is in chapters four and five. From chapter six to eighteen, the struggle of the Church and the judgments of God on the world are portrayed. The book closes with the destruction of Babylon, symbol of Rome and the dominion of evil, and the coming down from heaven of the city of God. There is a device connecting these many visions which gives order, suspense, and dramatic climax, as well as suggestion of the length of the struggle. In the fifth chapter, we see a book, written within and without, and sealed with seven seals. It is a book in which the destiny of the world is fully written, for all things are in the foreknowledge of God — yet they are sealed from man. The Lamb only is able to break the seals and make known the future. Six seals are broken, and then, when we are expecting the breaking of the seventh seal and the revelation of the consummation, there is a pause, and the reader is given a consolatory vision of what is taking place in heaven; then the seventh seal is broken, but, instead of the end, seven angels are revealed with trumpets. One after another they sound their proclamations of woe. Just before the final angel lifts his trumpet, the reader is again fortified by a vision of the heavenly blessedness; then the seventh angel sounds,,only to usher in the angels with the seven bowls, whose woes are successively to be emptied upon the earth. Then comes the end. It is all as Milton says, 'A majestic image of a high and stately tragedy, shutting up and intermingling her solemn scenes and acts with a sevenfold chorus of hallelujahs and harping symphonies.' In splendor of diction and in lofty rhythm it is superior to Daniel.

The power of the book lies in its appeal to the imagination. It is the gospel to the imagination. It puts its truth into unforgettable pictures, so majestic, so shining, yet so suggestive of infinite mystery and glory, that they quicken the deep emotion both of writer and of reader. The vividness of the picture in the mind determines the liveliness of the feelings. And these brilliant and awful pictures cause the author to speak with the musical cadence of deep emotion.

Hence these magical sentences, which are among the most precious in the Bible: 'Be thou faithful unto death and I will give thee the crown of life'; [1] 'Blessed are the dead that die in the Lord from henceforth; yea, saith the spirit, that they may rest from their labors; for their works follow with them.' [2] It is full of glorious similes: 'And his voice as the voice of

[1] Revelation 2:10. [2] Revelation 14:13.

many waters';[1] 'His countenance was as the sun shineth in his strength';[2] Jerusalem shall come down from heaven as a bride adorned for her husband. Then how many are the sonorous sentences whose musical cadences bear great thoughts with ever-mounting power: 'Amen, Blessing and glory, and wisdom, and thanksgiving, and honor, and power, and might: be unto our God forever and ever.'[3]

The principle of contrast is used most artistically. Above the scenes of woe on earth is the joyous calm of heaven. Set over against each other are the New Jerusalem and Babylon; the Harlot and the Bride; the Dragon at the head of the forces of evil, and the Father at the head of the forces of righteousness; the redeemed bear the name of Christ upon their foreheads, the followers of the Beast are stamped with his mark; there is the trinity of the Dragon, the Beast, and the False Prophet against the Father, the Son, and the Holy Ghost.

A revelation of the Supernatural intimately concerned in human affairs, a sense of mystery and impending doom, strange and flaming imagery, sweet and contenting pictures of the blessedness of the redeemed, sentences glowing with enchantment, the rhythm of deep and impassioned emotion, all appealing to our intuitive conviction that right will triumph ultimately over wrong, our eagerness that the victory shall come speedily — this is the unique power of apocalyptical writings.

[1] Revelation 1:15. [2] Revelation 1:16.

[3] Revelation 7:12.

NOTABLE EXPRESSIONS OF SPIRITUAL TRUTH

These are so many that it is possible to point out only a few of the most striking. In the fourth chapter is revealed the throne of God, with a green rainbow in a complete circle about it — symbol of hope without beginning and without end. In the next chapter John looks for the Lion of the Tribe of Judah to break the seals of the book, and, instead of a lion, behold a lamb as it had been slain! — and the lamb stood in the center of a throne! Is there anywhere a more powerful presentation of the truth that sacrificial love is the supreme power in the universe? That deep, infinitely deep truth which Isaiah has so pathetically stated in that wonderful fifty-third chapter is here disclosed in a picture.

Sorrow and pain, so necessary here for discipline and guidance, will some day no longer be required, 'for God shall wipe away every tear from their eyes.' [1] The sea of glass mingled with fire [2] is a memorable symbol of a perfect character — fiery energy under complete control. John beholding an angel standing in the sun [3] — the spiritual in the physical, and outshining it in glory — is the antithesis of Peter Bell, who sees only the material things. Again the seer exclaims, 'I saw the dead, both small and great, stand before God, and the books were opened.' [4] In this world we are judged by the tribunals of fashion, expediency, profit; ultimately we must pass beyond these and confront Reality. Then the deathless

[1] Revelation 7:17. [2] Revelation 15:2.

[3] Revelation 19:17.

[4] Revelation 20:12 (King James Version).

beauty of the Holy City coming down from heaven, adorned as a bride: the city of God is not erected on this earth by human wisdom, it comes as divine grace; its gates open to the four quarters of the earth, its gold where it ought to be — trodden under foot — and its citizens those who have identified themselves with the spiritual life of the world.

Note the pathos and profound significance of the final words: 'Surely I come quickly. Amen: even so, come, Lord Jesus.' The early Church expected the Master to come in power and great glory to restore all things in their own generation. But he did not come, and two thousand years have passed and yet their vision has not been fulfilled. Instead of manifesting himself suddenly, dramatically, he has come as the morning comes, silently, and with slowly increasing glory. There is a lesson here to be taken to heart. Our most ardent expectations, the forms of our most vital faiths are never satisfied in the way we anticipate. The reality is different from our dreams. Abraham looked for Palestine as a permanent possession of his race, yet four thousand years afterward his descendants have but a precarious hold on a land ruled by a foreign people. The nation looked for the Lion of the Tribe of Judah to restore all things; instead of a lion, a Lamb came to be crucified. They expected him to return as king, but he is coming slowly as an invisible God. The universe in which we live is not what our fathers thought it to be, but is vaster and infinitely richer in treasures of help than they imagined in the hours of their most exultant hope. So humanity is led on from step to step by illusions, the Reality is too stupendous to be grasped in our childish thoughts, the form of our vision fails, but the substance transcends by infinite distances our hope. Abraham's expectations were petty compared with the reality, the Christ who came was greater than the Davidic Messiah expected. Our own future and probably that of the race will not be what we prevision. We shall never see the God our imagination now envisages nor enter into the bliss of the heaven of our dreams. The Reality will be other and not less than our largest thought.

THE END

INDEX

INDEX